o

Published By Cane Creek Baptist Church
6901 Orange Grove Road
Hillsborough, NC 27278

and by

Edward S. Johnson
6000 Buckhorn Road
Hillsborough, NC 27278

2024

Cane Creek's Mission Statement

Our mission as a church under the lordship of Jesus Christ is:

WORSHIP:	Celebrate God's grace and active presence in our lives
DISCIPLESHIP:	Prepare people to live Christ-centered lives
EVANGELISM:	Lead people into a saving relationship with Jesus
FELLOWSHIP:	Show God's loving care through interaction
SOCIAL CONCERN:	Be actively involved in our community as we have since 1789

Our Church from 1880 until 1950

INTRODUCTION

This is not the first history of our church. One of our renowned members from an earlier generation, A. G. Crawford, wrote a history in 1933. The Minutes of the Mt. Zion Association for 1951 contain a brief historical sketch. Both are given in Appendix 1. Other histories have been written but are lost. The Sandy Creek Association minutes of 1830 refer to a historical committee that investigated the origins of all its churches and our Church Minutes of 1904 refer to the preparation of a history. It is sad that neither of these can be located, for they may have referred to matters still lodged in the memory of our ancestors that otherwise never made it to the written page.

I decided to expand the scope of this history beyond the confines of Cane Creek Baptist Church. I could have done otherwise and created a thoroughly acceptable and much shorter history, one that would look like many other church histories. But the Cane Creek community is too old and too steeped in history for me to ignore. The things that are recorded in our minutes reflect political, social, and economic forces at work both in the community and across the state and nation. To really understand what went on in Cane Creek, it is helpful to know what was going on elsewhere. For example, the coming of Stephen Pleasant to be our pastor in 1831 set Cane Creek on a new course. Pleasant never would have come had the members of our congregation had a different opinion of the role of the church in mission work. Cane Creek participated in the great debate on missions and helped direct North Carolina Baptists along the road that led to the formation of the Southern Baptist Convention.

I want to begin by reflecting on what it means to be a Baptist. When a modern-day member of our denomination ponders what it is that makes a Baptist church different from a Methodist, Presbyterian, or Episcopalian church, several principles may come to mind. The first is the idea that everyone should be able to read and interpret the Bible as he sees fit. This is sometimes called, the "priesthood" of the individual. Such a notion was foreign to long established Catholic principles. The old Roman Catholic Church thought that the Bible need only exist in its traditional Latin form, which few other than Priests knew how to read. That was what priests were for, to tell peasants what the Bible said and what to believe.

This practice took a hit with the first translation of the Bible into a modern language, English, by John Wycliffe in 1382. This was before the invention of the printing press so the few copies that existed were hand-written. This was a tiny opening of the door of the Bible to ordinary citizens, and it stirred some interesting discussions in England. But the floodgates opened when the first vernacular (German) translation was produced by Martin Luther in 1534. The invention of the printing press allowed for many copies to spread throughout Europe so that for the first time, ordinary people could read for themselves what the Bible had to say.

This development led directly to the principle, first enunciated by Martin Luther, that priests were unnecessary. Each person could now be his own priest. This became a general Protestant position but, to this day, it remains of particular importance to Baptists. As George Washington Paschal, the great historian of North Carolina Baptists, put it, "There is no room for priest, prelate, or pope; the one rule for faith and practice is the New Testament which each member interprets for himself and usually without getting so much at variance with his brethren as to become obnoxious to them."

The second Baptist principle is perhaps today the most basic and distinctive Baptist belief. It is that only believers should be baptized. That is, a person should know what he is doing when he accepts Jesus as Lord and Savior. A baby cannot do this. Baptists believe that baptism ushers a person into the brotherhood of believers. And, of course, we Baptists baptize by total immersion. This is how we first became known as "Baptists" in the 17th century. It was a derisive nickname (like "quakers" and "shakers") that was used to describe a particular Protestant sect.

A third principle is that each Baptist church is a bastion of self-rule and local autonomy. Seldom does some higher authority look down on local churches to see if they are doing things "right." No Bishop decides what pastor is to go to what church. There is no official creed or confession of faith that is recited every Sunday to remind members of the approved position on theological issues. Baptists leave it to each individual, with God's inspiration, to interpret the Bible's message.

A fourth Baptist practice is that individual churches associate themselves with like-minded churches in the support of mission work, Sunday school education, and other voluntary enterprises. Other than this there is virtually no central authority.

Finally, a fifth practice that Baptists have historically supported is religious liberty. We have opposed any interference of government in church affairs and the church in governmental affairs. When Baptists in Rhode Island became concerned, in 1802, that the new U.S. Constitution might allow for interference of the state in church affairs, they wrote to Thomas Jefferson, who replied with his now famous statement:

> "I contemplate with solemn reverence that act of the whole American people which declared that their legislature should 'make no law respecting an establishment of religion, or prohibiting the free exercise thereof,' thus building a wall of separation between Church and State."

But where did these principles come from? How, where and when were they forged? As we shall see in the chapters that follow, our beliefs about baptism, freedom of religion, and local church autonomy hark back to the earliest days of Protestant churches in the 17th century, which later were seen by historians as forerunners of today's Baptists. Our traditional support of missionary work arises from a great debate during the early years of the 19th century, a debate that profoundly affected the church at Cane Creek. The origins of this debate go back to England in the 17th century. Traces of this difference of opinion are still present among southern Baptists.

The pillars of Baptist belief and practice that I have mentioned above are not often discussed at Cane Creek. They are like the air we breathe. They are taken for granted as how a church should be. But if one really wants to know what the church at Cane Creek is all about, there is no better place to begin than with our mission and vision statements. Our mission statement is given on page ii. Our vision statement is below:

Our vision at Cane Creek Baptist church is to be a Christ-centered church made up of people who:

... are lovingly devoted to God and caring for others:

> **Goal:** Our focus on Sunday morning is to worship God in spirit and truth involving as many people as we can as we communicate the message of Jesus Christ through the spoken word, music, drama, and other media.

> **Goal:** Jesus taught in the great commission (Matthew 28:19) to "go" and "make disciples." We want everyone who comes to Cane Creek to believe in Jesus as their Lord and Savior. That's how you begin to become a disciple. Being a

disciple means we must be in a relationship with others, those who have long been with us as well as those who have just walked through our doors. We will take advantage of all opportunities to minister in word and deed, involving everyone in the life of the church.

Goal: We will deepen our understanding of God's love for us and strengthen our love and commitment to God.

... are committed to family-centered ministries

Goal: Our children and youth are the future leaders of the church. We seek to provide activities that communicate God's word, are fun, and are open to all students in the area. As we minister to these students, we will make ourselves available to the rest of the family.

Goal: We will provide ministries that address the special needs of young adults and parents, incorporating fun, support, and understanding.

Goal: Our senior citizens offer wisdom, experience, and a unique ministry perspective. We will continue to minister to their needs while providing them with outlets to serve others.

Goal: We will give all ministries at Cane Creek the highest level of commitment both individually and collectively. As we do this, we will continue to look for new ways to come together as a congregation in shared effort for the kingdom of God.

... are dedicated to growth in our spiritual lives:

Goal: We will make every effort to assist members in their spiritual growth incorporating traditional and innovative methods.

Goal: We want every person to discover and utilize their gifts for spiritual growth.

Goal: Prayer is our principal means of communicating with God. We will implement prayer into all aspects of life.

... actively support mission work in our world:

Goal: We accept missions as an imperative from God. We will increase and expand the scope of our mission effort within and beyond the community. We will also continue to address needs in our own congregation. We will provide opportunity for all members to be involved in service projects.

Author's Note (2022)

I was born a Methodist and in early adulthood became a "backslid" Methodist. I moved with my family to Orange Grove in 1973 and decided that the best way to participate in the life of my new community would be to check out the local church. I was a bit skeptical because it was Baptist and not Methodist. But my wife and I liked what we saw and became members in 1974. Since then, I have found that our church was filled with loving and caring people who were a joy to be with regardless of denomination.

I began to poke into local history when I became curious about the origin of the old gristmill site that I had bought and where we built our home. Over the years, this interest has spread to a curiosity about the entire community and what life may have been like at its beginning.

I was inspired to dig more deeply into our history at our 1989 bicentennial celebration of the founding of our church. I became a member of the church's Historical Committee when it was in the able hands of Rebecca Crawford. She was, more than any member of the congregation, interested in preserving the historical heritage of the church. Most of the pictures of our former pastors that appear in Appendix 2 were collected by her. When she died, I became the new committee chair, and the committee has tried its best to keep her interest in our heritage alive and vibrant.

The material in this book comes from many sources. The bibliography mentions most of them. Many of them are in our own library for the use of anyone in the community. I must acknowledge the help and encouragement of several people. Rebecca Crawford, our previous church historian, was my constant encourager and inspirer. Through her, I was able to contact others, such as Banks Cates of Charlotte and Tad Cates of Nebraska, who have helped me sort out the problem of which of the many Thomas Cates was our first preacher. Karen Sexton, our church office manager, dug up many details for me, such as names and birth dates. To these and all the others who have helped me, I want to express my sincerest thanks. At the same time, I must absolve them of all blame for any errors that remain. For these, I must take full responsibility.

Author's Children's Note (2023)

The author of this book, our father, passed away on December 7, 2022, a few months short of his 90th birthday and having only recently completed this history, a labor of love for him for many years. He was grateful for the love and support he received during his final days from members of Cane Creek Baptist Church and the Cane Creek community (aka, the Orange Grove community; *see* Chapter 18). Dad was eager to have this book published and offered to the church and community and any others who might be interested in their history.

Cane Creek Baptist Church was founded in 1789. Here are other events of that year:

January 7:	The first election day under the new U.S. Constitution.
February 4:	The Electoral College unanimously elects George Washington to be president.
March 4:	The United States Constitution officially replaces the Articles of Confederation.
April 6:	The Senate and the House officially certify George Washington as president.
April 28:	Fletcher Christian, aboard a British warship, leads the 'Mutiny on the Bounty."
July 14:	A Paris mob storms the Bastille and starts the French Revolution.
August 21:	The Bill of Rights is added to the Constitution.
September 22:	The US Postal Service is established.
September 29:	The Department of War establishes the US Army.
November 21:	North Carolina ratifies the Constitution, having waited for the Bill of Rights to be added.
November 26:	Congress observes a national Thanksgiving Day.
December 11:	The first state university is chartered in North Carolina.

Contents

This is the oldest community photograph I have been able to find. It was probably taken around 1910 at an Orange Grove School event, perhaps graduation. The original belongs to Margaret Miller. On the back is written, "Remember Orange Grove."

1: BAPTIST BEGINNINGS IN EUROPE

For centuries there was only a single Christian faith, a single "official" way to worship, a fixed doctrine, and a single church authority and hierarchy: the Roman Catholic Church. The Roman papacy had begun in the fifth century and after a thousand years had grown immensely. Its doctrines and practices had ossified, and abuses were growing.

The birth of the Protestant Reformation is traditionally dated to October 31, 1517 (the eve of All Saints Day) when Martin Luther nailed his 95 theses to the door of the church at Wittenberg, Germany. The theses were meant as debating points, and, like previous theses, were intended to be debated by Catholic theologians in an austere academic setting. No debate took place, however. It was clear that Luther's theses were more than mere debating points. They called into question the traditional practice of selling what were known as "indulgencies."

MARTIN LUTHER

Catholic theology of the time taught that when a person sinned but confessed the sin, he could be forgiven and would not be subject to an eternity in Hell. But these lifetime sins had to be atoned for before one became worthy of entering Heaven. At death one's soul was thought to reside in Purgatory, a way station on the way to Heaven, where one was punished and purified for all his minor sins. Purgatory was a sad and gloomy place, perhaps like being in the suburbs of Hell. If a person, during his lifetime, had done enough good deeds and acts of mercy, he had what could be called a get-out-of-jail-free card and quickly moved on to Heaven. But if he had not done enough, then he would be punished by a lengthy stay in Purgatory. There was no official Catholic doctrine on how long the stay was but in the popular mind it was reckoned to be thousands of years.

Indulgences could be issued by a priest or bishop that would shorten one's stay in Purgatory for a specified length of time. For praying a hundred Hail Mary's or Pater Noster's one could earn an hour's indulgence. For visiting a holy shrine, one might get a year's indulgence. But for the really big sins, one must make a donation to the church. No wonder people wished to obtain indulgencies for themselves and also for deceased loved ones who were already languishing in Purgatory. The sale of indulgences helped support worthy causes such as hospitals., but by Luther's time abuses had become commonplace.

What aroused Luther's ire was that in 1515 Pope Leo X wanted to build a new palace (now called St. Peter's Basilica). Luther's Thesis 86 read:

> "Why does not the Pope, whose wealth today is greater than the wealth of the richest Croesus, build the basilica of St. Peter with his own money rather than with the money of poor believers?"

The Pope issued his own special high-powered indulgencies (good even for adultery and murder) and forbade the selling of any other indulgences for eight years until he has raised enough money to build his basilica. Luther was particularly incensed when Johann Tetzel, the Pope's representative, traveled throughout Europe with a large wooden coffer containing the money he had collected. Tezel's famous saying was, "as soon as the gold in the coffer rings, the rescued soul to heaven springs."

Luther thought that indulgencies degraded grace and that they should be granted only for true repentance. He was also outraged by his parishioners who claimed that since they had bought the Pope's special indulgencies, they no longer needed to repent and change their lives for the better.

Luther went on to develop a radical theology that denied the traditional teaching that salvation depends on good works. Luther believed that salvation was dependent only on God's grace, which was granted because of the believer's faith in Jesus Christ. He also denied that the Pope was a trustworthy source of divine authority. He taught that the Bible is the only source of divine knowledge. Indeed, later in his life, he translated the Latin Bible into German so that ordinary people could read God's word for themselves.

JOHN CALVIN

Luther's 95 theses fell on fertile soil. There were already discontented clergy throughout Switzerland and northern Europe. John Calvin wrote _Institutes of the Christian Religion_ in 1536. Jacob Arminius preached a new doctrine of salvation in Holland in the 1620s. I will amplify on each of these below because they all influenced how the Protestant Reformation worked out and how the Baptist denomination evolved.

The young John Calvin, as a teenager, had set his mind on becoming a Catholic priest. Instead, Calvin's father sent his son to law school because he thought that a lawyer would make more money than a priest. But Calvin left law school and lived a life devoted to spiritual pursuits. He is best known for his doctrine of predestination. As he put it, "All are not created on equal terms, but some are preordained to eternal life, others to eternal damnation; and, since each has been created for one or the other of these ends, we say that he has been predested to life or death." Predestination is now a belief that we associate with the Presbyterian denomination.

Now I will repeat a little story that will never be found in any treatise on theology. It was relayed to me by my brother, who devoted his life to the sociological study of religion. He had heard it from one of his many colleagues who was a student of Presbyterian origins. The story explains how Calvin came up with the idea of predestination.

Calvin's first flock was composed of traditional Catholics in Geneva, Switzerland. They believed that one could store up a heavenly bank account by doing good works, bringing gifts to the Church, and by buying indulgences. Calvin felt that this excessive preoccupation with avoiding a long period of torment in Purgatory caused one to neglect his Christian concern for his fellow man. Calvin sought to alleviate this excessive concern for salvation with the simple assertion that the matter of salvation was already decided. Since God was all-powerful and knew exactly how everything would turn out, why worry since you couldn't do a thing about it?

Calvin hoped that believers would be relieved of a crippling anxiety, would relax, and would turn their attention to genuine good works. The actual result was somewhat different. Some of those who believed themselves to surely be included among God's elect, relaxed into self-satisfaction and did not see the necessity of doing good deeds or winning new souls to Christ since the fate of one's soul was in God's hand, not man's. Others would accept that they were doomed to eternal punishment and make no effort to reform themselves.

Calvin's basic points are wrapped up in the acronym TULIP and are as follows:

   Total depravity: another name for original sin;
   Unconditional election: God has predestined certain "elect" individuals to salvation;
   Limited atonement: Christ's sacrifice on the cross was limited to the elect;
   Irresistible grace: God's chosen elect cannot resist God's grace;
   Perseverance of the Saints: The elect cannot lose their salvation.

Calvin's idea of predestination became quite popular and was adopted by one group of early Baptists.

Another of the early dissenters against the Catholic Church was Jacob Arminius (1560-1609) of Holland who was a Dutch preacher who had studied at Leiden University and the University at Geneva. Arminius taught that Calvinistic predestination and unconditional election made God the author of all evil (since he created people who would never make it to Heaven and who he knew would do evil things and then roast in Hell). To him, God's election was conditioned on one's faith. Furthermore, Christ's sacrifice on the cross was atonement for the sins of anyone who professed belief in his teachings, not just a few special elected people. Arminius' beliefs were condemned and put down on the continent for a while but eventually Holland became  more religiously tolerant and Arminian churches were allowed to exist. Arminian ideas later migrated to England and found favor with the Crown. We will see that some of the earliest Baptists in England were sympathetic to Arminianism while other Baptists were more Calvinistic. This is the root of the debate that rocked our own church in 1831 and that will be discussed in Chapter 10.

Before we focus on Baptist origins, I would like to discuss a related topic, the origin of the Anabaptists. Despite the similar sounding names, there is little or no connection between the Anabaptists and what was soon to develop into the first Baptist churches. The origin of the Anabaptists, according to one popular theory, occurred on January 21, 1525, in Zurich, Switzerland. On this date Conrad Grebel (who had decided that only believers could be legitimately baptized) baptized one of his colleagues, George Blaurock, who in turn baptized several others. All had originally been baptized as infants in the Catholic Church.

The word "Anabaptist" means re-baptism. It was a disparaging word that steadfast Catholics applied to all who rejected their own infant baptism and instead had themselves baptized again as adult believers. They were, however, not a single group. Instead, there were several groups that practiced believer baptism. The various groups shared a belief in a strict interpretation of the Sermon on the Mount (Matthew 5-7). In particular, they emphasized these points:

- The believer shall not swear oaths to any authority except to God;
- The believer must not bear arms or forcibly resist wrongdoers;
- Civil government belongs to the world. True believers belong to God's kingdom and so may hold no office in any government;
- Sinners will be excommunicated unless they repent.

The Anabaptists foreswore contact with civil society. They kept themselves apart from the rest of society, shared property in common, and avoided conflict with any branch of government. There are a few small groups today that still consider themselves to be within the Anabaptist tradition. Among these are Mennonites, Hutterites, and the Amish. All three exist today in the United States in small enclaves.

Origin of the Baptists

Now we can return to the main subject of this chapter, the origin of what came to be known as the Baptists. We will begin in England. There, a secular and fleshy matter set the Protestant revolt going in that country. King Henry VIII, later to be known for his many wives, sought to be rid of his first wife, Catherine of Aragon, and, in 1525, asked papal permission to divorce her. The Pope refused, but Henry divorced her anyway, and the Pope responded to that by excommunicating him. To get around this, King Henry renounced the authority of the Pope and proclaimed himself the head of what he now called the Church of England. In doctrine and form of worship, it remained Catholic; but now, in England, Henry was in charge, not the Pope. His intention was to be able to marry Ann Boleyn who, he hoped, would bear him the son that Catherine had been unable to. Little did he know where this would lead.

Many people in England were already familiar with the religious ferment brewing across the channel. They felt that the Catholic Church had committed abuses and had not been responsive to their needs. Now, spurred on by the religious turmoil across the channel and King Henry's rebuff of Roman authority, they felt encouraged to explore new possibilities. When the Church of England turned out to be only a slightly different version of the Catholic Church, some daring souls, inspired by Calvin and others, sought to establish new forms of worship. Upon Henry's death in 1547, his young son, Edward VI, ascended the throne. He had been raised by Protestants and so was content to allow Protestant ideas to flourish.

Edward's grip on the crown was tenuous, however, and his sister Mary (later known as Bloody Mary), who was raised as a Catholic, seized power in 1553. Turbulent times ensued as Mary tried to put down not only the new Protestant groups but also the Church of England in order to restore Roman Catholicism. Her often violent efforts failed and she was overthrown in 1558 as Elizabeth, still another of Henry's children, took power. She re-established the Church of England.

By this time religious fires were burning brightly as Protestant agitators sought more radical reform. Those who opposed the Church of England came to be called Dissenters. At the same time faithful Catholics were agitating for the return of their Church. All the while, Queen Elizabeth attempted to steer a middle course between these warring factions. Some Dissenters did not want to abandon the Church of England. Instead they wished to cleanse and purify its doctrine and rituals. These came to be known as Puritans. Eventually many decided that their efforts to reform the Church of England were a waste of time. They separated entirely from the official Church. One group landed at Plymouth Rock in 1620.

Those who wished to establish their own forms of worship outside the Church of England became known collectively as Separatists because they wanted to separate entirely from the "official" Church. Although these groups were called Separatists, they differed among themselves on doctrine and procedure. Separatists were active as early as 1550. They formed underground churches. They were either tolerated or persecuted depending on who sat on the throne.

Later in the century several Separatist pastors led their congregations out of England because of religious persecution. One of these Separatists, John Smyth, had been imprisoned for criticizing, among other things, the Church of England's practice of baptizing infants. He had joined a Separatist church in London that eventually became large enough to cause the Crown to take notice. For safety's sake the congregation split in two to avoid attracting too much attention, and, in 1609, both congregations moved to Holland, which was known as a haven for Protestant congregations.

So much did Smyth rebel against the Church of England's highly formalized ritual that he forbade prayer books and even Bible reading during the service. He encouraged a free and spontaneous form of worship that sprung more from the heart than from bookish ritual. The only form of church government was the pastor and the deacons (who could be either male or female). Smyth was also greatly influenced by the teachings of Arminius. No outside influences, especially governmental, were tolerated.

It is to this time, about 1609, that we can date two cherished Baptist traditions: autonomy of the local church and a growing belief in the separation of church and state. These beliefs sprang from a natural reaction to religious persecution from the Crown. Although these two Baptist beliefs date to this time, it was well before the name, "Baptist," was applied to these churches.

Now another cornerstone Baptist belief was about to be set in place. Smyth was a man of strong principles. Since his days as a Separatist in England, he was convinced that only believers could be properly baptized. Because he and most of his congregation had been baptized as infants, he now believed these baptisms to be illegitimate and that his flock was not a legitimate Christian church. Accordingly, he dissolved the church so that its members could come together again at a mass baptism ceremony. Smyth led off the ceremony by baptizing himself. Then he baptized all the rest. At this early stage in Baptist history, baptism was done by sprinkling.

Within a few months Smyth had second thoughts about the validity of his own self-baptism. He came to believe that one could be legitimately baptized only by someone who was himself legitimately baptized. Once again, he dissolved the church. Smyth had received a baptism from some Mennonites because of their tradition of baptism only by one who was himself properly baptized. Presumably, this implied an unbroken chain of baptisms back to John the Baptist. With an authentic baptism, Smyth felt that he would be able to return to his flock and properly baptize them.

Unfortunately for Smyth, some of his original flock balked at being "unchurched" twice. In 1611 they returned to London under new leadership. This church prospered and by 1624 there were five churches in London that shared the same basic beliefs. By 1650 the five had grown to 47. Historians refer to this group of Separatists as General Baptists because of their Arminian belief that Christ's suffering and death on the cross atoned for the sins of mankind in general. They held that any human being could accept Christ and be saved.

In contrast, another group of Dissenters became known as Particular Baptists because of their adherence to Calvin's notion that God, even before he created the world, had determined the fate of every man and woman who would ever live. Some were predestined to be saved and others were predestined to be damned. The father of this branch of Separatist Baptists was Henry Jacob. Although he had also begun as a Separatist and had also fled to Holland to avoid persecution, he did not disavow the Church of England. He acknowledged it as the one true church and only wished to set up his own version of it to correct what he saw as deficiencies. He returned with his flock to London in 1616 and formed a new church that viewed itself as a purer form of worship than the Church of England. Within about twenty years this became the mother church for the Particular Baptists. In 1644, one branch of Particulars published a *Confession of Faith*. Here we find the first indication of baptism by total immersion. Soon mass baptisms in rivers and lakes became a common sight in England.

Although historians refer to these two groups as General and Particular Baptists, the church members at that time did not use these names. Instead, they used the terms "Believers," "the Baptized Churches," or "Churches of the Baptized Way." Their public baptisms were now attracting attention, and this caused them to receive what was then considered a contemptuous nickname, "Baptists." Eventually they themselves began to use this name.

The Particular Baptist practice of total immersion caused much discussion. Opponents declared the practice to be unscriptural, unnecessary, unhealthy, and immodest. This last criticism is perhaps justified because a few preachers demanded that those they baptized be totally naked regardless of the weather. But before long baptism came to look much like it does today.

The 17th century in England was one of religious turbulence. Both King James, who took the throne in 1603, and his son after him, proclaimed the Church of England to be supreme and sought to suppress any other form of religious expression, both Catholic and Protestant. In 1640 a power struggle between the King and Parliament broke into open warfare. When the dust had settled, the King had been defeated and the monarchy abolished. Oliver Cromwell was in charge, and the Church of England was no longer the "official" religion. Many new sects formed, and Baptists used the new freedom to expand their influence.

While it would not be accurate to speak of a Baptist "denomination," it was true that like-minded churches in the same region might band together in a loose sort of association. General Baptists were more willing than the Particulars to form a structure that could exercise some authority over local churches. By 1654, General Baptists had formed a nationwide assembly.

By 1689, Particular Baptists were following suit. One hundred and seven churches sent messengers to a convention. Unlike their General Baptist brethren, the Particulars were careful not to create a central authority that would challenge local church autonomy and they also refused to make any pronouncements of official Baptist belief, believing that this should be left to the individual churches to work out.

Oliver Cromwell held his Republic together by sheer force of will, and when he died in 1658, things began to crumble. By 1660 the monarchy had been restored. King Charles (whose name was later to be given to the Carolina Colony) ascended to the throne promising his people that he would tolerate as much religious freedom as Parliament would allow. When it turned out that Parliament restored the Church of England as the one and only religion, Separatists, with many Baptists among them, openly rebelled and were forcefully put down. Many were put to death. The more hotheaded among the Separatists were not to be easily suppressed however, for they saw the return of the British monarch as the final sign leading to the Second Coming of Christ.

The authorities were alarmed at the unrest created by the Separatist sects and the average English citizen was also greatly concerned. The government ruthlessly suppressed religious rebels and crowds rioted against any Separatists, including Baptists, who harbored the radicals. Parliament passed strict laws against all dissenting religious groups and it became a time for Baptists to grimly hold on and simply try to survive. Things only got worse when James II, a Catholic, was crowned in 1685. His efforts to suppress religious dissent were so ruthless that he was deposed only three years later. William and Mary, Protestant rulers of Holland, were invited to accept the crown. The next year Parliament passed the great _Act of Toleration_, which finally put an end to the religious persecutions. From this point onward, all forms of worship in England were to be tolerated by the Crown.

One would think that after so many decades of hardship, the new freedom from persecution would have led to a golden age in the development of a Baptist denomination, and, for that matter, all other Protestant denominations. But it was not to be. It was as if all the years of struggle had worn Baptists out. With their freedom secured, Baptists actually went into a long slow decline. There were still two major branches, the Generals and the Particulars. Some of the Generals began to relax their principles, even to the point of not insisting on the deity of Jesus. The Particulars went in the other direction. They had always been noted for their Calvinism but now their beliefs became extreme. Through all of this, membership declined and the interest of the average person in religion waned. England was now a major world power. New lands beckoned to be explored, subdued and exploited. Europe was now in what came to be called the Age of Reason. The energy and attention of the people turned to science, commerce, and politics.

Already we can see the beginning of a controversy over the issue of whether Christ's sacrifice atoned for all mankind's sins (the General Baptist's view) or just the sins of a select few (the Particular Baptist's view). Nevertheless, characteristics that we regard as typically Baptist (believer baptism, baptism by immersion, local church autonomy, separation of church and state) were already present in one or the other of these two early branches. I use the term "typically Baptist" instead of something like "doctrinally Baptist" because Baptists are to this day not entirely unified in their beliefs. Indeed, it may be impossible for people who so passionately believe in the autonomy of the local church to ever come together over the broad reach of doctrinal issues. This is both the strength and weakness of Baptists. In what follows, I will trace the development of that branch of Baptist belief that eventually came together to form the Southern Baptist Convention.

Before I leave this topic, I would like to say something about doctrine. Most of what you have read above is about religious doctrine and people's quarrels about it. It seems that each denomination required a strict adherence to its particular beliefs and these beliefs often concerned things that we, today, would consider trivial. For example, are musical instruments to be allowed in a worship service? Shall there be any singing? Shall weekly worship be done on Saturday or Sunday? These were all hot issues in the early days of Protestantism.

Even today, in Baptist affairs at the state convention or national convention level, one can hear remarks that this or that person advocates Calvinistic or Arminian ideas. But you don't hear these ideas discussed at Cane Creek. In my memory we have never had a preacher that advocated one position over the other. For us it has been a non-issue.

It seems to me that these theological details matter less to modern church goers. What is of more importance is belonging to a caring and compassionate group of people. We leave quarrels about doctrinal issues to the higher ups in all our denominations and wish that they would not so frequently get bent out of shape over issues such as Calvinism or Arminianism.

Next, we will turn our attention to how Baptists established themselves in America.

2: BAPTIST BEGINNINGS IN AMERICA

The first Baptist Church in America was formed in 1639 by Roger Williams. In England, Baptists were becoming stronger, more numerous, and more confident. Yet they did nothing to encourage the spread of the denomination to America and most definitely, they did not send missionaries. Baptists came to America as individuals and formed churches on their own initiative. Others, such as Roger Williams, came as Separatists and only later became Baptists.

ROGER WILLIAMS

Roger Williams was raised in England as an Anglican and was educated at Cambridge in preparation for the ministry. At the time of his graduation, he had given little indication of the fiercely independent and anti-establishment positions he was to take later in life. He had, however, ample opportunity to observe religious persecution during his childhood and youth. Dissenters were active near his boyhood home, and he may well have witnessed their public executions. As a lawyer's scribe the teenage Williams witnessed many proceedings against dissenters that could well have left an indelible mark on his character.

Upon graduation he accepted a job as a minister at a large private estate in the English countryside. Here he fell in love with a young woman far above him socially and when there was a forced breakup of the romance, Williams despaired and took sick, only to be nursed back to health by the loving ministrations of the woman who was to become his wife. At some time before 1629 he began to exhibit sympathy for religious dissenters to the extent that he was threatened with prosecution. He decided that he would be better off in another country. He therefore accepted a call to head a church in Salem, Massachusetts, a colony composed entirely of a variety of Dissenters known as Puritans.

Immediately upon landing in Boston in 1631, the handsome and dynamic Williams was offered a position at a prominent Boston church. By this time, however, Williams' Separatist sentiments were so strong that he decided that he could not serve the Boston church that seemed to him to be of such mild and timid beliefs. The main sticking point was that the Massachusetts Bay Colony adhered to a strict partnership between church and state. It was the state's duty to see that everyone obeyed the approved religious practices. Other forms of worship, especially Quaker, Baptist, and Anglican were forbidden. (The term, "Anglican" is synonymous with "the Established Church,' and "the Church of England." The Anglican Church evolved into present day Episcopalians.) Williams declined the Boston church's invitation and proceeded on to Salem leaving behind some insulted and angry Bostonians who were later to exact revenge for William's rebuff. The Bostonians exerted such pressures on the church at Salem that Williams soon had to move on, settling with a church in the Plymouth Colony (in southeast Massachusetts) where the Pilgrims had landed in 1620. Here, he interacted with the local Indians, learning their language and many of their customs.

It was not long before Williams was summoned to Boston by colonial authorities and charged with several offenses, among them claiming that the land belonged to the Indians and not the King, claiming that the oath of allegiance to the Colony, sworn in God's name, was improper, and, most importantly, claiming that civil magistrates had no right to enforce what was then known as the "first table" of the ten commandments. Like others of the day, Williams divided the commandments into two tables, the first being duties to God, the second being duties to one's fellow man. He recognized the authority of the magistrate to enforce the second table but denied that they had any authority to enforce the first. These, he claimed, were only within the jurisdiction of the Church, and the state had no business meddling in them. This was another manifestation of what was already a cherished Baptist principle, the separation of the affairs of the church from those of the state.

Williams stood trial, was found guilty and was given six weeks to leave the Massachusetts Colony. When the authorities learned that Williams was using these six weeks to continue preaching his radical message, they ordered his arrest, with the intention of sending him back to England for trial and punishment for violating the terms of the royal grant. But Williams was warned, and he escaped into the wilderness in the dead of winter. Only his friendship with the Indians saved him. They sheltered him and hid him from the authorities.

In the following spring, 1636, Williams and a few supporters left the Massachusetts Colony, found a spot along the coast, and settled down to carve out a colony to be called New Providence (later Rhode Island). They drew up a compact providing for a democratic form of government, official toleration of all religious beliefs, and a rigid separation of church and state. By 1639 Williams had established a Baptist church, the first one on American soil.

Curiously, Williams soon disassociated himself from the very church that he had helped to establish. Undoubtedly the strong and passionate beliefs that had driven him to establish the church in the first place now created such doubts about his own legitimacy that he felt compelled to withdraw. The point at issue was the legitimacy of his own baptism. Upon forming the first Baptist church in America, he and his flock were baptized by a man whom he soon came to doubt lay in an unbroken line of believer baptism back to the Apostles. Although Williams withdrew from the church, he did continue as a religious man and afterwards wrote stirring and convincing treatises on religious liberty and the separation of church and state.

The Church Williams founded went on without him, neither failing nor especially prospering. The church faced the problem that many of the later New England churches were to face and the same one that had proved to be so troublesome in England: the doctrinal differences between those church members who were more in the General Baptist camp and those who were more Particular.

The second Baptist church in America was formed in Newport, Rhode Island by John Clarke around 1644. Although second to the church at Providence, it was more vigorous in its organization and evangelistic outreach, which resulted in the formation of a Baptist church in Maine (then a part of the Massachusetts Colony) in 1682 by William Screven. This church would soon influence Baptist expansion into the South.

The principles that were dear to the hearts of the early New England Baptists were no mere debating points or issues for abstract discussion around the supper table. The points that they insisted upon were considered radical and treasonable by the authorities in other colonies. This is illustrated all too graphically by a visit of the Baptist preacher, John Clarke, and his assistant, Obediah Holmes, to Boston in 1651. Both were arrested for preaching in a private home and were sentenced to a public flogging. Clarke escaped punishment when a citizen paid a heavy fine on his behalf, but Holmes was savagely administered 30 lashes. Bravely, he restrained himself from crying out and instead preached to the crowd during the punishment. But he had been so grievously injured that he could not leave Boston for several weeks and spent much of the time crouching on the floor trying to find a comfortable position for his scarred back.

Eventually, Baptist sentiments began to be felt even in the Puritan stronghold of the Massachusetts Colony, particularly on the matter of infant baptism. In 1642 three women were hauled into court for refusing to have their infants baptized. In 1654, Henry Dunsten, President of Harvard, lost his job for refusing to let his son be baptized and most particularly for refusing to keep quiet on the matter. By 1665 a few brave souls dared to establish a Baptist church in Boston itself, the primary point of doctrine being a belief in the baptism of believers, not infants. Although they endured persecutions, this church persisted.

Baptists experienced a different situation in the middle colonies. In 1681 Charles II granted William Penn a charter for a new colony to be called Pennsylvania. Penn was a devout Quaker and thus championed the Quaker notion of religious freedom for all. It is understandable, then, that religious dissenters of all sorts should have found a safe haven in the "city of brotherly love." The first Baptist church in Pennsylvania was established in Philadelphia under bizarre circumstances in 1688 by Elias Keach.

ELIAS KEACH

Young Keach was the son of Benjamin Keach, a prominent Baptist preacher in England. This strapping young man landed in Philadelphia and was described as "exceedingly wild" and "a stranger to divine grace." And for some reason other than piety, he took up the practice of going about dressed in preacher's clothing. One day he chanced by a gathering of Baptists and was stopped and asked to preach to the throng. Having heard his father preach on numerous occasions, this was no problem and Keach, as a prank, began preaching. He had just launched fervently into the high point of his oration when he suddenly stopped, seized with the enormity of his sin. Shocked and shaken, he confessed to his deception and was converted to Christ on the spot, the only recorded case of a person converted by the strength of his own preaching. Keach devoted his life to Christ and within a year had established a church that exists to this day.

Keach proved to be a boon. He was vigorous and energetic in his efforts. He refused to become bogged down in the narrow doctrinal issues that plagued the northern Baptist churches. Instead, he engaged in vigorous outreach and helped to organize many churches. These churches soon were meeting together several times a year and, by 1707, had formed the nucleus for the first Baptist organization in America, the Philadelphia Baptist Association, which was to play such a prominent role in the future of the Baptists in America.

We think these days that the Baptist denomination is primarily a southern phenomenon and yet Baptists came to the South rather late. One reason was that in Virginia and in parts of South Carolina, the Anglican Church was "established," that is, it was the official church of the Colony and was supported directly out of tax funds. Dissenting churches were discouraged if not outright banned. This, of course, did not prevent other churches from organizing but it did put a damper on them.

The first outpost of Baptist belief in the South occurred in South Carolina. Charleston had been settled in 1680 after a group of settlers, who had come ten years earlier, moved to a more favorable location where the Ashley and the Cooper Rivers meet and flow into the Atlantic. It was to this town in 1696 that William Screven moved his Baptist congregation from Maine. Family tradition is that Screven and his small flock were driven out of Maine by Puritans who told him that if he ever returned, he would be hanged. Screven's church was the first Baptist presence in the south. To this day the church marks its time of origin as 1682 in Maine rather than 1696 in Charleston.

By 1700, Baptists were present throughout the Colonies but nowhere in great abundance. Indeed, the best estimate of their numbers in America at that time is fewer than 900 compared to a total white population of about a quarter million. The denomination could be considered neither prominent nor influential. Most of the early Baptist preachers in America worked for a living. There was no financial support from their church. Indeed, some churches considered it an important doctrinal point that they not pay their pastors. Most congregations were small and met in private homes with no more than ten or a dozen souls; few had separate church buildings, and many congregations went long periods without the services of any pastor at all.

One reason that the early Baptists were so obscure was that doctrinal disputes still plagued local churches, with the result that many congregations had little energy to put into outreach and evangelism. The issues that lay at the heart of these disputes were primarily the following.

First, the British dispute between the Particular and the General Baptists spilled over into this country. Particular Baptists were highly Calvinistic and General Baptists, who were followers of Arminian thinking, were not. In this country, strict Calvinist principles were somewhat muted at first so that there was a degree of toleration for religious outreach. But Calvinist thinking did establish a foothold among the Baptists in Philadelphia, and, as we will see in several of the chapters that follow, this would come to have a profound influence on some North Carolina Baptists and to cause ruptures among the Baptists.

Second, there were other more narrowly focused issues that separated General Baptists and Particular Baptists such as the rite of the laying on of hands for new converts. General Baptists did not do this; Particular Baptists did. For Particular Baptists, becoming a member of a church was a three-step process. First, one confessed his/her faith, second came baptism (by now it was total immersion), and third came a laying on of hands by the congregation.

Another dispute concerned the role of singing during church worship. Benjamin Keach had introduced hymn singing into English Baptist churches in the 1680s, but it had not caught on, especially among General Baptists. Some churches did allow the singing or chanting of scriptural verses, such as the Psalms, but not "man-made" songs. Many congregations split over this issue.

Finally, there was a dispute over the proper day of worship. The choice was between worshiping on the first day of the week, Sunday, or the seventh day, Saturday, or the Sabbath. Seventh day churches clustered mainly around Rhode Island. Some Baptists regarded the Sabbatarians with a degree of suspicion since, in England, Sabbatarians had sometimes been associated with the radical millennial movement that insisted that the present world was about to end and Christ would make a triumphant return.

The Land Rush South

We have now brought our history up to the middle of the eighteenth century. The northern colonies were filling up with new settlers from Europe. Many, especially those who had settled in Pennsylvania, began to look elsewhere for land. Inland sections of the Virginia and Carolina Colonies were wildernesses and offered vast unclaimed stretches for anyone bold enough to venture forth. The land was only sparsely settled, and these original settlers had a rough reputation. They were prone to drinking, fighting, gambling, and rough treatment of their wives and children. But word was abroad that in North Carolina land was available at a price that anyone could afford. This was enticing to residents of Pennsylvania, which was rapidly filling up so that new land was hard to find. So now, it is time to turn our attention to our own state.

3: BAPTIST BEGINNINGS IN NORTH CAROLINA

The Carolina Colony was chartered in 1663 by King Charles II to eight men who had helped him gain the throne after the death of Oliver Cromwell. Because, unlike other colonies, virtually all authority was vested in these men, the colony is referred to as a Proprietary Colony and the eight men were called Lords Proprietors. In its original charter, Carolina extended from the vaguely defined Virginia border on the north to about present-day Cape Canaveral to the South (well into Spanish territory) and as far west as "the South Seas," i.e., the Pacific Ocean. In 1665 a second charter was issued that clarified some territorial questions and resulted in bringing the southern border northward. In 1669, the great British philosopher, John Locke, wrote the _Fundamental Constitutions_ (_see_ Parker, 1963) as a model for the government of Carolina. Locke's writings later became the inspiration for our country's founding fathers as they wrestled with issues of liberty and freedom in their struggle against the British crown.

At this time there were only scattered European settlers anywhere in North Carolina. Most of these were clustered in the extreme northeast part of the territory and had come south from the Virginia Colony. Indeed, because of the vagueness of the Virginia border, some of these early settlers had actually obtained land grants from Virginia colonial authorities. Others had purchased land from local Indians. The precise location of the border was not determined until it was surveyed in 1729.

Many of the early Carolina settlers were Dissenters fleeing oppression in other colonies. Some were Quakers who had fled persecution in Massachusetts in the early 1650s and had settled in the southeastern part of Virginia. When colonial authorities in Virginia moved against them, for example, by fining them up to 20 pounds a month for failure to attend the Anglican Church, they moved farther south into North Carolina. The church at Cane Creek may owe its existence, at least indirectly, to this Virginia persecution of Quakers.

In 1663 The Lords Proprietors worded the first Carolina charter to provide religious freedom. The charter was revised twice, in 1665 and again in 1669. Each revision made religious liberty more explicit. The last charter said, "any seven or more people agreeing in any religion shall constitute a church" and, "no person shall use any reproachful, reviling or abusive language against the religion of any church." Indeed, freedom of religion was made a selling point for the colony by the Proprietors in hoping to attract a flood of immigrants from England. More immigrants would, of course mean more money for the Proprietors, who were eager to sell them land.

The Proprietors had every right to expect religious freedom to be a strong selling point because religious persecutions in England were still fresh in everyone's mind. But the hoped-for flood of immigration failed to materialize. There were several reasons for this. First, the cost of immigration was about a year's wages, far too much for an ordinary person to afford. Second, wildly exaggerated tales had reached England of fearsome death tolls in Carolina due to disease, Indian attacks, and wild animals. And it certainly did not help that the British courts frequently sentenced its convicts to a choice of going to jail or going to America.

The Carolina colony thus grew slowly. In 1663, at the time of the first charter, there were only about 1,000 European settlers in the portion of America that would become North Carolina. By 1700 it had risen to only 5,000. Thereafter, the rate of influx picked up and in 1730 the population had multiplied to about 30,000, virtually all of which was in the eastern part of the state. The interior was still a wilderness populated only by scattered Indian tribes.

Most of the population was spread throughout the northeastern coastal area. There were few wealthy settlers and few towns. In 1730, there were only five towns in the northern part of the colony, Bath, Edenton, New Bern, Beaufort, and Brunswick, all small ports. The main settlement in the southern portion of the colony was at Charleston, which quickly became a thriving port. One reason for the absence of a wealthy planter class in the northern part of the Carolina colony was the presence of the Outer Banks and, consequently, the absence of a good deep-water port. Access to the mainland was through treacherous inlets accessible only by shallow draft boats. Without a suitable deep draft port, North Carolina suffered by comparison to its neighbors to the north and south. The map below shows the colony in 1667. (Turn it 90 degrees to the left to make sense of it.)

The Carolina Colony in 1667

The original home of the Carolina governor was in Charleston. It was hugely inconvenient for him to have any control over the northern part of the colony because the roads were so treacherous, as they had to traverse many swamps. In the early years, the colony was informally divided into northern and southern sections, called "Albemarle" and "Clarendon," with no clear dividing line. There was only one governor, but each province had its own colonial assembly. There was a formal separation in 1719 following a rebellion against colonial authority around Charleston. When the dust had settled, the British crown had control of the southern part of the Carolina colony while the northern part remained in the hands of the Proprietors. In 1729 the colony was officially divided into North and South, and the first colonial governor was appointed for North Carolina.

In its earliest days, North Carolina was destitute of religious influence. Historians generally agree that only about 10% of the population was associated with any church. The single greatest religious presence was that of the Quakers. Some historians suggest that of the 10,000 inhabitants in 1715, perhaps as many as 2,000 were Quakers. In 1672 George Fox, founder of the Society of Friends (the Quakers) visited the region and soon had gathered a powerful group of ardent Quakers. They became so influential that they virtually ran the colony. Aside from them, there was very little religion of any sort in North Carolina.

Considering what was happening in the other colonies, this was a rather curious state of affairs. Massachusetts was firmly in the hands of the Puritans; Rhode Island had been founded by Baptists, Pennsylvania by Quakers, Maryland by Catholics, and Virginia by Anglicans. But neither North nor South Carolina had any particular religious orientation, due to provisions in the Charter of the Carolina Colony. Events were moving in England, however, that would soon influence the religious life of North Carolina.

In 1700, with the lack of an established church in the Carolina Colony becoming something of an embarrassment, the British Society for the Propagation of the Gospel pressured the Proprietors to do something about it. The Proprietors responded by sending a new Governor, Nathaniel Johnston, with specific orders to establish the Anglican Church. The legislatures of both sections of the colony obediently passed the Vestry Act. This act allowed for the establishment of parishes whose citizens would be taxed to support a local Anglican church. Under its provisions several churches were begun. Various Anglican ministers were sent to the Carolina Colony in the early 1700s and were uniformly met with a chilly reception. They found the citizens unwilling to support an official church with their tax money. As one Anglican minister ruefully put it, "this paying of money [to support the Church] puts them quite out of humor. They cannot endure to be charged for what they value so little as religion" (Paschal, 1930, p. 114). The coming of Anglican influence also led to conflict with the established Quakers. Soon there was a Quaker faction and an Anglican faction in the colony.

Quakers all but ran the colony and Thomas Cary, appointed Governor in 1708, had their full support. The Anglicans struck back by maneuvering to have one of their own, Edward Hyde, appointed governor in 1711. Hyde made the mistake of arriving in North Carolina without his official credentials of office and Governor Cary refused to yield his office to him. A civil war of sorts broke out, but Hyde was eventually able to secure aid from the Virginia colony and Cary fled.

These events were followed closely by an uprising of the Tuscarora Indians, in which many settlers were massacred. Hyde did not discourage the rumors that Cary and his Quakers had encouraged the Indian rampage. As a result, popular feeling began to run high against all Quakers. Soon the Colonial legislature had passed laws forbidding Quakers from holding any public office, from sitting on a jury, or from being allowed to testify as a witness in court. Within a few years Quakers had all but disappeared from the eastern part of the state.

There is no firm evidence to date the first appearance of Baptists in North Carolina. Morgan Edwards, writing in 1772, states that Baptists were present before 1700. Since there were scattered underground Baptists in Virginia in the early 1700s, it is natural to suppose that some of them migrated into North Carolina to escape persecution. The earliest reference to Baptists is in a letter by an Anglican minister in 1714, who complained that two of his vestrymen in Chowan Precinct "were professed Anabaptists." Indeed, he felt that one reason that the Anglican Church was not well received in the colony was because too many of the vestrymen were like these Anabaptists and really cared little for the Anglican Church. (Recall that Anabaptists endorsed believer baptism but may not have otherwise been Baptist.)

The first actual Baptist Church was established around 1727 in Perquimans Precinct on the Chowan River. It was the work of Paul Palmer, a Maryland native, who had been ordained as a General Baptist in Connecticut and who had done missionary work in New Jersey and Maryland before coming to North Carolina. At first, he seemed content to manage his sizable land holdings acquired partly through his marriage into a prominent local family. But by 1727 he had established a church. Although this first Baptist church did not endure, his second one, at Shiloh in Camden County in 1729, did. Soon it became a center of vigorous activity. Within fifty years it had spun off six "arms" that themselves became established Baptist churches. In 1736 the Shiloh church ceased meeting in private homes and moved into its own meeting house and, in 1757, into a larger meeting house. These were the first Baptist church buildings in North Carolina.

Palmer worked diligently to convert souls to the Baptist faith and managed to do in a few years what the Anglican missionaries had failed to do in twenty-five years. In 1729 Governor Everard wrote that he regarded Palmer's work with wonder (and, no doubt, chagrin).

One reason for the swift conversion of the citizens was that the General Baptists did not require any experience of grace or personal salvation prior to baptism. Indeed, it appears that Palmer and his associates simple baptized anyone who came forward. This reckless baptizing was later to lead Morgan Edwards to remark scornfully that of all the Baptists in America, those in North Carolina were "the least spiritual minded." The efforts of the General Baptists certainly led to the conversion of numerous individuals, but for all the conversions, few churches were actually established. Edwards lists only 16 by 1755. One reason was that by this time the colonial authorities required that a meeting house that wished to allow dissenting worshipers had to secure a license.

It is at this point, in the 1750s, that the General Baptist point of view in eastern North Carolina came under siege. The confrontation was due largely to Rev. Robert Williams, a North Carolinian who had been deeply influenced by his association with the Church at Welsh Neck in South Carolina, an outpost of the church at Charleston (the one that had moved to Charleston from Maine). This was a church with a pronounced Particularist leaning. Upon returning to North Carolina in 1750, Williams began to preach the Particularist doctrine wherever he could. But of perhaps more importance, he contacted the Philadelphia Association, the center of Particularist sentiment in America. They sent John Gano, a young traveling minister, to survey the situation. Gano reported back to the Philadelphia Association that the Baptist churches of North Carolina were in a sad state of affairs and that help was needed urgently. The Philadelphia Association sent ministers who spread throughout eastern North Carolina wherever they could convince a local congregation to allow them to minister to their needs. This intrepid band of young ministers then set about to redirect their new churches along Particular Baptist lines.

The process was not a harmonious one. The General Baptist Churches often had large loose memberships, sometimes numbering in the hundreds. The Particular Baptist ministers usually began by convincing a small portion of their congregation of the truth of their Calvinistic ideas. Then they would rise up and, usually with much animosity, take control of the meeting house and remove anyone who did not meet their Calvinistic principles.

Once the Particulars were in control, baptism and church membership could only follow a born-again experience of regeneration, and the Church was to pay strict attention to the personal conduct of its members and excommunicate those who did not conform to the rules. Within a period of about fifty years, from 1750 to 1800, this Particularist revolution led to a hyper-Calvinistic narrow-minded point of view throughout eastern North Carolina. Paschal estimates that during these tumultuous years many Baptist churches were reduced to barely five percent of their former membership.

Calvinism is a doctrine of predestination. That is, in the beginning God knew who would be saved (called "the elect") and who would be condemned to eternal torment. If you push the notion of predestination to the extreme, you come to the belief that God not only knows but has fore-ordained *everything*. Here are two 19th century quotes from hyper-Calvinistic authors that make it clear that hyper-Calvinists did not believe in missionary work.

"God has made a decree by which he has rejected some of the race of Adam from his favor, not because they sinned, for all have sinned, but just because he decided to do so. The cause of their election to damnation was not sin but the good pleasure of his will."

"Since the non-elect are persons foreordained to condemnation, whose names are left out of the book of life, it would hardly make sense to preach the gospel to them or urge them to repent their sins. At best it is a waste of time and at the worst, it violates the sovereignty of God. "

JOHN GANO

Another aspect of hyper-Calvinism was the doctrine of perseverance of the saints. This means that an elected person is forever elected, and no sin is too great to change that. If one of the elect were to defraud another person of his life savings, it would be understood that, to put it bluntly, "God made him do it," and he himself was not responsible.

A few General Baptist Churches in the eastern part of the state held firm against the rising tide of Calvinism and eventually came to refer to themselves as Freewill Baptist. Today, Freewill Baptists still cling to a precarious existence in the eastern part of North Carolina.

The western-most outpost of the Particular Baptists was the so-called Jersey Settlement. Although its exact origins are in dispute, it seems that a Baptist minister, Benjamin Miller, led his congregation from the Scotch Plain Church in New Jersey and settled on the Yadkin River in Davidson County in 1754. Miller soon moved on and his place was taken by the same John Gano who had brought Calvinistic practices to eastern North Carolina. Gano had some claim to fame. He had been instrumental in the founding of Brown University, had established the First Baptist Church of New York City, and, according to family tradition, had baptized George Washington in the Potomac River. One member of his flock will be mentioned in the discussion on the Regulators in Chapter 6. He pastored the church for about two years during which time he led it into the Charleston Baptist Association. In 1759 Gano became alarmed by Cherokee uprisings associated with the French and Indian War and feared for his family's safety. He took his family back to the safety of New Jersey. Early in 1760 his worst fears were realized: Indian attacks scattered the settlers and the Church disbanded.

The Great Awakening

While the Particularist-Generalist confrontation was significant, a new movement was under way elsewhere that was to shape the future of southern Baptists far more. The spiritual resurgence known as the Great Awakening had taken hold in England under the guidance and inspiration of John Wesley and his brother. The Great Awakening was a religious response to the tenor of the times. I have already mentioned the turmoil of religious dissent in England in the 1600s. There was much religious passion in response to religious persecution from the Crown. But when religious persecution ended about 1690 and Protestant groups were allowed to prosper, there developed a sort of religious lassitude. Passions subsided and interest in religion waned.

The Great Awakening began around 1740. In addition to John Wesley, George Whitfield (who was instrumental in establishing the Methodist denomination) began preaching a new set of ideas. Whitfield came to America and preached up and down the colonies, persuading people everywhere to accept his new style (or "method") of worship. His manner of preaching was electric. He shouted and trembled with emotion as if filled with the Holy Spirit.

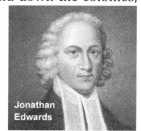

Jonathan Edwards

Soon, the new religious excitement spread to America. In New England, the Anglican minister Jonathon Edwards preached a similar theme. Here is a rough synopsis of their teachings:

- Everyone is a born sinner;
- Sin without salvation will send one to Hell for all eternity;
- Everyone who confesses sin and accepts God's grace can be saved;
- Everyone can have a direct and personal connection with God;
- Religious services shouldn't be strict and formal; they should be casual, personal, and emotional.

Edwards' preaching became powerful among the Congregationalists in New England and came to cause a split of ministers into two camps. The "New Lights" followed the teachings of Edwards and the "Old Lights" wished to continue the traditional methods that had seemed to work for such a long time. This division would come to have a great influence on Shubal Stearns, the man who spread a new brand of Baptist belief throughout the South.

We next turn our attention to this remarkable man, for it may truly be said that without Shubal Stearns there would be no Baptist church at Cane Creek and there would be no Southern Baptist Convention. Just imagine what could happen in North Carolina when a hugely evangelistic movement came up against another movement that did not believe in evangelism and had a practice of throwing out those who were not considered "pure." We will follow Stearns on his spiritual journey from New York to North Carolina. But first we will pause to draw a picture of Orange County as it was first being settled.

GEORGE WHITFIELD

4: CANE CREEK: THE LAND AND ITS SETTLERS

We have traced the history of Baptists in Europe, America, the south, and finally in North Carolina. Now we must place our ancestors and our part of Orange County into the stream of history. First, we will inquire about Orange County as it was originally and see when, how and why the first settlers arrived at Cane Creek.

With the exception of Sir Walter Raleigh's ill-fated attempt on Roanoke Island in the 1580s (what is known as "the Lost Colony"), there was no effort to colonize this part of the Atlantic seaboard until the middle 17th century. To the north, the British had staked out claims throughout New England and as far south as Jamestown. Far to the south, the Spanish had long since colonized throughout the Caribbean and Central and South America. They had ventured as far north as Saint Augustine, Florida, but between there and Jamestown there was virtually no European presence. Indeed, without the protective shield of a fleet of ships, it would have been foolhardy for anyone to set down a colony. The British crown felt that it had a valid claim to this part of America based upon Sir Walter Raleigh's colony at Roanoke, but actually putting down a colony would have invited Spanish raiders like honey draws flies. As late as 1749, there was a Spanish raid on the little coastal town of Beaufort in 1747 and at Brunswick in 1748.

As discussed earlier, in 1663 the King had chartered the Carolina Colony to eight noblemen known as the Lords Proprietors. He had two purposes in mind. One was to reward them for their help in regaining the throne. The other was to validate the English claim of ownership of lower America by locating a settlement there. For the Proprietors, it was primarily a money-making venture. It was hoped that the colony would prosper and that the individual Proprietors would make enormous fortunes selling land to English settlers and collecting "quit-rents" (more about this later) from the settlers. Land offices were established in the principal coastal towns to allow settlers and speculators to lay claim to tracts of land. Surveyors would be sent out and Land Patents, as the deeds were called, would be drawn up and issued, for a fee, to private citizens.

As the century closed, the hoped-for riches had not materialized. To stir up English interest in the new colony, the Proprietors hired John Lawson to trek through the Carolina wilderness and write a book extolling the virtues of the land. They hoped this might stir more interest and bring in more settlers.

JOHN LAWSON (perhaps)

In December 1700, Lawson departed from the settlement of Charleston with a small group of men and an Indian guide with the intention of trekking inland along Indian trading paths into unknown territory, swing north, and then trek back east to the coast. In January 1701 Lawson had reached Haw River at about the current location of Swepsonville with the next stopping point being the Indian town of Occoneechee near what is now Hillsborough.

"As soon as it was day we set out for Occoneechee Town, it being, by estimation, 20 miles off, which I believe is pretty exact. We were got about halfway (meeting with gangs of turkeys) when we saw, at a distance, 30 loaded horses, coming on the road, with four or five men on other jades, driving them. We charged our guns and went up to them, inquiring whence they came from. They told us from Virginia. The leading man's name was Massey, who was born about Leeds in Yorkshire. He ask'd from whence we came. We told him. Then he ask'd whether we wanted anything he had, telling us we should be welcome to it. We accepted two wheaten biscuits and a little ammunition...

"The Virginia men asked our opinion of the land we were then in. We told them it was a pleasant one. They were all of the same opinion and affirmed that they had never seen 20 miles of such extraordinary rich land, lying altogether, like that betwixt Haw River and Occoneechee Town...

"About three O'clock we reach'd the Town and the Indians presently brought us good fat bear and venison which was very acceptable at that time. Their cabins were hung with a good sort of tapestry, as fat bear, and barbecued or dried venison, no Indians having greater plenty of provisions as these. The savages do, indeed, still possess the flower of Carolina, the English enjoying only the fag-end of that fine country."

Our vision of an Indian village has been shaped by western movies that show Indians as nomads who set up temporary camps with teepees. The eastern Indians did a bit of hunter-gathering, but many formed semi-permanent or permanent villages and planted crops. Below is one 17th century representation of a village from the eastern part of the state.

AN INDIAN VILLAGE
From the De Bry Engravings of the John White Paintings.

17th Century Depiction of an Indian village

Even earlier than Lawson, we have the first recorded report of this part of the state from a German doctor, John Lederer, who passed through an Indian town, probably a predecessor of Occoneechee, in June 1670:

> "The country here, by the industry of these Indians, is very open and clear of wood. Their town is built round a field...They plant an abundance of grain, reap three crops in a summer and out of their granary supply all the adjacent parts (Lefler & Wager, 1953)."

In these days, the colony of North Carolina had only about 5,000 citizens. The two main towns were Bath and Edenton. Most people were independent settlers who farmed and lived near the two towns but were within just a few miles of the coast. The map below was made in 1733 by Edward Moseley of Edenton. This is a section of the map that shows our part of the state (present day Orange County and surroundings).

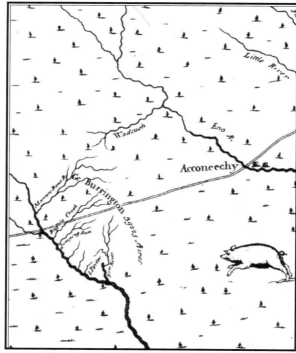

A Section of the 1733 Moseley Map

Moseley knew almost nothing about our part of the state beyond the name of some rivers and creeks. He did know that there was an Indian village that he called Acconeechy on the Eno River and that there was a trading path through the area. The Haw River is at the lower left and the lowest creek running in to it is labeled New River. This was later to be called Cain Creek, then Little Cain Creek, and eventually Cane Creek. It was also known that the land, from the Haw River crossing and to the northeast was very rich and desirable. According to Lederer, the Indians had cleared much of the land. This would later make it very desirable to eastern land speculators.

The Fry-Jefferson map of 1753 below shows just slightly more than the Moseley map. It laid out the Indian Trading path and where it crossed the Eno River (and became the site of Hillsborough). It also shows Haw Old Fields, which the trading path passes through. The Jefferson who helped create this map was Thomas Jefferson's father, Peter. The dark circle toward the center is labeled "Haw Old Fields," which borders Cane Creek on the west.

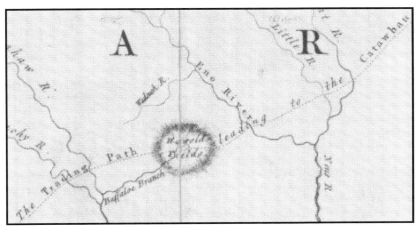

A Section of the 1753 Fry-Jefferson Map

The only counties that existed in 1740 were coastal. The colonial legislature created new counties as settlement spread westward. Beginning around 1750, the central part of the state began to be populated with settlers. The maps below shows what the new counties looked like in 1740 and 1760.

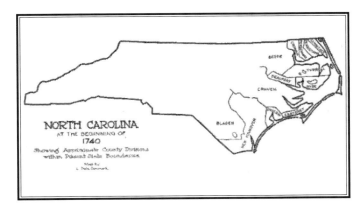

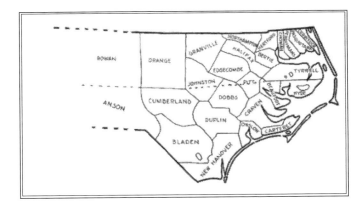

Orange County was established in 1752 and soon afterwards so was Rowan County. This gave Orange County established boundaries on all sides. The county was named after King Willian III of the House of Orange, who ruled England from 1689 to 1702. In those days Orange County was about ten times its current size. Over time, the county was carved up as shown below.

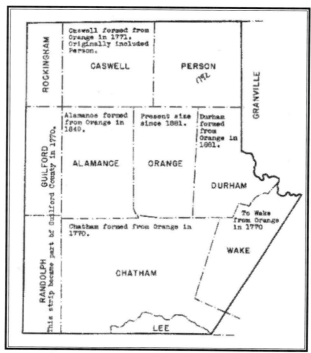

The Division of Old Orange County

The town of Hillsborough was established in 1754 and designated as the seat of the county's government. The town was initially called Corbin Town in honor of Francis Corbin, a member of the Governor's Council. The name was later changed to Childsburg to honor Thomas Child the colony's Attorney General. It became Hillsborough only in 1766. This name honored the Earl of Hillsborough, an official in London. It was located at a key river crossing, about where "Acconeechy" is shown on the Mosely map.

Before Orange County was formed, a set of events occurred that greatly influenced later developments around the area that came to be known as Orange Grove. These involved a transfer of ownership of the entire colony. The Proprietors sold North Carolina back to the British Crown. There were two basic causes for this.

One reason for this sale was that the Crown began to have second thoughts about having granted such a large chunk of America to the Proprietors. The King thought that perhaps he should find a way to get it back into official Royal hands. After all, the colony was huge, extending all the way to the "south seas." It was about 25% of the present-day lower 48 states of the U.S.

The other reason was that the Proprietors (and their heirs) began to have second thoughts about the wisdom of trying to run a colony. The hoped-for riches had not materialized. The colony had few settlers and they turned out to be an independent and unruly sort. Indeed, in 1719, residents around Charleston rebelled against the governor. The rebellion led to the division of the colony into North and South and the Crown's acquisition of the southern part.

To make matters worse, the Proprietors had a hard time collecting quit-rents. This fee was a hold-over from feudal times, when the King or the local Lord claimed ownership of all the land. In this system, residents owed certain things to the Lord in return for being able to live on his land. This could include a portion of the crops they grew, armed service in conflicts, or labor on any project conducted by the Lord. By the 16th century, it became possible for a peasant to get out from under these obligations by paying a fee to the Lord. This fee was called a quit-rent. This system was especially prevalent in England and the Proprietors tried to extend it to their American colony.

Collecting quit-rents was a problem for the Proprietors. Colonial authorities would come after you if you failed to pay the annual poll tax (a "poll" was any adult white male), But quit-rents were another matter. They were owed to the Proprietors and not to the colonial government. If a landowner did not fork over the money, there was no governmental authority to come after him.

The agreement to transfer ownership to the King neared completion in 1729. One of the sticking points was the exact location of the Virginia-North Carolina border. A swath of land about 15 miles wide was in doubt. The two colonies at one point agreed not to make land grants in the disputed area until the matter could be resolved, but for those who owned property or were settled there anyway, there was ambiguity about taxing rights, tax payment obligations and other jurisdictional matters.

Virginia and North Carolina settled on a surveying crew to establish and mark the exact location of the dividing line between the two colonies. A Virginian, William Byrd, headed the crew. The Carolinians were Edward Moseley (who made the map shown earlier), John Lovick, and William Little. This survey begins a peculiar tale that winds up affecting events in our neighborhood.

In March 1728 the survey crew sank a post on the coast north of the little village of Duck and proceeded west. When they got to about where I-85 now crosses the state line, they encountered the last settler as they trekked west. When they had gotten to about where US15-501 now crosses the Virginia line in Person County, a dispute broke out. The Carolinians wanted to leave off surveying. The Virginians countered by saying that their orders were "to survey to the mountains." The Carolina crew pulled out the official document and pointed out that it said, "*toward* the mountains" not "*to* the mountains."

So, they left while Byrd continued surveying westward. Later, Byrd wrote two books, the official _The History of the Dividing Line_ and, for his friends, _The Secret History of the Line_. In the latter, he was very critical of the North Carolinians. Among many other unfavorable comments, Byrd wrote that the real reason the Carolinians had abandoned the survey was that the whiskey had run out.

But there is another theory about why the Carolinians left Byrd's survey crew. They knew that they were due a handsome sum of money from the colonial government for their work on the survey. But they also knew that the colonial treasury was short of money, meaning that rather than being paid in cash, they would be paid in land. In this theory, the Carolinians left the survey party and trekked southwestward on the Indian Trading Path. They came to Haw Fields, where they surveyed the tracts that they wanted as payment for their work on the Virginia line survey. It is easy to presume that they had heard of the rich cleared land described by Lederer and Lawson in the area known as Haw Felds. Below is a rough map of the surveyed tracts.

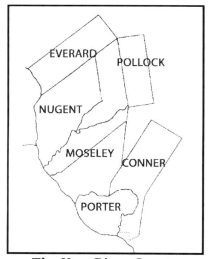

The Haw River Grants

The Carolinians, Moseley, Little, and Lovick, carved out huge tracts for themselves (and others) as shown above. The dark wiggly line on the left side is the Haw River. These tracts went to:

Edward Moseley:	18,400 acres
Richard Everard:	9,000 acres (the last Proprietary Governor)
John Lovick:	4,200 acres
William Little:	4,200 acres
Robert Forster:	2,425 acres
Lewis Connor:	10,000 acres

Thomas Pollock :   10,000 acres

John Porter: 8,000 acres (which later went to James Moore. (Members of the Moore family belonged to our church.)

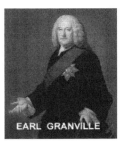

The Lovick, Little, and Foster tracts later were combined to form the Nuggent tract. In order to give a better impression of the extent of these tracts, I show below the tracts with current roads, Cane Creek, and the location of our first church roughly sketched in. Please remember the three shaded tracts. They will play a role in our history later.

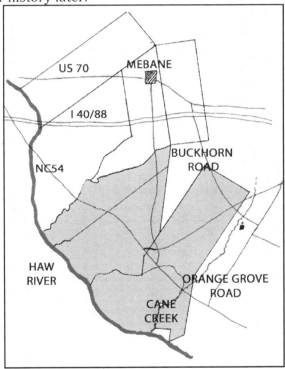

The Haw Fields Tracts Superimposed on a Map of Current Roads

In 1729, after years of negotiations, the King succeeded in reaching an agreement with seven of the eight Lords Proprietors to buy back the Colony. Only Sir John Carteret (who later became the Earl of Granville) refused to sell his undivided share. Eventually, the King agreed to carve out a one-eighth portion of the Colony (north and south) and turn it over to Lord Carteret as his personal property to dispose of as he saw fit (this did not actually become official until 1744). The grant to Lord Carteret, often called the "Granville tract" or "Granville District", is shown on the map below (it comprises far more than one-eight of current North Carolina because it was that fraction of the original North Carolina grant):

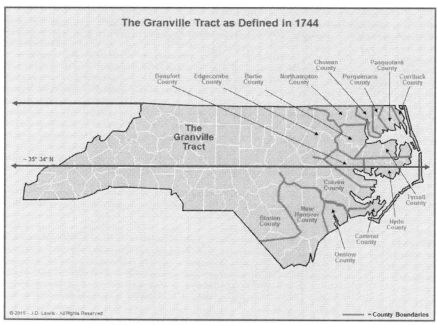

The Granville Tract

After the agreement with Carteret was finally hammered out, a stake was driven into the Outer Banks at about the present location of Rodanthe and a line was surveyed westward. By April 1744 the survey crew had reached the Haw River. The result was a strip of land, the Granville District, extending southward from the Virginia border about sixty miles and reaching indefinitely to the West. The remnants of this line can still be seen in the southern boundaries of Chatham, Randolph, Davidson, and Catawba Counties. Curiously, it is also the lower border of Rowan and Iredell counties, though at a slightly different latitude. Carteret took possession of all land in his Granville District that had not already been deeded to private citizens by the Proprietors. The previously deeded land includes all the Haw Fields tracts described above.

When George Burrington, the King's new Governor of the colony arrived in America in 1729, there were even more curious happenings. It was not long before he became the new owner of Moseley's two Haw Fields tracts as well as the Connor tract. These are the shaded ones in the above map. In the case of the Moseley tracts, it would appear that there was a "quid pro quo" arrangement. Moseley had become a defendant in a criminal case, and one might suspect that the Governor saw to it that Moseley was found innocent in return for his land. The three tracts amounted to about 30,000 acres.

Governor Burrington was described as "abusive, insolent, and dictatorial." When his term ended in 1733, he returned to England expecting the King to pay him handsomely for his service. On the strength of this expectation, he borrowed a considerable amount of money from a Scot businessman, Edmund Strudwick. But the King never paid up and Strudwick sued Burrington to recover his money. The debt was settled in 1761 by Strudwick's gaining ownership of the 30,000 acres in Hawfields. This was a time when settlers were streaming into Orange County looking for land.

Meanwhile, with his Granville District surveyed, Carteret sent land agents to North Carolina to set up land offices. By 1746 he was granting tracts of land to the earliest settlers. The process was not complicated in theory although in practice there could be many difficulties. A potential settler would identify a vacant tract of land of up to 640 acres (a square mile), stake it out, preferably using simple north-south and east-west lines, and then travel to the nearest Land Office to file a claim. This was not difficult since the land agents moved around the territory following the court as it moved from one county seat to another. So from time to time, they would be in Hillsborough, which was established in 1754, as a lonely outpost in the wilderness. The Land Agent would check to see if there were any prior claims to the land and then write a warrant directing a surveyor to map and describe the tract. The surveyor would convey the metes and bounds of the tract back to the land office and eventually the land patent would be drawn up, money would change hands, and the new owner would come away with a deed. The whole process could take several years. A copy of the deed was kept by the Granville District land office, and many were rescued during the Revolutionary War. They are kept in Raleigh at the Department of Archives and History.

Life in Orange County for the Early Settlers

Now that we have covered some of the "business" details of early Orange County, what was life like for the incoming inhabitants? A description has come down to us through oral tradition in the Nash family, which settled north of Hillsborough. Some of these were set down on paper in 1903 by Francis Nash in _The North Carolina Booklet,_ which includes this excerpt:.

> "This territory was a paradise for the hunter and trapper, abounding in bear, deer, beaver, wild turkey, and all the smaller varieties of game. It was the habitat and hunting grounds of the Haw, the Enoee, and the Occoneechee Indians..."
> "In 1750 huge forests spread in billows across the tops of the hills and down their sides and over the valleys. Along the creeks and larger brooks were to be found rich bottom-lands needing but to be cleared and planted to yield abundant harvests.
> "
> "This section was exempt from Indian raids. The only tribes remaining in the limits of the province of North Carolina at this period (1750-1755) who

were at all formidable were the Cherokees and the Catawbas. The latter tribe was fast disappearing from disease and contact with the whites, and the Cherokees were formidable only to the scattered settlements outlying toward their own hunting grounds. So, safety, fertility, convenience, and a mild and healthy climate all invited the adventurous Scotch-Irish of Pennsylvania to this section"

"It is probable that one or two families had already settled there as early as 1745 but the migration was at a flood-tide from 1750 to 1775. These immigrants were by no means pioneers, blazing the way for permanent settlers to come after them, but they were citizens of one province moving to another to improve their condition. They had already accumulated some property, owned lands and horses, cattle and sheep.."

"Let us take one family as a sample and follow them in their migration. The winter of 1750-51 had been severe in Berks County [Pennsylvania]. A killing frost had come unexpectedly early and had seriously damaged the crops of Mr. T. His oldest child had sickened and died with pneumonia, and his wife had been desperately ill. He had heard of the success of some of his neighbors in the beautiful and fertile Valley of Virginia, but the bloody-minded Shawnees were on the warpath and were threatening the outlying settlements. Some of his acquaintances ... however had pressed on farther south to the province of North Carolina, had settled on the Eno River, and had sent back glowing accounts of the climate and of the country. He determined to go himself and spy out the land with the view of moving his family to a less hostile climate. In the late fall or early winter, he sets out on horseback for this distant land of promise. Bearing to the west that he might strike the streams and rivers where they are fordable, he passes across Maryland and through the Scotch-Irish settlements in the Valley of Virginia and after a lapse of about thirty days, enters North Carolina into what is now Caswell County. He pauses for a while, on Hyco Creek, but finally rides on to the Eno River"

"He is pleased with the country, selects his future home, sends for William Churton, one of Earl Granvi'le's surveyors, and has it surveyed. After this is done, he pays Churton his fees for the survey and also three shilling sterling, consideration money for the deed which Churton is to provide for him from Francis Corbin, one of Earl Granvi'le's agents, and have ready for him on his return with his family from Pennsylvania. Then, with the aid of neighbors, he builds a log cabin on a suitable site, and with the same aid clears and fences a small parcel of land near it. The spring advancing, he plants corn in this little clearing, and leaving it to care for itself, he returns to Pennsylvania for his family. There he sells all his property which he cannot carry with him to North Carolina, purchases three or four sturdy horses... or perhaps two yoke of oxen and a heavy, unwieldy, but commodious wagon. In this are to be carried the household goods and in it the wife and the younger children are to sleep. A milk cow or two are to be tethered to its axle, and perhaps a small flock of sheep are to be driven by the children behind it ..."

"During the week-days they made on average ten miles a day, so they would arrive at their new home about the first of August. As they would pass through the settlements in Maryland and Virginia, they would be met with words of cheer, and there they would replenish their supply of food. When, wearied and footsore, they arrived at the end of their long journey, the neighbors flocked to welcome them and to aid them in establishing their new home ..."

"Hawfields, or Haw Old Fields as it was first called, had a certain unique characteristic, which makes it worthy of a more extended notice. Here had been the home of the Saxapahaw Indians. These Indians, like nearly all the tribes in central North Carolina, were less nomads and more agriculturalists than the northern and western tribes. These old fields had been cleared by them and cultivated by them. Thirty thousand acres of these lands were patented by Edward Mosley. From him they passed to Governor Burrington, and from him to Samuel Strudwick. As early as 1731, Colonel Byrd wrote to Governor Burrington of the": "but no place has so great a character for fertility and beauty of situation as the Haw Old Fiel"s."...The Mebanes and others settled there as early as 1745 and possibly earlier. The activity of the northern and western Indians, in the period commencing in 1750 and ending at Bradd'ck's defeat in 1755, not only vastly increased the migration from Pennsylvania, but also from the Valley of Virginia to North Carolina. It was during this period that the Hawfields and the region about it was settled...
"

"The Hawfields were on the east side of Haw River. The Quakers and Germans, however, settled on its west side, the Quakers on Cane Creek [that other Cane Creek that confuses historical research!!] and the Germans, in the region of Stinking Quarter and Alamance Creeks..."

"Further west on Sandy Creek, the home of Herman Husband [of Regulator fame], Baptists from Virginia, under Shubal Sterns, organized a church and erected a meeting house in 1755".."

What sort of dwelling did the early settlers construct? Since the available tools were mostly axes, adzes, and chisels, the first houses were crude. Trees would be cut and limbed. Then they would be stacked to form a square. On one side there would be a large hole in which was built a fireplace made of stone and clay. The opposite side would have another opening for a doorway that may have been left open or else closed in by crude cloth. There might also have been a window, but it would not have had any glass. The cracks between logs may or may not have been sealed with clay.

As the years went by, homes improved only slowly. Johnson (1937) gives this description:

"A common type of log house of the better sort was that which had four rooms, two rooms separated by a partition with a loft above which was reached by a narrow stairway or ladder, and a small lean-to at the end of the back porch. The chimney, which was usually built of fieldstone, was frequently ten feet wide and high enough for an ordinary man to stand in.

"In 1851 the *Southern Weekly Post* of Raleigh declared that that the average house in North Carolina was neither attractive nor comfortable and that the people of the state had not improved in their way of living of their ancestors. 'How often do we see houses set on the brow of a sandy hill, with not a tree or shrub or patch of green grass to relieve the eye or refresh the imagination. In summer they look like places of penance, bake ovens whose inmates are suffering all the tortures awarded to the martyred Saints. In the winter, fires roared in the immense chimneys and the family crowded around, scorching and sweating on one side while the other is shivering with the keen blasts that sweep through open doors and a thousand yawning crevices. Why do you not make your houses tight, and in the winter close the doors and keep the windows full of glass?'

Land Grants in the Cane Creek Area

The first Granville District land grants in the Cane Creek area that I have been able to locate were to Thomas Cate in 1756 (556 acres on "a branch of Cain Creek" and 640 acres "on the main fork of Cane Creek" – i.e., on Toms Creek); Alexander Mebane, the County's first sheriff, in 1757 (356 acres on the east bank of Cain Creek just below Cecil Crawford's, now Felton Johnson's farm); Thomas Lindley, later a mill operator on the Haw River, in 1757 (356 acres just south of the Mebane tract); and Sackfield Brewer in 1760 (570 acres on Watery Fork containing the present Snipes farm). Undoubtedly these lands were thought to be the best ones because they were the first to be claimed. Quite a few other Granville grants exist for the Cane Creek watershed. It is not always an easy task to discover precisely where they were located.

The grants I have mentioned above are shown in the map below. The shaded area is the upper portion of the Connor tract, which, by this time, has been transferred to George Burrington and then to Samuel Strudwick. A fairly complete map of original land grants can be found in Mark Chilton's 2015 book.

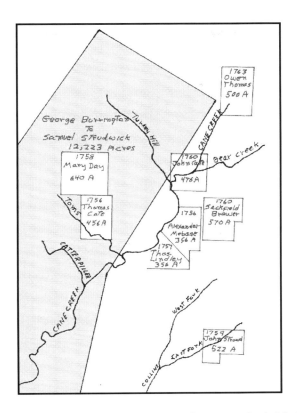

Some Cane Creek Grants Near and in Strudwick's Tract

Land agents for the Granville District issued grants from 1746 until Carteret's death in 1763, which threw the District into turmoil. Difficulties in settling Carteret's estate led to the closing of the land offices at just the time when settlers were flocking into this area in droves. With land offices closed, new settlers had no way to get deeds for the land they had settled on. Before the squabbling over the estate could be settled, the Revolutionary War broke out. After the Revolution, Carteret's heirs tried to re-establish claim to the Granville District land that had been vacant in 1763. This land was now considered by the North Carolina State government to be confiscated Tory land, hence the property of the State. The Carteret heirs' court case languished for years before being dealt a final deathblow in 1806 by the State Supreme Court.

Recall that Edward Strudwick had obtained 30,000 acres just to the west of Cane Creek. About this time Edward Strudwick's son, William, had come into ownership of his father's Hawfield holdings. He undertook to have his land surveyed and this was accomplished in 1763. He then boarded ship for America and landed at Brunswick in 1764 on the same ship that brought William Tryon to be the next Colonial Governor. Upon arriving in Hillsborough and riding out to inspect his holding, Strudwick found to his horror that what he assumed to be his land was filled with squatters and settlers, some of whom claimed to hold valid grants from the Granville land office. Attempts to evict the squatters met with varying success and eventually he took the matter to court in an effort to eject what he termed "intruders." This legal action was interrupted by the beginning of the Revolutionary War in 1776.

Strudwick's political position was, to say the least, awkward. He was a refined British gentleman whose principal wealth was land far in the interior of a newly developing country. He was more than friendly with the British Colonial officials and indeed had become a member of Governor Tryon's Council, was Secretary of the Colony, and was Clerk of the Pleas Court. Fortunately for him, he also had influential friends on the patriots' side. He did not flee the country when the Revolution broke out and so his property was not confiscated. He took an oath of allegiance to the cause of liberty around 1778 while the war still raged but it is likely that his neighbors in Hillsborough still viewed him with suspicion.

During the war the British Colonial government retreated to Wilmington and set up headquarters on a British warship. While the war raged on, some men on the patriot side set up the semblance of a state government to maintain the day-to-day operation of the colony. By decree, this hastily put-together North Carolina government confiscated all lands owned by the Earl of Granville. One important function of this early state government was the re-opening of the Land Offices. In 1778 the State opened up the books for land claims. For those who resided in the Granville District, this was the first opportunity since 1763 to lay claim to land. Many new settlers had arrived and set up homesteads during the fifteen years that Granville Land Office had been closed and so there was a huge rush to lay claim to land that they had already settled on. In the confusion several new grants were awarded within the borders of Strudwick's Haw Fields land.

The Strudwick "ejectment suits" dragged on in the courts for years but eventually Strudwick had his way with most of the intruders (although he did lose cases covering about 5000 acres) and settlers had to either pay him for the land they occupied or else move elsewhere. John and Henry O'Daniel, for example, had extensive holdings up and down Toms Creek. They stayed and paid Strudwick. Some families, among them, the Craigs, Blackwoods, and Freelands, all Presbyterians, picked up and moved eastward. They established a new church on New Hope Creek. Other familiar names involved in the ejectment suits were Thomas Cate, Lewis Kirk, and Thomas Thompson. I have not yet discovered the outcome of these suits.

The Vale of Humility

Before we move on to other matters, I should take a moment to characterize the history of how our state compared to our neighbor states. These days, we are proud to be natives of North Carolina. It is a strong and prosperous state. We have good farms, industry, schools, and roads. We are more prosperous than many of our neighboring states. But it was not always so.

To begin with, geography dealt North Carolina a bad hand. Virginia to the north and South Carolina to the south had excellent ports with which to import and export goods. North Carolina, instead, had the outer banks. Getting through them in a sailing ship was a precarious task. The ports at Beaufort, Morehead City, Bath, and Wilmington were small. As a result, our neighbor states prospered, and North Carolina struggled in their shadow.

When the Virginian, William Byrd led the survey team that established the Virginia-Carolina border in 1728, he referred to North Carolina as "Lubberland." This is a reference to an old English song about a land where the creeks flow with wine, the crops grow themselves, and the inhabitants are supremely lazy. Here is one quote from Byrd:

> "To speak the truth, 'tis a thorough aversion to labor that makes people file off to N. Carolina, where plenty and a warm sun confirm them in their disposition to laziness for their whole lives.

> "Indian corn is of so great increase that a little pain will subsist a very large family with breads and then they may have meat without any pains at all, by the help of the low grounds, and the great variety of mast that grows on the high land. The men impose all the work upon the poor women. They make their wives rise out of their beds early in the morning at the same time they lie and snore 'til the sun has run one third its course and dispersed all the unwholesome damps. Then, after stretching and yawning for half an hour, they light their pipes and under the collection of a cloud of smoke, venture out into the open air, though if it happens to be ever so little cold, they quickly return shivering to the chimney corner. When the weather is mild, they stand leaning with both arms upon the corn-field fence and gravely consider whether they had best go and take a small heat at the house."

We North Carolinians reacted by calling ourselves "a vale of humility between two mountains of conceit" (an aphorism sometimes attributed to Civil War governor Zebulon Vance but that may have older origins). There is truth to this characterization. Virginia was rich with prosperous plantations and produced many of America's early political leaders. South Carolina's coastal region was also a land of rich agricultural plantations.

By the early 1800s, things were no better. We were known by the nickname, the "Rip Van Winkle state" after Washington Irving's character who went to sleep under a tree and did not wake up for twenty years. We earned this reputation rightfully. Other states of the new nation were engaged in a program of "internal improvements," that is, the building of what we now call "infrastructure:" roads, bridges, and canals. Money from the government in Washington was granted for these projects but some in our legislature considered it unconstitutional to accept such money.

We fell behind for several reasons. One was that the state constitution, quickly drawn up in 1776, apportioned representatives to the legislature just as the English colonial government had. Each county was allowed two representatives to the lower house. Since the western counties were large and the eastern ones small, the easterners had a large advantage even though, by 1830, the center of population had shifted well to the west. This method of apportionment to the legislature allowed the eastern part of the state to continue its domination of the back country. Additionally, the eastern planters were not enthusiastic about letting back country farmers compete with their own farms. Why build roads and canals to help the westerners ship their crops to the coast to compete with the eastern plantations? These conditions set up a serious rivalry between the eastern and western parts of the state. We will amplify on this in Chapter X. For now, we will turn to the arrival of a new form of Baptist worship that led to the founding of our church.

5: SHUBAL STEARNS AND THE SEPARATE BAPTISTS

Now that we have looked at the history of early Orange County, we return to the story of Shubal Stearns, who was so vital for Baptists in the South. His name is unfamiliar to most Southern Baptists today, yet without him it is likely that there would never have been a Cane Creek Baptist Church. Since our church is a "granddaughter" of Stearn's church, we need to know more about this amazing man.

Stearns, born in 1706, was a member of a New England Congregational Church. When the "Great Awakening" reached American shores from its English birthplace in the 1750s, it sparked a spiritual response among some of the Congregationalists that became known as the "New Light" movement. The New Lights embraced a highly emotional style of worship that emphasized a "born again" experience. One could become a devout Christian in a flash, as if struck by a spiritual thunderbolt. The "Old Lights," in contrast, preferred the traditional style of worship in which one slowly and methodically became a Christian by studying the Bible and listening to numerous sermons.

Stearns became strongly attracted to the New Lights after hearing a sermon by George Whitefield in 1754. Conflict between New and Old Lights within his church congregation soon drove Stearns to a more congenial home among a New Light group of Congregationalists who had already split off from their traditional "Old Light" church and who called themselves "Separates." This name was based on Corinthians 6:17 "Come out from among them and be ye separate." Still later, Sterns decided that his views on baptism (i.e., that only believers should be baptized) was closer to those of Baptists. He became a Baptist and an ordained preacher but held on to the designation "Separate." He became the founder of a branch of Baptists known as the Separate Baptists.

Soon Sterns felt God calling him to spread the gospel to the south and west in the "waste places" inhabited by frontiersmen and Indians. He persuaded a small group, including his two sisters and their husbands, to sell their property and move with him to do the Lord's bidding. This was a dramatic life change for a man of almost fifty years and it was at least in part motivated by a feeling that the Second Coming was at hand. In 1754 they landed in Opekon, a small town in northern Virginia, and joined the local Baptist congregation. But from the start they ran afoul of two circumstances. First, was the fact that Virginia had an "established" church under the direct control of the British crown, the Church of England. This was the only religion allowed to be publicly practiced. Failure to pay the "vestry" tax that supported the Established Church was a crime, as was persistent failure to attend weekly church services.

The second circumstance was that the local Baptist Church belonged to the Philadelphia Association, which was highly Calvinistic. Since Calvinists were only lukewarm to evangelism and Stearns was highly evangelistic, there was a conflict that soon led

Stearns and his little band to pack their belongings once again and head farther south to a land where, they had been told, the people were destitute of religion and were so eager to hear the gospel preached that they might ride forty miles to hear one sermon.

The little group arrived in 1755 at Sandy Creek near present-day Liberty (about fifty miles southwest of Cane Creek) and set about building a small meeting house even before building dwellings for themselves. The great Baptist historian, Paschal, states "I make bold to say that these Separate Baptists have proved to be the most remarkable body of Christians America has ever known." It is hard to deny his words. Today the largest Protestant denomination in America is the Southern Baptist Convention. The General Baptists did not create this enormous movement nor did the Particulars. It all began with the Separates at Sandy Creek under the stewardship of Shubal Stearns.

In 1755, North Carolina had a white population of about eighty thousand, and a slave population of about twenty thousand. The state was growing rapidly and much of the growth was due to a southward migration from Pennsylvania and Virginia into the fertile piedmont. It was a propitious time and Sandy Creek was a wisely chosen location, sitting at the intersection of three old Indian trading paths. The colonial governor, Gabriel Johnston, was bemoaning the passage of yet a few more dismal years failing "to civilize a wild and barbarous people." The time and the place were ripe for the planting of a new spiritual seed.

At about the same time Shubal Stearns and the Separates were developing a presence in piedmont North Carolina, other groups were flocking to the area. A large group of Quakers settled around Snow Camp and along the other Cane Creek, which flows into the Haw River from the west. They established their first meeting house in 1751 and within six years had built four more, including one just northeast of Hillsborough. There were probably Quakers in our Orange Grove neighborhood. Alexander Mebane, who held one of our earliest land grants, was a Quaker, as was the father of our first preacher.

Moravians arrived in 1753 and settled in a community they called Salem. Germans of the Lutheran faith came about 1750, settling in what is now northern Alamance County. They kept to themselves and continued to speak German. Travelers passing through the lands just west of Hillsborough often complained that they could find no one who spoke English. This continued well into the 19th century. Scotch Highlanders speaking only Gaelic settled in Cumberland County beginning in the 1730s and continued to follow their Presbyterian faith.

These groups came with established religious leanings and were all the harder to evangelize because they did not speak English. But others were coming into the state as well. Among them were many English, Welsh, Irish, and Scotch-Irish settlers who settled throughout central North Carolina including Orange County. It was among these less religiously oriented settlers that Shubal Stearns experienced his greatest success.

Not long after Stearns and his group built their meeting house, they began to make their presence known in the surrounding countryside in the most forceful of ways. As Morgan Edwards, writing in 1772, notes:

> "Soon after, the neighborhood was alarmed and the Spirit of God listed to blow as a mighty rushing wind in so much that in three years' time they had increased to three churches and upwards of 900 communicants... [Sandy Creek] was a mother church, nay a grandmother and a great-grandmother. All the Separate Baptists sprang hence... The word went forth from this Zion and great was the company of those that published it, in so much that her converts were as drops of morning dew" [Paschal, p271].

What sort of person was this Shubal Stearns, a man who, at the age of fifty, settled in a strange new territory to begin an effort that was to result in the creation of the nation's largest Protestant denomination? According to Morgan Edwards:

> "Mr. Stearns was but a little man, but of good natural parts, and sound judgment. Of learning he had but a small share, yet was pretty well acquainted with books. His voice was musical and strong, which he managed in such a manner, as at one while to make soft impressions on the heart, and fetch tears from the eyes in a mechanical way; and anon to shake the nerves, and to throw the animal system into tumults and perturbations."

Stearns and his following brought strange and unfamiliar ideas with them. Religion was not simply the practice of routine ritual and the obeying of commandments. Stearns wanted everyone to feel conviction and emotion and to experience a born-again revelation. This was the style of the New Lights that had so captivated him at the beginning of The Great Awakening. He brought with him this new style of preaching, which Benedict (1860) describes as:

> "a very warm and pathetic address, accompanied by strong gestures and a singular tone of voice. Being often deeply affected themselves when preaching, correspondent affections were felt by their pious hearers, which were frequently expressed by tears, trembling, screams, and acclamations of grief and joy. All these they brought with them to their new habitation, at which the people were greatly astonished, having never seen things on this wise before."

As reported to Morgan Edwards (1772) by Tiden Laner, a resident of central North Carolina:

> "When the fame of Mr. Stearns' preaching had reached where I live, I felt a curiosity to go and hear him. Upon my arrival, I saw a venerable old man sitting under a peach tree with a book in his hand and the people gathered about him. He fixed his eyes upon me immediately, which made me feel in such a manner as I never had felt before. I turned to quit the place but could not proceed far. I

walked about, sometimes catching his eyes as I walked. My uneasiness increased and became intolerable. I went up to him, thinking that a salutation and shaking hands would relieve me. But it happened otherwise. I began to think that he had an evil eye and ought to be shunned. But shunning him I could no more effect than a bird can shun the rattlesnake when it turns his eyes upon it. When he began to preach, my perturbations increased so that nature could no longer support them, and I sank to the ground."

A Recent Artist's Depiction of Shubal Stearns

Another description from Morgan Edwards concerns Elnathan Davis, who would later establish a church at Haw River and ordain our founding preacher, Thomas Cate. Davis was born in Maryland in 1743. His parents were seventh Day Baptists, i.e., they held services on Saturday. Davis is described as being a youth who was wild and reckless. He moved to North Carolina in 1757. After his conversion, he was ordained in 1764. He was probably first connected with Deep River Baptist Church. The Haw River church was a "daughter" church of Deep River and Davis became its minister. Soon it was the largest church in the region. Purefoy notes that, following the death of Shubal Stearns, Davis was the leading minister of the Sandy Creek Association.

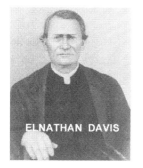

Here is Morgan Edward's description of Elnathan Davis' conversion by Shubal Stearns:

"Elnathan Davis had heard that one John Steward was to be baptized by Mr. Stearns. Now this Mr. Steward being a very big man, and Stearns of small stature, he concluded there could be some diversion if not a drowning;

therefore, he gathered about eight or ten of his companions in wickedness and went to the spot. Shubal Stearns came and began to preach. Elnathan went to hear him, while his companions stood at a distance. He was no sooner among the crowd but he perceived some of the people tremble, as if in a fit of the ague; he felt and examined them, in order to find out if it were not a dissimulation; meanwhile one man leaned on his shoulder, weeping bitterly; Elnathan, perceiving he had wet his new white coat, pushed him off and ran to his companions, who were sitting on a log at a distance. When he came, one said, "Well, Elnathan, what do you think now of these damned people?" He replied, "There is a trembling and crying spirit among them; but whether it be the spirit of God or the devil, I don't know; if it be of the devil, the devil go with them, for I will never more venture myself among them." He stood for a while in this resolution; but the enchantment of Stearns' voice drew him to the crowd once more. He had not been long there before the trembling seized him also; he attempted to withdraw; but, his strength failing and his understanding being confounded, he, with many others, sank to the ground. When he came to himself, he found nothing in him but dread and anxiety, bordering on horror. He continued in this situation some days, and then found relief by faith in Christ. Immediately, he began to preach conversion work, raw as he was, and scanty as his knowledge must have been. He was later pastor at Haw River."

A Recent Artist's Depiction of Fervent Baptist Preaching

One of the first of Stearns' little band to venture out to spread the word was his brother-in-law, Daniel Marshall, who joined an arm of Sandy Creek at Abbots Creek in Davidson County and only needed ordination in order to properly minister to his flock. Since proper Baptist procedures required at least two ordained ministers to perform Marshall's ordination, Stearns sent word to one of the Baptist ministers along the Pee Dee River in South Carolina. The request was stoutly refused, according to Benedict, because the Separates were considered "a disorderly set, suffering women to pray in public, and permitting every ignorant man to preach who chooses, and that they encouraged noise and confusion in their meetings."

Nevertheless, Stearns succeeded in ordaining Marshall and others after him. These dedicated men set out both in North Carolina and in Virginia to spread the Gospel as the Separates saw it. Others spread the word into South Carolina and Georgia.

Within three years of the establishment of his church at Sandy Creek, so many arms of churches and arms of arms had been established that Stearns decided that an association was needed to encourage and direct their efforts. He visited each Church, explaining his ideas with such persuasion that they sent delegates to Sandy Creek in January 1758 to form the Sandy Creek Association. Although the early records are lost, we have the recollections of James Read, who was present:

> "At our first Association we continued together three or four days. Great crowds of people attended mostly through curiosity. The great power of God was among us. The preaching everyday seemed to be attended with God's blessing. We carried on our Association with sweet decorum and fellowship to the end. Then we took leave of one another, with many solemn charges from our reverend old father Shubal Stearns to stand fast to the end" (Paschal, 1930, p, 283).

Benedict (1813) commented on the success of the new association in spreading Baptist influence throughout the state:

> "By means of these [Association] meetings, the gospel was carried into many new places where the fame of the Baptists had previously spread ... Many became enamored of these extraordinary people and petitioned the Association to send preachers into their neighborhood. These petitions were readily granted, and the preachers as readily complied with the appointments. These people were so much engaged with their evangelical pursuits that they had no time to spend in theological debates, nor were they very scrupulous about the mode of conducting their meetings. When assembled, their chief employment was preaching, exhortation, singing, and conversing about their various exertions in the Redeemer's service, the success which had attended them, and the new and prosperous scenes which were opening before them."

The annual association meetings were given over mostly to singing and preaching and prayer. The style and enthusiasm of the preaching attracted settlers from miles around. But some of the time was devoted to business. Here the delegates would discuss matters of church organization and issues of theology. Individual churches that had wrestled with a thorny issue would send a "query" to the Association in hopes that a proper answer could be found. Here are two examples given by G. W. Purefoy (our preacher in the 1840s):

1805: Shall the new exercise, called dancing, be a bar to communion? The answer given was simply "no." ["Dancing" here refers an emotional response to fervent preaching.]

1812: Is it right for a member of the Baptist church to live in the bounds of one church, and hold his membership in another a distance off? The answer was, "No, unless under particular circumstances."

Because the early Sandy Creek records were lost to a fire in 1816, we do not know precisely the original member churches of 1758. From a list dated in the 1770s, we know that the churches closest to Cane Creek were:

Tar River (in Granville County) established in 1753;
Grassy Creek (in Granville County) established in 1754;
Deep River (in Chatham County) established in 1757;
Lockwoods Folly (in Caswell County) established in 1759;
Haw River (at Bynum, now Rock Spring) established in 1764; and
Rocky River (in Chatham County) established in 1776.

All these churches were located in Orange County as it was then constituted but none was closer than a day's ride from Cane Creek. There was no Baptist church in what is now Alamance County, probably because of the overwhelming presence of Quakers in the southern part and of Presbyterians and German Lutherans in the central and northern part. There was also no official Baptist church in what is now Orange County, a matter that we will inquire about later.

The early Sandy Creek Association was very much the creature of Shubal Stearns. The first dozen annual meetings were held at his church although, by 1769, member churches extended into eastern North Carolina, northward into Virginia, and southward into South Carolina and Georgia. Stearns set the agenda. He approved the young men who wished to be ordained, and he visited the member churches to inspire them and to see that they were "orderly." Stearns also visited "waste places" in an attempt to establish new churches.

Perhaps it was inevitable that, in time, Stearns should come to exercise too heavy a hand in the affairs of the local churches. One can imagine the chagrin that a local church might feel when Stearns disagreed with their hopes of ordaining a promising young member of their own congregation. When the Association responded to local church queries, it undoubtedly left a few members disgruntled.

At the 1769 annual meeting, held as usual at Sandy Creek, the growing dissatisfaction came to a head. Two issues arose that began to shatter the blissful unity of the earlier meetings. The first issue had to do with the Separate's relationship with the other Baptist groups in the state. As already mentioned, there were other Baptists present in North Carolina, so-called General Baptists and Particular Baptists. There was considerable animosity between these two groups that had gone on for years. Eventually some cooler heads tried to bring the two groups together. Some of the Particulars, who had aligned with the Charleston Association, broke away and renamed themselves "Regular" Baptists.

So, this first divisive issue to come up at the Sandy Creek Association meeting was the possibility of a union with some of the new Regular Baptist churches to the east. After a long debate, the Association decided against the union. The Separates were just too evangelical, and the new Regulars were still seen as Particulars in disguise. With the possibility of a union gone, the Regulars formed themselves into the Kuhukee Association.

The divisiveness of the 1769 meeting set the stage for the turbulent meeting in 1770. Divisiveness was so much in the air that for three days the delegates could not even decide upon a person to lead the meeting. about it seems the only thing that they could agree on was that it was time for the Association to divide itself. Accordingly, the Virginia churches and the South Carolina churches withdrew and formed themselves into their own associations. The North Carolina churches retained the Sandy Creek name. Perhaps a lesson had been learned. After 1770 the Sandy Creek Association abandoned some of the authority it claimed over local churches.

The estrangement between the Separates and the Regulars continued until 1789 (the same year our church was founded), Finally, the Separates and the Regulars signed a reconciliation agreement that ended with the statement, "we are united and desire hereafter that the names, Regular and Separate, be buried in oblivion and that from henceforth we shall be known by the name of the United Baptist Churches." The term "United Baptists" never took off, but the term "Separate" was seldom used after that year.

Returning to the issues debated at the 1769 Association meeting, the second divisive issue that came up had to do with the so-called Regulator movement that had seized every settler's attention. The movement became a matter of concern for the Association. After much debate, the Association passed a resolution calling upon local churches to excommunicate any member "who takes up arms against legal authority." Such a course of action may have seemed justified in many quarters, but in locations where sympathy ran in favor of the Regulators, chiefly in Orange County, this action must have seemed an improper interference in the affairs of the local churches.

The Regulator movement, or, as some would have termed it, this insurrection, will be the topic of the next chapter. Suffice it to say here that the settlers were aroused by the abuses of their local county officials and were at the point of resorting to violence to do something about it.

6: CANE CREEK AND THE REGULATORS

The Regulator movement, variously called a "war," a "rebellion," an "insurrection," and an "uprising," covers the period 1766-1771 and occurred in the back country of both North and South Carolina. But it was centered in old Orange County. I have so far been unable to uncover any record of Cane Creek involvement with the Regulators but, because of the involvement of North Carolina Baptists in general, I will recount the gist of its history. It is quite possible the there was some Cane Creek participation or at least some Cane Creek sympathy for the movement. And it is also possible that the Regulator troubles influenced Cane Creek attitudes about Baptists before the founding of our church.

The Regulator movement had several underlying causes. One was an unequal balance of influence in colonial affairs between the older wealthier east and the newer more upstart western frontier where Orange County was located. Another cause had to do with the way county officials went about exercising the power of their offices.

In the 1740s, there were scarcely 100 fighting men to be found in the then western portion of the colony, but the population began to grow rapidly so that by 1755 Orange County alone had 2,825 taxable white persons and ten years later had 3,573. When established as a county in 1752, the citizens of Orange County were allowed to elect two representatives to the colonial General Assembly. By 1766, Orange County was the most populous of North Carolina's counties, with a population that exceeded the eastern counties of Pasquotank, Chowan, Currituck, Perquimans, and Tyrell added together. Yet each of those older eastern counties was allowed five representatives in the Assembly and could easily overwhelm any initiative from the western counties. And whenever it became necessary to create a new county in the west, the Assembly was careful to split an eastern county into two new counties to maintain their voting advantage.

The main purpose of governing a colonial county lay in keeping the peace and collecting taxes. The most important government official was the Sheriff. The county court was important since all local matters were decided there(there were no County Commissioners then). The Register of Deeds, the Clerk of Court, Magistrates and Justices of the Peace also held important positions. None of these office holders were elected by the people. All were appointed by the Governor. They performed necessary duties and charged fees for doing so. The only officials that the people were allowed to elect were representatives to the North 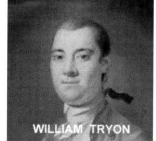 Carolina Assembly, but the Assembly had little power and anything it decided could be overruled by the Colonial Governor, who was then William Tryon.

One especially galling practice of the Governor and of the Colonial Assembly was the levying of a poll tax. A "poll" was a taxable individual and generally it referred to white males. A poll tax, unlike a property tax, fell on each man to the same extent regardless of his wealth or poverty. This became an issue when, in 1766, Governor Tyron decided to locate the colony's capital in New Bern and to build a "palace" for the government and for himself. Prior to that, the capital was wherever the governor happened to be. It moved where he moved. Tryon wanted to find a permanent home for the government. Below is a contemporary drawing of the palace.

Tryon's Palace on a £5 note

The palace cost £15,000 and was to be paid for by a poll tax. This fell most heavily on the populous western frontier counties where the citizens complained that few of them would ever live to see the ornate and luxurious building they were being asked to pay for. They had already paid a poll tax for Tryon's treaty with the Cherokees (which put a damper on settler-Indian conflicts) that cost £20,000. Still another poll tax had financed North Carolina's participation in the French and Indian War. A new tax for a governor's palace was a step too far. It was also widely suspected that a lot of the money would land in the Sherriff's pocket.

At the local level there was ample reason for many of the citizens to hold grievances against those who held office and exercised control over the affairs of the county. The office holder was not paid a salary but instead was paid out of the fees he levied for rendering his service. Fees were established by the Assembly, but they were not published, and it was a common practice for county officials to double or triple the allowable fees and pocket the difference. The county officers were appointed by the Governor and were men who were in his favor and who could be trusted to carry out his wishes. It was also common for the same man to hold several offices. Thus, in Hillsborough, Francis Nash was an Assemblyman, Clerk of Court, Justice of the Peace, member of the County Court, and a Militia Captain. Edmund Fanning was a lawyer, Assemblyman, Register of Deeds, a judge, and a Militia Colonel.

Since Edmund Fanning will play a role in what follows, I will take a moment to describe him. Fanning had no local ties. He was born in New York, graduated from Yale College with a law degree, and was a man of culture and refinement. He loved good clothes and had a fine library in a fine Hillsborough house. He was there to help administer governmental duties in the county. He was well liked within a small group of well-to-do locals, but he shared the aristocratic view that the local settlers were his inferiors. Indeed, he considered them to be rude ignorant savages. He despised them and they returned the favor.

EDMUND FANNING

Another problem had to do with the general lack of currency in the colony. Farmers would send their produce to the eastern part of the colony to a warehouse and receive a receipt in lieu of currency. A warehouse receipt could almost be treated as currency in Orange County, but taxes had to paid in hard cash; a warehouse receipt would not work. And when a settler could not produce the currency to pay his tax, the Sheriff and his deputies could "distrain" (seize) any of the man's property they liked and auction it off to pay the tax. Needless to say, these actions by the Sheriff outraged the settlers.

One of the earliest of the settlers' grievances was over the actions of the Granville's Land Agents, Francis Corbin and Thomas Child. It was suspected that they deliberately deeded the same tract of land to more than one settler and collected fees from all of them. In the Granville District it was important for a new landowner to prove and register his deed within one year of its issuance. Corbin and Child were well known to charge excessively for seeing that the required paperwork was done in a timely manner. In Hillsborough, Edmund Fanning was known to regularly charge four times the legal fee to register a deed. Those who complained about taxes and exorbitant fees were jailed and charged with libel. No wonder there were general complaints against, "the courthouse ring" and "the Sheriff and his bums."

The wrath of the settlers can be seen in the fact that the name of the county seat, originally called Corbinton (in honor of Francis Corbin), was changed in 1759 to Childsburg (in honor of Thomas Child) and in 1766 to Hillsborough. This change was made on order of Governor Tryon, Who wanted to salve some of the local outrage at having the town named after despised men. But he also wanted to make the town into a "borough," which entitled the town to have its own representative in the Assembly. Edmund Fanning was appointed to this position. Of course, this created more resentment.

There were also grievances of a more religious nature. When Tryon took office as Governor in 1765, one of his primary goals was to spread the Church of England throughout the colony and to check the spread of dissenters. Francis Corbin sponsored the Act for Establishment [of the Church of England] in the Assembly, which divided the colony into "vestries" and authorized each to levy a tax to pay the salary of a minister. In the face of general non-compliance by the population, Tryon appealed to London – to The Society for the Propagation of the Gospel – for financial support to establish the Church of England. By 1770 he was able to place Anglican ministers in 18 of the colony's

32 vestries. Tryon well knew that his actions were wildly unpopular with dissenters. The hotbed of resentment was in the back country. Tryon referred to the protestors as ruffians and labeled them a bunch of Quakers and Baptists.

Another grievance concerned marriages. It was particularly galling that only ministers of the Church of England were allowed to conduct marriages that were considered legal in the eyes of the law. A special arrangement with Presbyterians allowed their ministers to conduct legal marriages but this privilege was withdrawn in the Marriage Act of 1766. The only way around this law was that local magistrates were allowed to perform marriages. Some Baptist preachers managed to get themselves appointed a magistrate.

The Orange County leaders of the protest group were located near Sandy Creek and some may have been members of Shubal Stearns' church. Herman Husband, a Quaker, was the intellectual head. He was well educated and was the author of several important publications called Regulator Advertisements. Another leader, James Hunter, was a more hot-headed man who advocated the use of force. Some of the violence that followed could be attributed to him and his gang of friends.

The first action taken by the disgruntled settlers centered near Sandy Creek. Tryon had just ordered the poll tax to pay for his palace. The Sandy Creek settlers knew well of Tryon's hatred of Quakers and Baptists and this section of the back country was a hotbed of both. They warned the Sheriff not to distrain them for failure to pay the tax. In August 1766 they printed and circulated "Regulator Advertisement Number One," which called for a general public meeting to "inquire whether free men of this County labor under abuses of power or not." County officials were invited to the meeting held near Deep River at Maddock's Mill, close to the home of Herman Husbands. Late on the day of the meeting an officer appeared from Hillsborough and said that Edmund Fanning considered the meeting an insurrection and would not tolerate it. The twelve assembled men thereupon issued "Advertisement Number Three," again calling for a general meeting and offering to meet with county officials anytime and anyplace.

In 1767 the disgruntled citizens petitioned Tryon and the Colonial Assembly concerning their grievances. This petition was rebuffed although Tryon did warn Orange County officials about charging illegal fees for their services.

In 1768 citizens, despairing of any official action on their behalf, came together to create an organization. They called themselves Regulators, so named because they sought to impose some regulation on the actions of County officials. They announced specific grievances in "Advertisement Number Four." In sum, they asserted that:

> "We will pay no taxes until we are satisfied that they are agreeable to law and are applied to purposes therein mentioned unless we cannot help it and are forced" and "we will pay no officer any more fees than the law allows unless we are obliged to it and then to show a dislike to it and bear open testimony against it."

Following this, in a masterstroke of bad timing, the Sheriff distrained a Regulator's horse for nonpayment of taxes. Seventy Regulators thereupon rode into Hillsborough, seized the horse, and fired shots into Fanning's house. Immediately, Fanning appealed to Tryon for help, saying that "the late orderly and well-regulated County of Orange is now the very nest and bosom of rioting and rebellion." Tryon's response was to issue two Proclamations, one to the Regulators to desist and the other to the militia in several counties to ready themselves to go to the aid of Fanning.

The Regulators responded by taking scores of depositions against the actions of County officials. A petition complaining about "paying fees more than the law allows" was circulated and got almost 500 signatures. All these were sent to Tryon, whose response again was to order the Regulators to disband, pay their taxes, and not molest county officers. But he also warned local county officials once more about illegal fees and ordered that a list of lawful fees be published so that all citizens could know the proper amounts.

In September 1768 matters appeared headed toward a bloody confrontation. Husband had been arrested for inciting a rebellion. Fanning had been indicted for taking excessive fees. Both were scheduled for trial in Hillsborough. Rumors began to fly that Tryon was raising the militia and negotiating with the Indians to attack from the west. County officials feared that the Regulators were arming themselves for a confrontation. On the day of the trials the town was packed, by Husband's estimation, with over 3,500 Regulators. Tryon himself was present with a small army of militia.

The expected battle did not materialize. Husband was acquitted. Fanning was convicted, paid a fine of one cent, and resigned as Register of Deeds. For a brief moment, it looked as if the Regulators had made their point.

Tryon Reprimanding the Regulators

But conditions were not remedied, and the Regulators did not desist. In the fall of 1769, they roused the citizens to elect men to the Colonial Assembly with strong Regulator sympathies in Orange, Granville, Anson, and Halifax counties. There was civil unrest throughout the western counties. In September 1770, Hillsborough again became the focus of attention as many cases both for and against Regulators were scheduled for trial. The town once again filled with angry settlers. When court convened, the Regulators marched in, announced that they could receive no justice from the court, and took over the bench. They severely beat the judge, and Edmund Fanning was dragged out by his heels with his head banging on every step. They then proceeded to try their own cases and left town, but not before burning Fanning's library, wreaking his house and running him out of town.

In response to this challenge to his authority, Tryon reacted by having the Assembly pass the Riot Act authorizing county officials to act ruthlessly against the Regulators. The Regulators, growing in numbers and audacity, declared Fanning an outlaw to be killed on sight, forbade any court session, and threatened all judges and lawyers with death.

Tryon ordered a special court session to be held in Hillsborough in the spring of 1771 and called out the militia to stand guard. The militia, with 1,452 men, camped along the Great Alamance Creek on May 16. About 2,000 Regulators appeared and asked for an audience with Tryon. He refused and gave them an hour to lay down their arms and disperse. At the end of the hour Tryon attacked and routed the Regulators in the so-called Battle of Alamance. (The battleground is now a park on NC62 south of I-40.) Both sides lost nine men killed and a larger number wounded but the fight was entirely one-sided. The militia was well armed and disciplined. The Regulators were a rag-tag untrained group with neither officers nor organization.

After the battle, Tryon marched to Sandy Creek, laying waste to Regulator farms, and then on to John Gano's Jersey Settlement on the Yadkin River. There, he arrested six Regulators and took them back to Hillsborough for trial as traitors. Garland Hendricks, in his history of the Jersey settlement written in 1964, tells us what happened to Benjamin Merrill, a member of Gano's Baptist church. Here is what the trial judge proclaimed (if you are the least bit queasy, you may want to skip over this quote):

> "You, Benjamin Merrill, shall be carried to the place from whence you came; that you shall be drawn from thence to the place of execution where you are to be hanged by the neck; that you be cut down while yet alive; that your bowels be taken out while you are yet alive and burnt before your face; that your head be cut off, and your body be divided into four quarters, and this to be at his Majesty's disposal; and the Lord have mercy on your soul."

REGULATORS HANGED
After the Regulators were defeated at Alamance, May 16, 1771, six of their number were hanged. 1/4 mile east, June 19, 1771.

Five other Regulators suffered a similar fate. The historical marker in Hillsborough commemorating this atrocity is above. For all practical purposes, the Battle of Alamance settled the issue. Tryon called for all Regulators to throw down their arms and sign an oath of allegiance and agree to pay lawful taxes. Six thousand four hundred and nine people did so. The battle won, Tryon departed North Carolina and headed north to become governor of New York. Interestingly, Governor Martin, Tryon's successor, was much more sympathetic to the Regulators. He took several tangible steps to address their grievances and soon had their grudging admiration, enough so that when the first rumblings of the American Revolution broke out prior to 1776, Martin enjoyed the support of the former regulators. When the revolution broke out, however, virtually all of the remaining Regulators took the patriot's side, so much so that when Cornwallis occupied Hillsborough in 1781 with the intent of restoring Governor Martin to power, he complained that "I could not get 100 men in all of the Regulator's Country to stay with us even as a militia."

The Regulators and Religion

The so-called War of Regulation had a profound influence on religion in the west. From the beginning, Tryon had considered that the trouble was centered among the Quakers and Baptists, "the first no friend, the latter an avowed enemy of the mother church."

What was the truth about Baptist participation in the War of Regulation? Was Tryon accurate in portraying the rebellion as being caused by a bunch of Quakers and Baptists? It is certain that the region was filled with members of both groups. But Morgan Edwards, who visited many Baptist Churches along the Atlantic seaboard, wrote in 1772 that he had examined the matter carefully and found only seven Baptists who had been dismissed from their churches for participating in armed rebellion. He pointed to a resolution at the annual meeting of the Sandy Creek Baptist Association in 1768. A motion was passed forbidding participation in the war on pain of excommunication. A similar resolution was passed in 1769 by the church at Haw River, the mother church of Cane Creek. Technically, the church resolutions said that participation in the Regulator movement **and** the practice of violence could lead to excommunication. The word "and" seems to mean that it was alright to be a member of the Regulators but violence was forbidden. Indeed, the _Biblical Recorder_ for October 16, 1889 presents an historical sketch of the Haw River church and reports that the church had once passed a resolution saying "Resolved, that any member of this church who shall fail or refuse to join the Regulators shall be excommunicated." This seems to be conclusive evidence that many Baptists were involved in the War of Regulation. There are also known Baptists, some at Haw River and some at Sandy Creek, who signed the Regulator petitions. The same might be said for the Quakers.

The Baptist historian, G. W. Paschal, writing in 1930, had this to say about Baptist participation:

> "... after the battle of Alamance, one would gain the impression that the entire Baptist population of the central and western counties belonged to the organization whose purpose was to secure redress of grievances and relief

from unjust taxes and extortion of officers. As many as belonged to this organization, whether they fought at Alamance or sought redress by peaceful means, must be regarded as Regulators. With the Regulator movement especially strong in Baptist communities it cannot be doubted that nearly the whole body of Baptists were in the organization ... After the battle of Alamance those who came into the different camps and took the required oath of submission numbered 6,049. Including participants and active sympathizers not sworn, and the women and children, the population involved must have been at least 50,000 ... the great body of the white people in the territory east of the mountains and west of what is now Wake County. As the settlers in that section between Haw River and Deep River and south of Cane Creek [that other Cane Creek] were for the most part Baptists in belief, there can be no doubt that they were among the supporters of the Regulation ... No other political movement in our history has had such a far-reaching effect on the development of the Baptists in the entire south as the Regulator movement."

After the Battle of Alamance many of those who had been forced to swear an oath of allegiance to Tyron, fearing that they could never escape persecution where they lived, packed their possessions and moved, some to Tennessee (then still a part of North Carolina) and Kentucky and some southward to South Carolina and Georgia. Wherever they settled they established Baptist churches of the Shubal Stearns variety. Stearns' own church at Sandy Creek was a particularly striking example of the effect of the Regulator defeat. Before the Battle of Alamance, the mother church of all Southern Baptists had a membership of 606. Afterwards it had diminished to fourteen.

And what of the settlers at Cane Creek? How did they stand on the matter? Undoubtedly, Cane Creek settlers were sympathetic to the complaints of the Regulators. Such sympathy was widespread throughout the county, so much so that Tryon had trouble raising militia troop anywhere in Orange County. But it is also true that the Regulators contained some unruly hotheads that were given to violence and rash action. It may be that Cane Creekers wished to steer a middle course through these several years of turmoil and civil unrest. A list of 883 known Regulators, published in 1942, contains no Kirks, Brewers, Cates, O'Daniels, or any other name of a landowner in the Cane Creek neighborhood. The only names that might come close to being community people are Joshua Edwards, Thomas Lloyd, Jacob McDaniel, Abraham Strowd, Robert Thompson, and Robert Woody.

It would be interesting to inspect the list of 6,409 residents to whom Tryon gave amnesty. Unfortunately, the list has never been found. It may no longer exist or it may still be in some musty archive in London.

As we turn back to the history of the early Cane Creek church, we might ponder what effect, if any, the Regulator turmoil had on our ancestors. Could it be that the reputation of Baptists as being Regulator agitators affected how local settlers viewed Shubal Stearns' Separate Baptists?

Our history has taken us up to the end of the Regulator movement in 1771. This is still 18 years before the creation of our church. Many of these years were filled with our war of revolution. We shall look at it next and learn of another notorious man named Fanning, who was no relation to the aristocratic Edmund.

7: CANE CREEK AND THE REVOLUTIONARY WAR

The first hostilities between the colonies and the British government broke out in New England, in 1775. In 1776, a Continental Congress was convened in Philadelphia. All the 13 colonies sent delegates. They produced a Declaration of Independence. This was a dangerous and radical thing to do. If the British had won the struggle, these men would have lost all their property and, like some of the Regulators in North Carolina, would have been hanged as traitors.

GENERAL CORNWALLIS

The early part of the war was fought in the north and for months things looked bleak for the patriots. This began to change when, on Christmas Eve of 1776, Washington crossed the Delaware River and caught a bunch of British mercenaries by surprise. He quickly followed up by marching on Trenton and defeating British Hessian mercenaries before retreating back across the Delaware and holing up for the winter. When these victories happened, the colonists began to take heart and hope that they might succeed after all.

But things dragged on for years with neither side gaining much advantage. It began to look like a war of attrition to see who could hold out longest. The British commanders decided on a new strategy. They would secretly set sail for Charleston and Savannah with a large army headed by General Cornwallis, and there they would take advantage of what they saw as an American weakness. They thought that in the South they would meet with many sympathetic settlers who would clamor to join the British army. In this way, with his army enlarged by southern recruits, Cornwallis would sweep northward through South Carolina, then North Carolina, and then into Virginia, the home of the most reviled patriots. This would surely break the Americans' spirit.

NATHANIAL GREENE

At about the same time, George Washington asked Nathanael Greene to take charge of the army in the south. Greene knew that he was at a disadvantage because he now had command of many disjointed militia groups that had never worked together. He decided to follow a guerilla style of warfare where he would strike suddenly and then retreat suddenly, hoping to wear down the British army.

Cornwallis' southern coastal plan worked for a while. In the spring of 1780, he took control of Georgia and much of South Carolina, and then set his mind on taking upstate South Carolina and then moving into North Carolina. Cornwallis recruited some Tory militias and won some minor victories. But things began to go sour for Cornwallis at the battle of Cowpens. Cornwallis had wintered in Charlotte and then opened the 1781 spring campaign in the South Carolina back-country. Here a patriot army of about 2,000 had a two-to-one advantage over the British and inflicted heavy losses on them.

Then came the battle of King's Mountain. British Major Patrick Ferguson had a detachment of about 1,100 men returning from a raid up to the North Carolina mountains and was planning to meet up with Cornwallis, whose army was in Charlotte. They encamped on top of Kings Mountain, thinking they had found the safest spot to be found. About an equal number of patriot soldiers knew where Ferguson and his men were. This was a ragtag bunch of individual militias. John Sevier brought his "over mountain boys" from northeast Tennessee (just beyond Boone), another group came from Virginia, and there was a strong presence of North Carolina men. Altogether they had about 2,000 men, but nobody was in charge. During a savage two-hour battle, General Ferguson was killed, his detachment suffered many losses, and many of the British surrendered. Patriot losses were light. The battle of King's Mountain and the next battle were turning points in the southern part of the war.

Despite his heavy losses at Cowpens, Cornwallis still had by far the greatest military force in the south. He took his main army and pursued General Greene northward, in what came to be known as "the race to the Dan (River)." Greene kept his forces just ahead of Cornwallis even though Cornwallis destroyed his own supply wagons to speed up his forward movement. He thought that defeating Greene would lead to a final British victory.

Greene's forces got to the Dan River just two hours before the British did. They commandeered all the boats they could find and crossed the river during a flood. Cornwallis, seeing that there was no way he could cross the river, took his army south to Hillsborough. Both armies were exhausted from the two-hundred-mile race and needed time to recoup and re-supply. In Hillsborough, Cornwallis thought that surely he would be able to recruit many of the old Regulators to his side, but this did not happen.

The next battle took place at the Guilford County Courthouse in March 1781. The Americans again had a two-to-one advantage in manpower, but the British were a better disciplined army and drove the patriots from the field. But this success came at a steep price as the British suffered much greater losses of men than the patriots – 25% to 6% – leading a member of Parliament to say, "Another such victory will ruin the British army."

Cornwallis then took his army to Wilmington, where the last remnants of the North Carolina colonial government were hunkered down in the harbor on a warship. He rested and resupplied his army and then marched off to Yorktown. Here he expected to meet up with the British naval fleet, be resupplied, and continue northward into Virginia. What he did not know was that the French navy had created a blockade to keep British ships away and that the patriot's General Washington was rushing his troops southward to cut Cornwallis off. These developments led to the final defeat of the British at Yorktown in October 1781.

How did the war affect our community? There is a faint community memory of a revolutionary war skirmish known as the battle of Kirk's Farm that happened just south of Cane Creek on Teer Road. There would be no way to learn more had not someone written about it. The Reverend Eli Caruthers was the minister at Alamance Presbyterian Church. He was an amateur historian who interviewed many Revolutionary War veterans. He also made use of the historical writings of Governor Swain. In 1854 he published _Revolutionary Incidents._ This book is the source of the information that follows. A copy of the book is in our church library.

Eli Caruthers

Soon after the Declaration of Independence in 1776, the colonial government of the North Carolina Colony (the Tories) removed itself to Wilmington for safety's sake. The patriots (the Whigs) set up a provisional state government and tried to keep basic governmental functions going. But the state sank into a dangerously lawless condition that led to the rise of various desperadoes and guerilla bands that thought, "Where there is no law, there can be no transgression."

In the countryside, things were in an uncertain status for much of the war's duration. The old cliché is that about one-third of the population were patriots, one-third were Tories, and one-third kept quiet until they could see how things were going. Locally, there was likely more sympathy for the patriot's side, but this sentiment was not unanimous. Our first preacher was Thomas Cate, who was married to an Estridge. The name Estridge is associated with the Tories. My understanding is that her father's land, located a mile or so northeast of the church, was confiscated by the State after the war. Also, there are Edwards on the Tory side mentioned in Caruthers's narrative. There were quite a few Edwards land grants located just south of the church around Highway 54. There was also an Estridge serving with a Tory guerrilla group.

During much of the war there were few outright battles between armies in the state other than the battle of Guilford Courthouse. Instead, both sides mustered local fighting groups that conducted raids from time to time. In between raids, these men tended their farms. The most notorious Tory fighting group was mustered by David Fanning. He had a solid core of about 30 or 40 men but could raise a larger force for an important conflict.

Fanning on Baby Joe

Fanning was born in 1754 and was trained in carpentry and loom making. Caruthers wrote that he thinks that, beginning at around age 16, Fanning stayed for several years with "John O'Deniell, who lived in Orange County." This may actually have been John O'Daniel, who had a land grant roughly in the vicinity of Apple Mill our early church rolls list several O'Daniels). Here, Fanning learned to read and write, became a craftsman, and picked up a reputation as a skillful breaker of wild horses. He suffered from "scald head" that cost him his hair, so he always wore a silk cap to cover his baldness. He had no known connection to Hillsborough's Edmund Fanning, who had provoked the ire of the Regulators .

Caruthers describes David Fanning as intelligent and resourceful but adds, "His powers were developed under the influence of poverty, disease, and neglect … without any moral or religious training." His actions earned him special notoriety, "and made his name, not only from that time to the present, but for generations to come, a reproach and a byword for infamy."

Fanning's notorious career began in 1776. He declared himself a Whig but while on a trading venture in South Carolina was beaten and robbed by a band who called themselves Whigs. So, Fanning changed sides and joined with a South Carolina Tory guerilla leader by the name of McGirth. He continued with McGirth for several years before returning to North Carolina early in 1781. For a while he lurked to the south of Deep River.

When Fanning carried out a small but successful raid across the Deep River, his actions caught the attention of British Major Craig, who thereupon made Fanning a Colonel and gave him a British uniform and a sword. Fanning soon acquired "Bay Doe," a mare of such special quality that her bloodlines are still traced among the very best racehorses of today.

James Cheek, a member of our church who was born in 1874, reported a story he heard from his grandfather regarding the attempted hanging of a rebel in Hillsborough during the war. He mistakenly calls the man a Regulator but this was after the Regulator uprising had been suppressed so Cheek's use of the term may have intended to identify a patriot:

> "A Regulator by the name of Andrew Hunter was on the gallows with the noose around his neck when Colonel David Fanning rode up and dismounted, leaving on his saddle a brace of pistols which had been given to him. Hunter, seeing his chance to escape, threw off the noose, leaped on the horse and galloped away, pistols and all. Seeing the soldiers preparing to shoot at the fleeing man, Colonel Fanning told them to shoot high, as he wanted to save his much-prized horse, Baby Doe, which had been given to him by a loyalist."

After being named a Colonel, Fanning carried out a number of swift and daring raids. He took the courthouse at Pittsboro and carried off prisoners to Wilmington, where the British colonial government was located. He raided and captured Fayetteville. In between, he fought several battles against superior numbers and always came out the winner. His name struck fear in patriot hearts.

Fanning learned that the North Carolina state government was going to settle itself in Hillsborough for a while. In September 1781 he hatched a plot to raid the town and capture Governor Burke. Fanning and his men joined Colonel McNeill's 600 Scotsmen, crossed the Deep River, and headed north. He received word from a scout that a party of patriots was encamped at Kirk's farm and that this was the only obstacle to a surprise raid on Hillsborough. This farm was located on Teer Road close to where Rebecca Crawford lived until recent years. In those days, I think that Clover Garden-Orange Chapel Road continued on north of Highway 54, went through the Kirk's farm and paralleled Cane Creek past where the Cane Creek Meeting House was to be built after the war.

Caruthers gives this account of the Kirk's farm skirmish:

> "They came up just as the day was dawning and killed the sentinel, a man by the name of Couch, who had been posted at the end of the lane ... then lay in ambush ... The [Whig] party moved out under Captain Allen ... The Tories emerged from their concealment and a severe conflict ensued in which some important lives were lost on both sides ...Captains Allen and Young (Whigs) were both severely wounded, the former recovered but the latter died."

Caruthers goes on to say that three of Fanning's men were Edwards – Richard, Edward, and Meredith. Richard was killed in the battle.

The skirmish did not deter Fanning and Colonel McNeil. They continued north, raided Hillsborough, captured the Governor, sacked the town, drank all the whiskey they could find, and headed back south to deliver Governor Burke to British authorities in Wilmington.

Along the way Fanning fought a battle at the other Cane Creek, on the south side of Haw River. Fanning's fifty men joined a band of about 800 Scots loyalists and engaged General Butler and his 600 patriots. It ended in a standoff and Fanning's prisoners were delivered to Wilmington in September 1781. On October 19, Cornwallis surrendered at Yorktown. This led to the release of Governor Burke but not to the end of the rampages of David Fanning. If anything, they increased in ferocity. He waylaid bands of patriot soldiers returning home from the war and continued to burn the farms of Whigs and to murder their owners.

In Hillsborough, several notorious members of Fanning's gang had been captured, tried and sentenced to be hanged. Among them were Meredith Edwards and Thomas Estridge. Edwards was one of the Edwards clan living on land grants to the south near NC54 and whose brother had been killed at the Kirk's farm skirmish. Another Edwards brother fell at the Battle of Cane Creek. Thomas Estridge may have been the father of our first preacher's wife, Sarah.

Fanning, hearing of the capture and trials of his men, wrote an enraged letter to Governor Burke threatening that if the men were hanged "I will retaliate blood for blood and tenfold for one." Thomas Cate and other prominent Orange County citizens petitioned to spare the life of Thomas Estridge, but the men were hanged.

Fanning was true to his word. He raided up Deep River. As the historian Caruthers put it:

> "For some weeks after, a state of suffering and distress existed in Randolph County, especially in the upper parts, which can hardly be conceived. Many of the most respectable men in the county, prominent Whigs, who had been active in the cause, and a number of peaceable inoffensive men, who had taken no active part on either side, were murdered in the most shocking manner. Houses and barns were burned with everything they contained. Beddings and comforts of every kind were destroyed, and many families, hitherto in affluent circumstances, were left to beggary and absolute starvation. All this was done from an insatiable spirit of revenge for the British had been driven from the country."

Once Cornwallis had surrendered, few patriots had the stomach to once again shoulder arms to go after Fanning, but eventually some patriots did get on his trail. In May 1782, seeing that the loyalist cause was lost, Fanning made his way to Charleston where, by treaty, the remnants of the British army and Tory sympathizers were allowed to gather and ship out.

Fanning left behind a fearsome reputation. Caruthers says, "Fanning inflicted more injury on the country, and was more dreaded at the time, than any other man and many of his crimes and deeds of violence would live in the traditions of people, from age to age." When the North Carolina General Assembly passed a general act of amnesty in 1783 in an attempt to put to rest any lingering antagonisms remaining between old patriots and old loyalists, David Fanning was mentioned by name as being exempt from amnesty.

Fanning went to Nova Scotia where he managed to work himself into a position of respectability. Maintaining the pretense may, however, have been too much of a strain. In 1800 he was tried and convicted of raping the daughter of an acquaintance. On hearing his death sentence, Fanning appealed for enough time "to make peace with my maker." Several months were granted. Fanning used this time to apply to the British crown for a pardon (and even a pension!). To support his petition, he sent an account of his exploits in North and South Carolina as a loyal supporter of the Tory cause. Fanning's petition was granted and he was pardoned. He lived out his life in Nova Scotia, dying in 1825. His writings passed from hand to hand and eventually were published (only 50 copies) in Richmond in 1861. I have recently obtained a copy and put it in our church library.

In his narrative, Fanning presents himself as simply a loyal British subject who fought nobly for his King against a wicked insurrection and who was unfortunate enough to wind up on the losing side. He quotes Psalms 37:37: "Mark the perfect man and behold the upright, for the end of that man is peace."

This is Fanning's account of the raid on Hillsborough:

> "At 7 o'clock on the morning of the 12th [of September] we entered the town in three divisions and received several shots from different houses; however, we lost none except one man wounded. We killed fifteen of the Rebels and wounded twenty and took upwards of two hundred prisoners; amongst them was the Governor, his Council, and part of the continental Colonels, several captains and subalterns, and seventy-one continental soldiers out of a church. We proceeded to the gaol [prison] and released thirty Loyalists and British soldiers, one of which was to have been hanged on that day. About 12 o'clock, I left."

Unfortunately, Fanning was not at the battle of Kirk's farm and does not write about it. Caruthers says that about 30 of Fanning's men engaged about 20 Patriots there and that about a third on both sides were killed or wounded.

Sam Crawford of our community passed the following remembrance to me. In his neighborhood there is the faint recollection of where the Battle of Kirk's Farm took place. There are said to be traces of graves of those who fell in the battle. He said that long ago a local resident dug up one of the graves and recovered buttons and buckles which she then proudly displayed on her mantle, much to the disgust of her neighbors. I wish someone would locate these graves.

Now that we have covered the major events of early Orange County, from its origin up to the Revolutionary War, we will return to the founding of our church after the war ended.

8: THE ORIGIN OF THE CHURCH AT CANE CREEK

The first settlers arrived at Cane Creek in the 1750s. Within 30 years virtually all land was in private hands and being cultivated by the families who resided on it. A road had been opened from Hillsborough to Woody's Ferry on the Haw River. It followed, approximately, the present route of Orange Grove Road and then onto Bradshaw Quarry Road. Another road would soon reach westward into Haw Fields and eastward toward what was to become Chapel Hill. It closely followed Dairyland Road and went across Cane Creek near where Cecil and Mae Crawford used to live.

By 1780 the best land had been in cultivation for a generation by families such as the Andrews, Kirks, Brewers, O'Daniels, Moores, Lloyds, and Cates. It is chancy to hazard a guess as to the size of the local population. If we assume that each land grant was occupied by a family of five then by 1780 there were about 500 individuals within a five-mile radius of the present church, not counting slaves. This seems a sizable enough population to support a church. Therefore, a question that we shall consider is why it took so long to establish a church at Cane Creek. Another question is why the church at Cane Creek, established in 1789 and led by a preacher who was an ordained Baptist minister, took until 1806 to become a Baptist church.

As far as we have been able to discover, the history of our church begins in 1789 when a small group of Cane Creek settlers came together to act as trustees to buy an acre of land from Thomas Durham for twenty shillings for "Cain Creek Meeting House."

To be truthful to the record, however, I must cite A. G. Crawford's history written in 1930 (*see* Appendix 1), which refers to a "local tradition" that the origin of the church is really 1785. In those days, people wishing to establish a church, often met in private homes. We are not told the source for this tradition and so must let it pass for now as only an interesting hypothesis. But we do not have to leave the matter exactly there.

In the old records in Hillsborough, I have located a couple of cryptic references to a "Meadow Meeting House" as early as 1785 in Orange County records of The Court of Pleas and Quarter Sessions. The references come in connection with the upkeep of roads in the community. In those days the presiding judge would appoint an "overseer" whose duty it was to recruit his neighbors to maintain a designated stretch of a public road. In this case, there are two stretches of interest, one from Woody's Ferry (on Haw River in Alamance County) to the Meadow Meeting House and another one from The Meadow Meeting House to a location closer to Cane Creek.

The clue that the Meadow Meeting House was in the community lies in the names of the overseers and his crew. They bear names of people who lived in the vicinity of Toms Creek. We might speculate that settlers involved in this meeting house later may have been involved in beginning our church.

This Indenture made the twentieth day August in the year of our Lord one thousand Seven Hundred and Eighty Nine Between Thomas Durham of Orange County of the one part and Thomas Cate preacher, Thomas Cate Robert Cate John Strother Richard Cate John Workman Barnerd Cate Joseph Cate, Mary Christmas Jointly Trustees of Orange County of the other part Witnesseth That for and in Consideration of the Sum of Twenty Shillings North Carolina Currency to the Said Thomas Durham in hand payed by the Said Thomas Cate preacher or either of the above mentioned Trustees at or before the Sealing and Delivery of these presents the Receipt whereof he doth hereby acknowledge and therefore doth Release acquit and Discharge the Said Thomas Cate Preacher or either of the above mentioned Trustees them or their heirs, Executors, and administrators by these presents he the Said Thomas Durham hath Granted Bargained Sold, aliened, and Confirmed, and by these presents doth Grant, Bargain Sell, alien and Confirm unto the Said Thomas Cate preacher & the Rest of the above mentioned names of the Trustees Jointly they or their heirs a Sertain piece or parsell of Land Sittuat Lying and being in the County of Orange and State aforesaid for the use of Building a meeting house to hold publick meetings in and Thanksgivings, for the for the Mearces and Blessings of Almighty God. Bounded as followeth, Begining at a Black oak at the old path joining John Strothers line, then along the old path to a Hickory adjoining John Strothers line, thence East along John Strothers line to a post Oak, Thence a Direct line to the Begining Containing [...] more or less, and all Houses, Buildings, ways waters, Watercourses, profitts

Tenements and appurtenances whatsoever to the Said premises, hereby Granted or any part thereof Belonging or in any ways appertaining, and the Reversion and Reversions, Remainder and Remainders Rents Isphues and Profitts thereof & all the Estate Right, title, Interest, use, Trust, property, Claim, and Demand whatsoever, of him the said Thomas Durham of in and to the Said premises and all [...] evidences, and writings Touchings, or in any ways Concerning the same. *To have and to Hold* the land hereby Conveyed, and all and Singular the premises hereby Bargained and Sold and every part and parcel thereof with their every of their appurtenances unto the Said Thomas Cate Preacher Trustee and the rest of the above named Trustees all jointly them and their heirs and of que for ever to the only proper use and behoof of him the Said Thomas Cate preacher trustee and the rest of the above named Trustees all jointly them and their heirs for ever, and the said Thomas Durham doth Covenant and agree that I have absolute authority to grant and convey the same to the above Trustees in maner and form aforesaid In Witness whereof the Said Thomas Durham hath hereunto set his hand and seal the day and year first above Written

Signed Sealed and delivered
in the presence of us   Thomas Durham (Seal)

Thomas Basket Iah s.
Mark Couper

1789 church deed recorded in Hillsborough

But there is a final clue as to the actual time of origin. In 1830 the minutes of the Sandy Creek Association (housed in the Southern Baptist Library at Wake Forest University) indicate the appointment of an historical committee to determine, among other things, the date of origin of the member churches. This was done on the spot. That is, the resolution was passed early in the meeting and a report was made before the final adjournment. Thus, it is probably the case that a poll was taken that drew on nothing more that the memory of the older delegates. The date indicated for Cane Creek was 1790, very close to the date on our original deed. Therefore, until solid evidence comes along to prove otherwise, we should stick with 1789 as the date of our founding, more particularly, August 20, 1789.

One reason why it took so long to establish a church may have been the terrible wrangling over land rights arising out of the Strudwick affair discussed in Chapter 4. The "intruders" that Strudwick attempted to throw off his land were properly indignant. Many of them held what they assumed to be legitimate land grants from the Earl of Granville and many others felt that although they had no official claim to the land, nevertheless they had done all they could to secure a proper title: they had applied for a grant and were waiting for the legal wheels to grind following the death of Earl of Granville and the closing of his land offices.

Another reason why the church at Cane Creek was so long in coming may have been the Regulator movement. The hotbed of Regulator sentiment was south and west of Cane Creek along that other Cane Creek where many Quakers settled and where Shubal Stearns' church was. Many Baptists were listed as Regulators. Could our community have been uneasy about the violence surrounding the movement?

Our first pastor was Thomas Cate. His name is given on the 1789 deed and shown on the last page (a readable transcription is given on the next page). We know just a bit about the religious development of our first preacher. He grew up in a Quaker family. When he and his two brothers arrived at Cane Creek there was no nearby Quaker meeting house so the family may have been without a spiritual home.

We know another interesting detail from a curious source. There is an 18th century index of American Baptist Churches that was compiled by John Asplund, who had an interesting life story. He was a Swede, probably born in the 1750s, who went to England and worked as a clerk. During the Revolutionary War he was abruptly impressed into service in the Royal Navy and served aboard a war ship along the American coast. Somehow, he was able to desert and wound up in eastern North Carolina. In 1782 he joined with a Baptist church near New Bern. He tried preaching but was not very good at it. He then decided to make a registry of America's Baptist churches. Here are his words:

> "I have long been desirous to see a publication like [the one I present here]. And though I was sensible that I could publish nothing of the kind without the

fatigue and expense of travelling over the greatest part of the continent; yet at the request of many, I have been prevailed upon to make the tour of the Baptist churches, to obtain necessary information. … I have travelled about seven thousand miles in about eighteen months, chiefly on foot, and have visited about two hundred and fifteen churches… Having been brought up with a view to the business of merchandize, I have been accustomed to keeping accounts; and I now keep accounts of souls with their faces set Zionward in preference to those which only respect money or trade. I have a natural turn for travelling, and I am convinced I could not better spend my time, than in itinerating to preach the gospel, and to collect materials which may assist future historians…"

1789 Deed of conveyance from Thomas Durham to Thomas Cate et al

This indenture made the twentieth day of August in the year of our Lord one thousand seven hundred and eighty nine between Thomas Durham of Orange County of the one part and Thomas Cate, preacher, Thomas Cate, Robert Cate, John Strother, Richard Cate, John Workman, Bernard Cate, Joseph Cate, Mary Christmas, jointly Trustees of Orange County of the other part.

Witnesseth that for and in consideration of the sum of twenty shillings North Carolina currency to the said Thomas Durham in hand paid by the said Thomas Cate preacher or either of the above mentioned Trustees at or before the sealing and delivery of these presents the receipt whereof he doth hereby acknowledge and therefore doth release acquit and discharge the said Thomas Cate preacher or either of the above mentioned Trustees, them or their heirs executors and administrators by these presents he, the said Thomas Durham, hath granted, bargained, sold, alined, and confirmed and by these presents doth grant, bargain, sell, aline and confirm unto the said Thomas Cate preacher & the rest of the above mentioned names of the Trustees Jointly they or their heirs a certain piece or parcel of land situate, lying and being in the County of Orange and state aforesaid for the use of building a meeting house to hold public meetings in and Thanksgivings for the mercies and blessings of Almighty God. Bounded as followeth, Beginning at a Black oak at the old path joining John Strother's line, then along the old path to a Hickory adjoining John Strother's line, thence East along John Strother's line to a post oak, thence a Direct line to the Beginning containing one acre more or less and all the houses, buildings ways, waters, watercourses, profits, heredaments and appertanances whatsoever to the said premises hereby granted or any part thereof Belonging or in any ways appertaining and the Revertion and revertions, Remainder and Remainders, Rents, tythes and profits thereof & all the Estate Right, title, Interest, use, trust property claim and Demand whatsoever of him the said Thomas Durham of, in, and to the said premises and all, and deeds, evidences and writings, Touching or in any way concering the same.

To have and to hold the bounds hereby conveyed and all and singular other the premises hereby Bargained and sold and every part and parcel thereof their and every of their appertanances unto the said Thomas Cate preacher Trustee and the rest of the above names Trustees all jointly them and their heirs and assigns forever to the only proper use and behoof of him the said Thomas Cate preacher trustee and the rest of the above named Trustees all jointly them and their heirs forever and the said Thomas Durham doth covenant and agree that I have the absolute authority to grant and convey the same to the above Trustees in manner and form aforesaid.. In Witness whereof the said Thomas Durham hath hereunto set his hand and seal the day and year first above written, signed and sealed and delivered in the presence of us.
(witnesses)   Thomas Basket   Mark Couper

Thomas Durham
(seal)

Asplund began his tour around 1787. He probably visited North Carolina churches early in his travels. In 1791 he published the first of four directories. Below is a portion of one page of the directory that shows he visited Haw River Baptist Church located near Bynum. Look closely at entry #15. You will see that Elnathan Davis was the pastor of a congregation of 320 people. Below his name are the names of his assistants. The third name is "Tho. Cate."

8	Burke,	Catawbo River,	Y.		John Chefter, Cleveland Coffey, Richard Ofgatharp,	159	1-8
9	Camden,		Ke.		Henry Abbot,	80	2-10
10		Sawyer's Creek,	Ke.	1790	David Duncan, Thomas Etheridge,	52	2-10
11	Carteret,	Hadnot's Creek,	Ke.		James Sanders, —— Johnfen,	35	2-10
12	Cafwill & Pir-fylvania,	Country Line,	R D		Thomas Mullins, Jofeph Bufh, *	160	3-10
13		Flat River,	R D		George Roberts,	161	3-10
14	Chatham and Randolph.	Bear Creek,	San		Sherwood White,	55	1-8
15		Haw River,	an		Elnathan Davis, Tho Brown, Jef. Buckner Tho. Cate, Solomon Smith, Ifaac Hailer, —— Ray William Weatherfpoon,	320	1-8
16	Chatham,	Rocky River,	San		Francis Dorfet,	45	1-8
17	Chewan,	Ballard's Bridge,	Ke		John M'Cabe, John Afplund,	80	2-10
18		Yoppim Creek,	Ke		Thomas Harmon,	60	2-10
19	Craven,		Ke.		William Phipps, Tho. Richard, Joel Willis	106	2-10
20		Goofe Creek,	Ke.		Jam. Brinfon, Jam. Roach	162	2-10
21		Newport River,	Ke		John M'Cabe, Jofeph Bell, —— Simpfon,	86	2-10
22		New River,	Ke		Robert Nixon, Job Thigpen, —— Wilkins Kittrill Mondine.	145	2-10

A page from Asplund's registry in 1791

Since Haw River is only about 20 miles south of the Cane Creek community, and since Cate was a prominent local name here but not there, we may conclude that Asplund's Thomas Cate was a Cane Creek resident who had to travel a day on horseback to find a church to his liking. He was probably baptized by Elnathen Davis (1735-1821) who in turn was baptized by Shubal Stearns himself. The dramatic scene of Davis' conversion was described in Chapter 5.

Who were these individuals who banded together in 1789 for the purpose of "building a meeting house to hold public meetings and thanksgivings for the means and blessings of almighty God"? Nine names appear on the deed: our first preacher, Thomas Cate, and eight others (and two witnesses, Thomas Basket and Mark Cooper).

I am indebted to Banks Cates of Charlotte for much of what follows. Dr. Cates (now deceased) generously shared with me his findings on the Cates family tree. As we will see, most of the trustees were bound together by family ties, being related to one another either by blood ties or by marriage bonds.

It is striking that six of the nine trustees bear the same family name of Cate. Banks Cates has traced the Cate family back to a shoemaker named Robert Cate, who would have been born around 1670. His name first appears in historical records in 1689 in Henrico County, Virginia when he was indentured for a four-year period to learn the shoemaker's trade. It is apparent from other records that Robert Cate was a Quaker, as were his sons.

Robert Cate, who died in 1728 or 29, had six sons, three of whom came to reside at Cane Creek. Captain Robert Cate, Jr. lived first on New Hope Creek, then Cane Creek. Thomas Cate also moved to Cane Creek. John Cate settled on the Flat River but owned much land around Cane Creek and may have lived here. All three appear on the first Orange County tax list in 1752.

The three brothers who settled on Cane Creek originated three lines of Cates. Robert's line produced four of our trustees: sons Robert, Richard, and Thomas, and son-in-law John Strother. Thomas' line produced three trustees: sons Bernard, Thomas (the preacher) and son-in-law John Workman. John's line produced Joseph. To complete the family connections, the grantor of the land, Thomas Durham, was married to Susannah Cate (a daughter of Thomas).

This simplified family tree shows the family connections. The trustees are shown in large bold type.

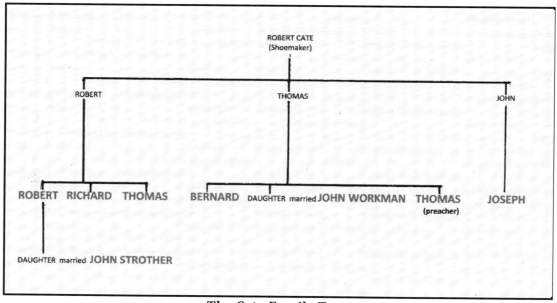

The Cate Family Tree

Below is what we know about each of the trustees.

Thomas Cate. Unfortunately for the historian, there were many Cates in the early days of Orange County and all too many of them were named Thomas. The ones who were not seem always to have had a son or a father by this name. So, keeping all the Thomas Cates straight is quite difficult. This Thomas was the son of Robert, one of the original settlers, and a cousin to the preacher. He had extensive landholdings and therefore must have been a prominent member of the community.

John Strother. He seems to have been a temporary resident of Cane Creek. Because his name also appears as "Struther" and "Stroder" on old deeds it is possible that he was of Pennsylvania Dutch origin like many others who settled farther to the west. He married Mary Ann Cate and in 1776 he bought a tract of 200 acres from his father-in-law, Robert Cate, located on both sides of Cane Creek just south of where the original meeting house was to be built. He sold this tract to Sackfield Brewer in 1790. He obtained a State land grant in 1798 a bit to the east of Cane Creek. He was a brother-in-law of the Thomas Cate above.

Richard Cate. Apparently, Richard Cate was the builder and owner of a mill on Cane Creek for which no trace remains. It is possible that the mill was never built. If it did exist, it was located about halfway between the old dam at Cecil Crawford's house and the old dam at Teer. Both are now below the surface of Cane Creek Reservoir. He seems to have married his cousin Emelia Cate. In the 1781 tax evaluation, Richard had the highest valuation of any of the Cates.

John Workman. His name does not appear on any deeds until 1799, when he bought 130 acres from his brother-in-law, Bernard Cate, along Cane Creek about two miles north of the Church. From other sources, we know that he was around earlier and owned land. The absence of his name from the official records is probably due to the loss of the land records in Hillsborough during the Revolution. We know that he staked a land claim in 1778 and is on the tax list of 1782. He was listed as "over 45" in the 1800 census. By 1801 his land holdings were over 500 acres. He may have therefore been a young man in 1789. He married Sylvia Cate, a sister of our preacher, Thomas Cate. Workman represented Cane Creek at the Sandy Creek Association meetings of 1807 and 1815.

Bernard Cate. He was a brother to our first preacher, husband to Jane ("Jennie") Sykes, and one of the three large landowners during the early days of Cane Creek (along with Sackfield Brewer and Lewis Kirk), owning well over a thousand acres. The bulk of his holdings were north of the Church and east of Buckhorn Road and extended into the Seven Mile Creek watershed. In 1813 he constructed the mill on Turkey Hill Creek where I now live.

Joseph Cate. I suspect that Joseph (and his brother Stephen) were the sons of the elusive John Cate who obtained a Granville land grant about 1755 for which all trace has been lost. It was located north of Buckhorn Road and south of Bradshaw Quarry Road and included about 500 acres. He was a son of John and Elizabeth Cate. He died in 1793.

Robert Cate. This is the eighth trustee. He was a son of Robert. Little else is known about him.

Mary Christmas. How amazing to have a person by this poetic name among our founders and how amazing to find any woman at all. (The phrase "merry Christmas" was not yet in vogue.) She is also the only trustee to have no known connection to the Cate family. The Christmas clan was an interesting group. The patriarch seems to have been John Christmas, a surveyor by trade and the man who laid out the original town of Raleigh. He obtained a tract of land on Toms Creek, which already had an interesting history. The Earl of Granville originally deeded it to a Mary Day in 1757. This is peculiar because it almost never occurred that a grant was made to a woman, who by law had quite limited rights to own property. However, a widow could own property. So, this may have come about when she became a widow during the process of obtaining the title to the land. In any event she soon sold the tract to a speculator. A few years later we find that the tract, which was located on Strudwick's land, was sold by him to Christmas. John Christmas died in 1783 leaving a widow, presumably Mary (we know that he married Mary Graves in 1738), and several sons, each of whom obtained large chunks of Strudwick land. Two of his sons, Charles, and Nathaniel, also became surveyors and their names appear as the official surveyors on some of the early State land grants in our neighborhood. Two of her sons, probably those just named, were delegates to the state convention held in November 1789 in Fayetteville that ratified the American Constitution. Ironically, throughout their tenure along Toms Creek, they persisted in referring to it as Cane Creek. By the early 1800s all the Christmases had migrated to the west and south.

Thomas Cate, Preacher. We know little about this man. We assume that he is the same Thomas Cate who was associated with the Haw River Church. From piecing together the old records in Hillsborough and Raleigh, it seems that he had a homeplace some two miles south of the church in the northern reaches of the Collins Creek watershed below present Teer Road.

In early Cane Creek history, there are three Thomas Cates who could have been our preacher. One was married to Martha and died in 1811. Another was married to Elizabeth and died without a will. The third was married to Sarah and died in 1814. It was not possible to learn from reading the wills which one had been our first preacher. None of them are recorded as having died owning a Bible.

Eventually a clue to which Thomas was our preacher came from out of the blue. One day, when answering a fire call at the dumpster site on Bradshaw Quarry Road, I chanced upon an old friend, Ken Hardy, who lives near where Caterpillar Creek flows into the Cane Creek. He asked if I were working on Cane Creek Church history and said that his wife, Nancy, had some information that might interest me.

Nancy told me of a trip she had taken with her father to his boyhood home in Juniata, Nebraska. While there, he had invited several of his old high school friends to visit him at their motel room. At that get-together, one of the visitors turned to Nancy and asked if she had ever heard of Cane Creek. She answered that she practically lived on its banks! The man, Thane Weeks, replied that one of his ancestors was known, through family tradition, to have been the pastor of Cane Creek Church. His name was Thomas Cate. He had no idea where in North Carolina it could have been and despaired of ever finding it. In his words, "I had wondered if that place might be like Camelot -- always off somewhere in the mist."

I could not wait to write to Thane Weeks. The materials he sent indicate that the Thomas Cate that I had been trying to identify was the one married to Sarah, the one who died in 1814. From his information and clues in our local records I put together the following picture of the man. (This has since been verified and added to by Banks Cates of Charlotte.)

Thomas Cate was born about 1747 and was the son of Thomas and Rebecca Sykes Cate, who had migrated to Orange County from Prince George County in Virginia. He was 42 years old at the founding of our church in 1789. He had brothers named Barnard, John, and Richard. He married Sarah Estridge about 1767.

Thomas Cate's will mentions eleven children: Moses born about 1768, who married Hannah Bradford; John B. born about 1770, who married Priscilla Lloyd and who died in Tennessee in 1840; Fanny, born about 1772, who married John Sykes; Martha, birth date unknown, who married William Moore; Winny, birth date unknown, who married William Roach; Huldah, birth date unknown, who married Elisha Cates, possibly a cousin; Tabitha, birth date unknown, who married William Smith; Elizabeth, born about 1784, whose marital status is confused; Thomas, born in 1784, who married Elizabeth Roach and later Martha Carroll, and who died in 1863; and Ephraim, born about 1778, who married Rebecca Lindsey and who died in Missouri in the 1850s. The name of the eleventh child is unknown.

Part of finding the real Thomas Cate was discovering that he owned two stills. This sounds shocking to modern ears, but it should be understood in the context of the time. Alcoholic beverages were distilled for two purposes. One was so-called "medicinal alcohol." It was thought that a bit of whiskey or brandy could treat ague, flu, and colds. The other use, of course, was recreational drinking. The shocking truth was that our ancestors were heavy drinkers. Drunken carousing was commonplace. Baptists did not begin to change their attitude toward whiskey until the birth of the temperance movement in the 1830s.

Thus, the church was officially established on August 20, 1789, and a meeting house was built shortly afterward. Its initial membership was small, perhaps the nine individuals just discussed plus their families – maybe 20 in all.

Now that we have seen the creation of the church, we need to consider what the church actually stood for, what its beliefs were and how its church services were conducted. This is the topic of the next chapter.

9: RITES AND BELIEFS

Beliefs are the basic positions on theological issues such as predestination. Rites are the actual practices carried out by the church members on special occasions. I will begin with rites.

Today we still practice a few rites including baptism, communion, and the laying on of hands. In the early days the list was much longer. Paschal (p. 409) states that Sandy Creek churches had some beliefs and practices peculiar to themselves in the early years. We are fortunate to have Banks Cates' description of the nine rites practiced by Shubal Stearns' church at Sandy Creek. Here is what he wrote (slightly edited):

> "In the early years of the Sandy Creek Association, its churches had some practices and beliefs peculiar to themselves. They had ruling elders, elderesses, deaconesses, and weekly communion. There were nine Christian rites. It should be noted that many of these rites, except for baptism and communion, soon fell into disuse.
>
> 1) **Baptism.** This was the crucial sacrament which distinguished Baptists from other Christians. It was performed by Immersion only, and only after an adult believer had made a public declaration of faith. Its purpose was to encourage the hope of salvation, to bind one to the laws of Christ, to admit one into the church, and to confirm the doctrine of the resurrection. The rite of baptism was followed by three others: the laying-on of hands, the right hand of fellowship, and the kiss of charity.
>
> 2) **The Lord's Supper**. This began with the minister's giving a short sermon explaining the significance of the supper, followed by a suitable scripture reading, then by a prayer giving thanks for the bread and what it represented. A single loaf of bread was then broken and distributed to the congregation. After it was eaten, the minister gave thanks for the wine and shared it from a common cup. A hymn was sung and an offering and benediction followed.
>
> 3) **The Love Feast.** This rite took place in a church member's house for the purpose of promoting brotherly love and relieving the poor. The host reminded his invited guests of the purpose of the feast and then invited them to enjoy the meal. On this festive occasion, songs were sung after the meal, and the host might perform the foot-washing rite. As guests left, the host gave each the right hand of fellowship and the kiss of charity.
>
> 4) **Laying-on of Hands**. This was a rite administered by the minister on several appropriate occasions. After a person was baptized, the minister laid hands on him to signify "a consequent receiving of the ghost." The rite was administered to new church officers "to encourage their expectations

of increase of gifts." It was performed when infants were brought to be dedicated to God. All recipients, except infants in the minister's arms, knelt during the rite.

(5) **Washing of Feet**. The purpose of the rite of foot washing was to remind Christians to be humble toward one another, and to signify the cleansing of post-baptism sins. Any Christian could perform the rite and it usually took place in the home. Each guest's feet were washed by the host, who repeated to each person the following words: "I love thee, my brother, better than myself and hereby plight willingness to serve and honor thee in love. Hereby also the Lord Jesus signified that he will cleanse thee from the sins thou art liable to since thy birth that thou mayest have a part in him. So be it, Lord Jesus. Amen."

(6) **Anointing the Sick with Oil**. This rite was initiated when a sick person called for the minister to administer it. The minister insisted that the sick one confess any sin which he knew or suspected he had committed. He then anointed the penitent one with oil and said that, in the name of the Lord Jesus, his sins had been forgiven. The rite was concluded with a prayer that healing would come.

7) **The Right Hand of Fellowship.** The purpose of this rite was to commence, improve, or renew friendship. It was administered on occasions when Christians met, but especially when a new member was received into the church.

(8) **The Kiss of Charity.** Its purpose was "to plight and testify brotherly love." The rite was observed on many occasions, but most often after baptism and the love feast.

(9) **The Dedication of Children.** Morgan Edwards stated that this took place at the parents' home. But Paschal says that "This rite was founded as the circumstances of parents binding their children to Christ. It was thus performed as soon as circumstances would permit, after the birth of the child. The mother carried it to meeting, where the minister either took it in his hands or laid his hands on it, thanked God for his mercy, and invoked blessing on the child, at which time it received its name. Many called this rite a dry christening. It prevailed not only in the Sandy Creek Association but in many parts of Virginia."

When Morgan Edwards visited North Carolina in 1772, he noted that various churches in the Sandy Creek Association practiced some of these rites, but that only two churches practiced all nine and had a slate of male and female officers. These two were Sandy Creek and Haw River. What rites Cane Creek practiced at its inception can only be surmised. Since it was a granddaughter of Sandy Creek and daughter of Haw River, and since Shubal Stearns was "grand mentor" of our first preacher, it is quite likely that Cane Creek followed its predecessor.

In addition, the early Sandy Creek churches had ruling elders and eldresses, deacons and deaconesses, and weekly communion. Benedict, writing in 1813, says that "the greatest part of the nine [rites] together with the offices of eldresses and deaconesses have fallen into disuse." But Paschal (footnote, p. 411) comments that the Haw River Church observed all nine rites and had eldresses and deaconesses. So, we might suppose that Thomas Cate was exposed to these ideas while serving there and might have incorporated them into the covenant at Cane Creek. This might also explain the presence of a woman on the list of trustees. Perhaps Mary Christmas was Cane Creek's first deaconess!

Beliefs

We have already mentioned the cornerstone beliefs of most Baptists: Only believer baptism is acceptable; each church is an autonomous unit; there should be a wall of separation between church and state; everyone is his own priest in interpreting the Bible; and evangelism is a must. In addition, churches of the 18th and 19th century had their own set of lesser doctrinal beliefs that distinguished them from other protestant groups. They may have even distinguished one branch of Baptists from another.

It is very likely that our original members, likely led by the people mentioned in the last chapter, inscribed their basic Christian beliefs on the first page of the official church book (I will call these types of statements, "Articles of Faith"). Unfortunately, our early history is lost. Our earliest records (consisting of beliefs and practices, roll, and minutes of monthly meetings) were destroyed in 1829 when Enoch Crutchfield, then our Clerk, lost his house to a fire. The roll was immediately reconstructed, and a new book of minutes was begun, but the loss was permanent. The new 1829 Minute Book does not contain any statement of belief.

Other clues about Cane Creek Church and its original Articles of Faith principles may be found by looking into the minutes of Antioch Baptist Church, located several miles to the southeast on White Cross Road. Antioch is a daughter church of ours.

Antioch Church was established as an arm of Cane Creek Church on the 20th and 21st of August 1806. It was located a few miles south of its present location and was then known as Haw River Mountain Church. The founders were Thomas Cate, our first preacher, and two men who were prominent in Sandy Creek Association affairs, George Pope and Jesse Buckner. These latter two helped establish several other Baptist churches in the region and were not local residents. We know that Jesse Buckner was a licensed minister associated with Haw River, as was Thomas Cate. I do not know anything of George Pope other than that he later became pastor at Abbott's Creek in Davidson County.

It is interesting to note (and indeed we shall have reason to inquire about this later) that neither Cane Creek nor Haw River Mountain church were officially Baptist Churches at this time. Some of the early family names at Haw River Mountain include Copeland, Michum, Caruthers, Durham, Pickard, Snipes, Lloyd, O'Daniel, Edwards, and Ivy.

On the first page of the Antioch Church Book we find the sort of Articles of Faith statement that may have been inscribed in the book at Cane Creek. It reads as follows:

> "The faith with which this Church was constituted respecting principles are these:
>   Election according to the foreknowledge of God;
>   The effectual calling;
>   Justification by Grace;
>   Baptism by immersion;
>   Washing of feet;
>   Final perseverance in Christ
>   A rule of government in which we take the Scriptures for our guide. The Lord directs us therein."

Of course, these principles may have been the work of Pope and Buckner more than Cate. Our church was organized at least 18 years before this and may have had organizing principles somewhat at variance with the ones above. It is also possible that our original principles were modified in 1807 to conform to what the Sandy Creek Association expected from its member churches.

Other models for the Cane Creek covenant might be those at Grassy Creek or at Abbott's Creek. At Grassy Creek in Granville County the covenant is said to have been written by Shubal Stearns himself. It lays out most of the nine rites mentioned above and goes on for several pages with the most profound and poetic language, alas, too long to quote here, but including as main points these doctrinal beliefs:

- Laying on of hands;
- Effectual calling by the Holy Ghost;
- Free justification through the imputed righteousness of Christ;
- Progressive sanctification through God's grace and truth;
- Final perseverance or continuance of the saints in grace;
- Resurrection of these bodies after death;
- Life everlasting.

At Abbott's Creek, the Covenant is much more succinct: "Believing the Old and New Testament to be the perfect rule for life and practice; and secondly Repentance from dead works; and thirdly, Faith toward God; and fourthly, the doctrine of baptism; and fifthly, laying on of hands; and sixthly, the perseverance of the saints; and seventhly, the resurrection of the dead, and eighthly, eternal judgment."

Terms such as "effectual calling" and "progressive sanctification" may sound foreign to modern ears. They are shorthand references to particular doctrinal beliefs. Here are the main ones.

Effectual calling is a Calvinistic notion. Only the "elect" can be effectively called to Christ. Those who are not among the elect may feel themselves called by the word of God but this calling has no effect. These are the damned.

Free justification: God's gracious acquittal of all sinners who believe in Christ.

Progressive sanctification: The spiritually reborn gradually attain moral and spiritual perfection.

Final perseverance refers to the idea that the elect cannot totally fall from a state of grace. They shall finally persevere and be eternally saved. Another way of saying this is that true believers persevere in their Christian walk and do not backslide.

Positional sanctification: God declared a person to be saved upon the instant of accepting Christ. This is an Arminian concept.

Thus, it seems clear that many churches within the Sandy Creek Association expressed somewhat Calvinistic views. This is interesting because Stearns is often described as having steered a middle course between Calvinism and Arminianism. This can be seen in churches that endorsed both "effectual calling" (a Calvinistic belief) and "free justification" (an Arminian belief).

When Cane Creek and Haw River Mountain sought admission to the Sandy Creek Association in 1806, our church had no difficulties with the Association on matters of doctrine. This was not the case with Haw River Mountain. There arose almost from the beginning a point of doctrinal difference, which kept the Haw River Mountain Church and the Sandy Creek Association at odds for many years.

The initial break came dramatically, according to George W. Purefoy. He was one of North Carolina's most influential Baptists and wrote the definitive history of Sandy Creek's first 100 years. He was also the preacher at our church from 1839 to 1852. His book reveals what happened at Antioch (then called Haw River Mountain).

Upon application for membership in the Association, Haw River Mountain was selected as the site for the 1806 Association Meeting. But the delegates, upon arriving there and inspecting the Church Book, found something to their disliking and refused to hold fellowship with Haw River Mountain. Inspection of Haw River Mountain's organizing principles given above suggests that the offending words may have been "election according to the foreknowledge of God." This is the most blatantly Calvinistic principle of all, one that might more commonly be associated with the Particular Baptists to the east. It is curious, to say the least, that a church organized by Thomas Cate and two Sandy Creek stalwarts could possibly have included such an extreme Calvinistic principle in the basic principles of a Church seeking entry into a Separate Baptist Association. I think that we may assume that Cane Creek had no such organizing principle.

Only one clue about the nature of the dispute remains to be discussed and it is a very tenuous clue indeed. It involves two individuals. One was the first preacher at Haw River Mountain, Mark Andrews, and the other was a person who very likely was a preacher at Cane Creek, Randolph Mabry. We know that Mabry was a delegate from Cane Creek to the Association Meeting of 1816 and according to Purefoy's use of italics, we are led to believe that he was an ordained minister, hence the pastor at Cane Creek. (He had earlier been the preacher at Bear Creek in Chatham County.) The first part of the clue is that there appears to be a link between Andrews and Mabry, a link that has to do with a shared belief on some issue of theological importance to the Sandy Creek Association. It was important enough that, in 1825, the Association saw fit to excommunicate both men and to have a public notice inserted into several newspapers stating:

BAPTISTS BEWARE OF IMPOSTORS!!

The Sandy Creek Baptist Association in session at Friendship Meeting House, Moore County, the 24th day of October 1825, having learned that Mark Andrews, Randolph Mabry, Leonard Prather, and Elisha Revel are pretending to preach the gospel in the regular Baptist churches in this state, deem it their duty to publish in these churches and to their brethren in general that said Andrews, Mabry, Prather, and Revel are excommunicants from churches within their body. By order:

Nat. G. Smith, Clerk
[The North Carolina Star, November 16, 1825]

But what was the nature of the dispute? Only one shred of evidence can be matched with the supposed connection between Mabry, Andrews, and a theological dispute. From the Cane Creek minutes of March 1833, we find:

"Randolph Mabry is restored."

From this entry we know that Mabry was firstly, a member of Cane Creek Church, and secondly, had been excluded for some offense. The nature of the offense becomes apparent in June 1835:

"A charge is brought against Randolph Mabry for drinking and for opposing the benevolent institutions of the day and refusing to give up his church letter when demanded by the church." (The next month Mabry was found guilty and excluded.)

The matter was thought serious enough to be published in the minutes of the Sandy Creek Association for 1835: "Randolph Mabry is excluded from Cane Creek for disorderly conduct." By 1835, exclusions for such reasons as intemperate drinking were routine in Baptist churches and were hardly deemed worthy of spreading across the minutes of the annual Association meeting. We may safely conclude, therefore, that Mabry's exclusion was for some theological reason having to do with "benevolent institutions."

The term "benevolent institutions" is a code word for a set of issues that began to concern Baptists in the early 180'0s. It was the latest and greatest conflict between two opposing camps within the Baptist belief system: the Calvinistic idea that God already had determined the spiritual fate of all humans versus the Arminian idea that Christ's sacrifice on the cross atoned for the sins of all mankind for all generations. Benevolent institutions were those practices, including missions, that sought to spread the faith to the irreligious. Calvinists thought that benevolent institutions were, at the very least, a waste of time, and at the worst, an affront to a God who needed no such help.

This idea reinforces the supposition that we have already considered. That is, the issue that kept Haw River Mountain at odds with Sandy Creek for so long was the former church's opposition to the so-called benevolent institutions, an opposition that would have been apparent to the Sandy Creek delegates upon inspection of the Haw River Mountain Church Book and its reference to "election according to the foreknowledge of God."

Could it be that the record of this dispute and its resolution has disappeared from Antioch's record? It is possible because Antioch's original minutes no longer survive? What remains at Antioch is a handwritten copy of the original minutes made in 1859 (when it was still known as Haw River Mountain). By this time, the divisive issues surrounding benevolent institutions had been thrashed out and such institutions as missions, Sunday Schools, associational literature, and theological schools were flourishing.

Our supposition is that Randolph Mabry, as our pastor at Cane Creek, attempted to spread the anti-mission sentiment to this community. He apparently failed and probably failed early on. After 1816, Mabry is no longer mentioned by Purefoy as a Cane Creek delegate to any Association meeting. Had he continued to serve Cane Creek he surely would have been a delegate. The final irony in the case is that Mabry presented himself for restoration at Cane Creek at precisely the wrong time. In 1833, Stephen Pleasant was our pastor and Pleasant's opinion about mission work was plain and straightforward. He was for missions, and he was willing to go to extremes for his belief.

Before we leave this topic, let us pause and contemplate once again the central mysteries of this chapter: Why did a church founded in 1789 with the help of a licensed Baptist preacher wait 17 years to affiliate itself with a Baptist Association? Several possibilities come to mind:

- a doctrinal difference between the Sandy Creekers and the Cane Creekers;

- a sentiment in the community that the Church should either remain independent or affiliate with another denomination;

- a difference of opinion within the community that kept affiliation with Sandy Creek from happening.

We will probably never know. But the historian is ever hopeful. Perhaps in the next tattered book from someone's attic or in the next folder of loose 18th century papers at the State Archives, the answer to these questions will be found.

Next, we will consider our church's experience under the pastorate of Stephen Pleasant. This is an important time in the development of Baptist practices. The modern Southern Baptist denomination was born with much controversy.

10: STEPHEN PLEASANT AND THE STRUGGLE OVER MISSIONS

Perhaps it was inevitable that the theological issue that divided Baptists into the Particular and General camps would eventually lead to a showdown. General Baptists had always believed in the potential salvation of all of mankind. One had only to spread the word of God to the "waste places" and souls would be saved. Particular Baptists had been inspired by John Calvin to believe that God, in his infinite wisdom, had laid out the course that the world and its inhabitants would take. This meant that it was pre-ordained who would be saved. The hyper-Calvinists believed that mission work was an insult to God's sovereignty and would not touch it. More moderate Particulars did engage in some mission work but not with great enthusiasm.

In the early days, when Baptists were simply a collection of individual congregations, it was easy to gloss over this doctrinal point, or at least to fight it out within a congregation. But when the first Baptist associations began to form, the stage was set for these theological matters to become a matter for large-scale dispute.

In the South, the Charleston Association had been formed in 1751. In 1769 some of its churches in the eastern part of North Carolina withdrew to form the Kehukee Association, which leaned strongly toward the Particular side. One of the first issues to face them was their relationship with the new upstart breed of Baptists who had settled to their west: Shubal Stearns and his Separate Baptists in the Sandy Creek Association. Eventually, they decided to compromise.

Roughly, the compromise went like this. The Separates insisted that it was proper to baptize only those who genuinely and sincerely had felt a "born again" experience. They wished each church to inquire of its members whether this was true and either re-baptize or dismiss those who failed the test. The Particulars, for their part, succeeded in incorporating into the Kehukee Association's Confession of Faith the following language: "We believe that God, before the foundation of the world ... did elect a certain number of men and angels to eternal life and that the election is particular, eternal, and unconditional on the creature's part" (Paschal, p. 477). Thus a union was effected and the Kehukee Association took in a number of Separate Baptist churches in Virginia. But it was probably an uneasy and unstable accommodation because the Separates were enthusiastic about evangelism and the Particulars were skeptical.

After the Revolutionary War, The Kehukee Association considered the matter of whether or not it should attempt to evangelize within the borders of the Association. One delegate expressed the dominant view by saying, "if God has any elect in Northampton or Gates [counties], in his own good time he will convert them without your help or mine." And, as if this attitude were not enough of an obstacle, there was the perennial problem of financing such an operation. Member churches had a hard enough time keeping up their own churches and taking up occasional love offerings for indigent members, much less contributing to missionary causes. Thus, little effort was expended on missionary work. Indeed, in the 1790s there seemed to be little enthusiasm anywhere for religious outreach. Religion seemed to be in a decline. In this decade, when eastern North Carolina had a population of 250,000, there were only about 4,000 Baptists. For many Kehukee Association meetings the total number of baptisms reported for the entire year was fewer than 100, barely enough to keep up with attrition.

This religious decline occurred not just in eastern North Carolina but across the land, and not just with Baptists but with all denominations. It was widely felt that a certain "coldness" had crept into America's churches and in many quarters the call went out to fast and pray for a revival of the spirit of the so-called "Great Awakening" of the 1740s.

The hoped-for spark was struck in an unlikely spot, in the Elkhorn Association in Kentucky in 1800. A huge emotional response swept throughout the South amid popular excitement bordering on hysteria.

All across the country people of many denominations came together in great camp meetings to hear impassioned preachers beg their listeners to abandon themselves to Christ and to accept his call. For a while, the old disagreements over evangelism faded away. Presbyterians united with Methodists in this "Second Great Awakening." Many individual Baptists felt drawn to the camp meetings but Baptist pastors and their Associations preferred to hold exclusively Baptist camp meetings. Benedict, in his History of the Baptists (Vol. II, p108) presents this picture:

> "In the progress of the revival among the Baptists, and especially at their camp meetings, there were exhibited scenes of the most solemn and affecting nature; and in many instances there was heard ... a mingled sound of prayer, exhortation, groans, and praise... Many were taken with these religious epilepsies, if we may so call them, not only at the great meetings where those scenes were exhibited, but also about their daily employments, some in the fields, some in their houses, and some when hunting their cattle in the woods... And besides falling down there were many other expressions of zeal, which in more moderate people would be considered enthusiastic and wild"

George Pope greatly encouraged the new movement within the Sandy Creek Association. Lemuel Burkitt, of the Kuhukee Association, is credited with single-handedly bringing the Second Great Awakening to eastern North Carolina. He traveled to Kentucky to see for himself what the excitement was about. Upon returning, he had such a profound effect on the 1801 Kehukee Association meeting that the new spirit spread like wildfire. Burkitt later wrote in the Association Minutes (Paschal, Vol. I, p. 540):

> "Old Christians were so revived that they were all on fire to see their neighbors, their neighbor's children, and their own families so much engaged. Their souls seemed melted down in love, and their strength renewed like the eagles. Many backsliders who had been run away for many years returned weeping home...

Some churches which had not received a member by baptism for a year or two, would now frequently receive, at almost every conference meeting, several members."

The revival of the spirit that accompanied the Second Great Awakening was destined to lead on, at the Association level, to a movement to keep the tide running among the unsaved. At the 1803 Kehukee Association the following query was put forth:

"Is not the Kehukee Association... called on ... to step forward in support of that missionary spirit which the great God is so wonderfully reviving amongst the different denominations of good men in various parts of the world?"

The Association answered with a thundering "yes!" This led to the creation in 1805 of the first state-wide Baptist organization, the Philanthropic Missionary Society. It was followed by The Baptist General Convention of North Carolina in 1812, the North Carolina Society for Foreign and Domestic Missions in 1814, and finally, the North Carolina Baptist Benevolent Society in 1829, which transformed itself a year later into the North Carolina Baptist State Convention.

These organizations did not spring up in response to popular agreement on the value of evangelism. Indeed, the very number of these organizations speaks to the difficulty of getting a mission effort going. As soon as one organization would get itself into operation, objections would be heard at the grass roots level and the organization would fail, only to be followed by another attempt under a new name. The enthusiasm felt at the associational meetings simply did not translate into action at the local church level.

Some Baptists said that they could find no justification in their Bibles for a state-wide organization of any sort, much less one that sponsored mission work. They objected when such organizations asked them and their churches for money to further their goals. Many churches refused to make contributions. Likewise, many individuals claimed that there was no Biblical authority to support Sunday Schools, Tract Societies, and the paying of ministers, or educating them in a seminary. All of these new efforts came to be known as "benevolent institutions,"

From the perspective of a hundred and fifty years of Baptist tradition in the missionary field, it is hard to see what the controversy was all about. But for about thirty years the issue was hotly debated within associations and within churches all across the south. At times the debate became so divisive that churches split and associations divided into pro-missionary and anti-missionary factions. When the dust had settled, mission-minded Baptists were set upon a new course and new statewide institutions had been established.

Under the influence and support of the mission-minded Baptists, the Baptist State Convention was organized in 1830, the *Biblical Recorder* began publishing in 1833 and Wake Forest College opened in 1834. Sunday Schools were promoted. The American

Bible Society received enthusiastic support. Religious tracts were printed by the thousands and circulated far and wide. The State Convention took a firm stand on temperance. Those Baptists who did not stand with these principles were left behind to stagnate with religious principles that doomed them to isolation and little hope for growth. We know them now as "Primitive Baptists."

Stephen Pleasant and Cane Creek Church

We have now about set the stage for the dramatic series of events that our former pastor, Stephen Pleasant brought about. To complete doing so, we must consider what was happening at about this time in Pleasant's home territory of Caswell and Person Counties, the home of the Country Line Association. In this Association of churches, and in most others, there was at first little opposition to the cause of missions. It is most likely that opinions on both sides of the issue could be found in all its churches. Then there appeared, in 1829, a catalyst in the form of one James Osbourn, an itinerant minister from Baltimore, who traveled about the countryside preaching the anti-mission cause and encouraging churches to rally to help him.

STEPHAN PLEASANT

At Bush Arbor Church in south-side Virginia, Osbourn's anti-mission message fell on fertile ground. Here he met an ordained minister (though not the pastor at Bush Arbor) by the name of John Stadler, who, under Osborn's influence, became the Association's leading proponent against missions. After the Stephen Pleasant affair to be related below, Stadler became the Country Line moderator and held this position for many years. After the pro-mission churches left the Association, Country Line held to a strong anti-mission stance, and still does to this day.

The split in the County Line Association occurred in 1832, when it went on record against all the new elements then coming into the Baptist church. That is, they expressed disapproval, officially, of: "all the societies of the day, namely Bible Societies, Temperance Societies, Tract Societies, Sunday School Societies, Missionary Societies, Baptist Conventions, Religious Newspapers, etc."

Stephen Pleasant, later to become our pastor during the rest of the 1830s, became involved in all these controversies and took a courageous stance in favor of missions and "benevolent institutions."

We know little of Stephen Pleasant's early life or what occupation he followed. He had joined Ebenezer Church in Person County in 1799 and a year later married Polly Brown, the daughter of the church's minister. As Elder Brown advanced in age, he came to rely on the assistance of Pleasant as an exhorter and song leader. Pleasant was doing this at least by 1824. One Sunday, Elder Brown suddenly realized that his text and the sermon he had prepared had "flown from his mind" and he could not remember a word of it. He called for his son-in-law to address the congregation. In doing so, Pleasant made such a profound impression that Brown arose and commended him to the church as his eventual replacement. Pleasant was ordained at Ebenezer in November 1826. He immediately began to serve this church and soon added Flat River and Wheeler to his circuit. All three churches experienced great success and increased in membership under his care. Ebenezer still exists and is located south of Yanceyville in Caswell County.

Our minutes for May 1830 record that Stephen Pleasant was asked to "attend church two days in every other month" (i.e., to serve as our pastor and to moderate a Saturday Conference meeting and Sunday preaching every second month). Pleasant sent back word that he would accept the call beginning in 1831.

The issue of missions had not come up in Sandy Creek Association meetings prior to this point. The Minutes of the 1832 meeting indicate that this was about to change. The Association's stand on missions is indicated in what was called a "circular letter," a sort of sermon in writing that was printed in the back of the annual minutes and sent to every member church. The 1832 circular letter concerned missions and reads in part:

> "Others of our denomination have not hesitated nor been ashamed to come forth before the world with an expression of their sentiments unfavorable to the cause of missions... We believe that they have erred sadly in their judgments and that if they would take an enlightened and unprejudiced view of the subject, they would ... be as zealous in behalf of missions as they are now against them."

The circular letter then goes on to review the major argument of the anti-mission forces:

> "There are some who think that all movements on the part of men to convert heathen... are presumptuous and imply that God cannot do his own work ... and that when he sees fit he will accomplish his own purposes without meddling interference."

And then the Association's circular letter concludes:

> "This kind of argument would prostrate all the activity of man and make him a mere drone ... It is incumbent on all Baptists that are favorable to the diffusion of Missionaries, of Bibles, of Tracts, and of Temperance principles, to proclaim it openly and boldly, to consent so that the whole Denomination shall not be disgraced by the ill-judged conduct of one or two misguided churches or associations."

When these same issues were addressed at the Country Line Association meeting in 1832, Stadler made a motion that the Association go on record against missions. Stephen

Pleasant vigorously opposed Stadler's motion and as a result was excommunicated by the Association. He thereupon led two of his churches, Ebenezer and Wheeler, out of the Association. Flat River did not support him, and he resigned as their pastor.

Difficulties soon developed in both Ebenezer and Wheeler. Anti-mission members worked to get their churches to withdraw their support for Pleasant. At Wheeler, the members voted to remain with the Country Line Association but also wanted Pleasant to continue to preach. He refused. At Ebenezer, Pleasant's home church, events took a nastier turn. Pleasant was charged, in February 1833, with holding an unchristian grudge against one of the anti-mission stalwarts. When Pleasant denied the charge and insisted that the real charge against him was his stand in favor of missions, the Ebenezer church excluded him from fellowship.

We are fortunate to have a letter written at just this time by Pleasant to Samuel Wait, an agent of the State Convention and later the first president of Wake Forest College. Excerpts from the letter, preserved in the archives at Wake Forest, dated April 23, 1833, follow: [dashes indicate words that I cannot make out]

"Very Dear Bro. Wait: I have just returned home from Cain Creek last evening and found you had wrote me a letter... I was much pleased at hearing that you and your family were well... The people about Cain Creek are well. I staid one night at Bro. Joel Parrish's and one with Bro. Stephen Justice and saw most of the brethren. Things go on quite comfortable there. But, oh my Bro., things are different in this region. Things have gone seemingly to their full length. The Church at Ebenezer has excluded me from them, and I expect they will have to exclude about 15 more that stand in sentiment with me. At Wheeler twenty-one have been excluded, not for any aggression or any Steps as Christian but for their benevolence and efforts to promote good...

"I will now try to give you some of the particulars that led to my exclusion. You know when you were with me at Wheeler's, I informed the church that I could not attend them any longer until they manifested a wish for it to do so. At their next meeting a vote was taken and a messenger sent to request me to attend them. I promised to give them an answer at their January meeting at which time there was a large church collected. When they came to that part of the business, I then rose and told the church I wished to ask them some questions before I could give them an answer. I wished to know if the church thought I had faithfully discharged my duty to the best of my ability. The reply was I had. I then asked if they had seen anything in me like lauding over the church. Some of the members ... said they thought they had, particularly in ---ing the Association. What they call lauding I call self-defense and I still stood there, was my reply. I then went on to tell them I had several objections against attending them... [then] Bro. McKee preached a sentiment I could not bear and that I did believe to be in --- with his text ... and that if he believed as he preached he ought not to unite with me and if he would act so un---- I would not for I did not fellowship the preaching nor would I have any connection with him as a minister until he confessed the wrong or convinced me of an error. For this --- alone he came to Ebenezer and laid in an accusation against me before that church and said I would not acknowledge that I was wrong; they declared me unworthy of fellowship. Sometime after this ---- took place, I went to Cain Creek. They, understanding the matter, declared their fellowship good with me and, during my exclusion, they have taken me into that church ... I will try to take care of them...

"I have gone through a scene of much trouble but I have come to a conclusion that ... I will now go and preach at the request of my brethren, find friends, and to form ourselves into a church and at some fit opportunity annex ourselves to some association... Farewell."

As indicated in his letter, Stephen Pleasant found a church home at Cane Creek and he continued to preach here during the 1830s. The Ebenezer Church felt ill will against Cane Creek and the matter came to the attention of the Sandy Creek Association at their annual meeting in 1833. A resolution was passed saying, in part:

"Whereas Elder Stephen Pleasant, who was a member of Ebenezer Church, ... has been excluded from that Church ... and whereas Cane Creek has received said Pleasant into that Church, from a belief ... that he was disowned by that Church, not for immoral conduct, but for being friendly to the benevolent institutions of the day:

"...Resolved, therefore that this association advise these two churches to get helps from other sister churches and meet in conference on this matter and endeavor to adjust the differences so that brotherly love may continue not only between them but likewise between the associations."

Our minutes for November 1833 tell what happened next:

"... to bring about a reconciliation between Cane Creek and Ebenezer Church which were at [odds] with each other on account of the Church at Cane Creek, having retained Elder Stephen Pleasant as their Pastor who had been excluded from the Church at Ebenezer and on account of his being in favor of the benevolent institutions of the day, namely Bible Societies, Temperance Societies, and missionary societies..."

Cane Creek selected four of its own members (John Reeves, James Morrow, Thomas Oldham, and Thomas Hunter) and called upon Mount Carmel, the Flat River Association, the Raleigh Association (who sent George W. Purefoy), and the Roanoke Association. This delegation then traveled to Ebenezer church in Yancyville to negotiate reconciliation. Our minutes record the results:

"The Committee from the Cane Creek attended but the Church at Ebenezer refused to hear them."

At their next annual meeting, the Country Line Association refused to receive any Sandy Creek delegates as guests because "Sandy Creek was friendly to all religious and benevolent institutions of the day and because Sandy Creek received Stephen Pleasant as a preacher."

Stephen Pleasant continued as the pastor at Cane Creek after his break with Ebenezer and the Country Line Association. Soon after his letter to Samuel Wait, he rallied his sympathizers from Wheeler and formed Clement Baptist Church. Those who had been excluded with him from Ebenezer Church helped him establish Beulah Church. In October 1834 these two churches and one other, with a combined membership of 131, joined together to form the Beulah Association. Undoubtedly, Cane Creek's old ties with Sandy Creek were still strong for we did not immediately join the new association even though Stephen Pleasant continued to serve as our pastor. But eventually, in May 1837, Cane Creek elected to switch to the Beulah Association and for the duration of its stay there, 1837-1870, was that Association's largest church.

And what became of Ebenezer, the church that had begun the difficulties by excluding Stephen Pleasant? They retained their anti-mission sentiment and wrapped themselves proudly and defiantly in the banner of the Primitive Baptists, a small sect of Baptists who do not choose to ally themselves with mainstream Southern Baptists because they continue to this day to believe that God, "when he sees fit, will accomplish his purposes without meddlesome interference."

In October 1839 our minutes state that "Bro. Pleasant requested the Church to release him from the Pastoral charge of the Church that he may apply his labors where they were more needed. The Church agreed to the proposition. On motion, the Church agreed to call Bro. Geo. W. Purefoy to the Pastorate of the Church." Purefoy was at this time one of North Carolina's most prominent Baptists and had been a member of the 1833 delegation from Cane Creek to Ebenezer Church. He later joined Cane Creek by transferal of letter in April 1838.

There was one final bizarre episode concerning Stephen Pleasant in Cane Creek's history. This concerned his friend Stephen Justice. It will be recalled that Justice was a Deacon at the original Antioch church and that when that Church fell into doctrinal difficulties with the Sandy Creek Association, he was declared by the Association to be the only member to be doctrinally "pure." He was advised to find a church home elsewhere. Nevertheless, Justice stayed and labored on at Antioch for many years before eventually coming to Cane Creek along with his wife, Anna.

Justice was apparently a successful planter whose plantation was several miles east of the church. The events surrounding his death read like a soap opera. Our church minutes give us only faint clues as to what really occurred. When Justice died, he left a considerable sum of money and, in his will, directed Stephen Pleasant to see to it that it was spent on missionary work. The will did not go undisputed. A member of Cane Creek, James Morrow, laid claim to some of Justice's money. This is puzzling. Why would someone else contest the will? We find the following entries in our Minutes:

March, 1840:
"It was stated to the Church that a difficulty was existing between Bro. James Morrow and Bro. Stephen Pleasant which had given rise to many false reports whereby his character and the character of this church is suffering. Wednesday before our next meeting was set apart to investigate the matter and Brethren Sidney Whitted and John Moore were appointed to see Bro. Pleasant and invite him to attend. [By now, Pleasant was no longer our pastor.]

"On the day appointed the matter was investigated. Bro. Morrow stated to the Church that he did wrong in attempting to break the will of Bro. Stephen Justice and that he was sorry that he ever attempted to. His acknowledgment was satisfactory to the Church and Bro. Pleasant. Bro. Morrow stated that he had relinquished all claim in the suit pending about such will.

"The Church unanimously agreed to give Bro. Pleasant an instrument of writing certifying that they were perfectly satisfied with the course he had pursued in relation to the will."

September, 1840:
"...Bro. Lemuel Carroll was laid under the censure of the Church for saying in a conversation with Bro. John Moore and Sidney Whitted that Bro. Pleasant had cheated the heirs of Stephen Justice out of $2000 and that Bro. Pleasant would keep the money left for missionary purposes if he could."

November, 1840:
"The Church met in conference. Bro. Carroll acknowledged that he was sorry for what he had said respecting Bro. Pleasant and the Church forgave him."

March, 1841:
"Bro. Oldham stated that Bro. Stephen Pleasant had left in his hand for the church fifty dollars of the money which Bro. Stephen Justice directed in his will to be given to the poor saints to be distributed among the needy of this church. On motion, Bro. Oldham was appointed treasurer of the church and Bro. Sidney Whitted, Sidney Lloyd, John Reeves, and Thomas Cate to direct the treasurer how to apply the money." (This marks the beginning at Cane Creek of the position of Church Treasurer.)

So, what was really going on? The real story lies in a set of notes sent to our then Clerk, Mae Crawford, in 1976. A collateral descendant of Stephen Justice had located court records in Raleigh for the Orange County Court of Pleas and Quarter Sessions. (In those days all county business was conducted out of this court. There were no county commissioners.) The story that emerges is this:

One night in 1835, Stephen Justice summoned our preacher and his good friend, Stephen Pleasant, to his house. Justice felt that he was dying and wanted to have Pleasant help him write his will. He was too feeble to write it himself, so he dictated it to Pleasant and was at least able to put his signature on the document. Justice had no surviving children, so he left money to various relatives and everything else for his wife's use during her lifetime. Then, at her death, he wanted to give $1,000, a huge sum in those days, to missions, with his friend Stephen Pleasant to manage the gift. (He also gave Pleasant an enslaved girl named "Hut.")

Things began to become complicated when, a year after her husband had died, Anna Justice married James Morrow. In those days, the property owned by the new wife became the property of the new husband, so James Morrow's wealth increased considerably. Things grew even more complicated when Anna Justice Morrow died in 1839. James Morrow was then faced with losing control of the old Justice plantation because Stephen Justice's will stipulated that $1,000 was to be placed in Stephen Pleasant's hands to be spent on missions. The only way to do this was to sell the plantation to raise the money (the sale ending up bringing in closer to $1,500.)

Morrow as a result went to court claiming that the will was invalid. It had not actually been written by Justice. The case was heard at the courthouse in Hillsborough. After some wrangling, the judge ruled in favor of Pleasant: The will was valid. At this point Morrow apologized to the church for contesting the will in the first place.

Stephen Pleasant then attended the annual meeting of the Beulah Association and offered it $1,500 for missions on the condition that the Association raise matching funds of $1,000. This proved impossible and Pleasant withdrew his offer the next year. I have a stray note in my records that Pleasant then may have offered the money to Bethel Baptist Church or he may have offered it to the Baptist State Convention. Cane Creek received only $50 of Stephen Justice's bequest.

Cane Creek was thus a focal point in the struggle over missions. Under Thomas Cate's leadership as our first pastor, we probably had a favorable attitude toward evangelism. But we also probably experienced the religious "coldness" that was felt far and wide in the late 1700s and early 1800s. The Second Great Awakening was no doubt felt here but we lack solid evidence as our records are missing for this period. Undoubtedly, though, we had some sympathy for the growing interest in "benevolent institutions" as otherwise, we could not have provided a good home for Stephen Pleasant, a determined advocate for them. Our good fortune continued because after Stephen Pleasant moved on, our pulpit was filled by one of the most prominent men in Baptist affairs in North Carolina, George W. Purefoy.

11: CANE CREEK AND THE CIVIL WAR

Today, when we think back to the Civil War, we recall the old stories about valorous and bloody fighting, about the suffering of the citizenry, and how it all came to an end locally on April 26, 1865, at Bennett's farm, then in Orange County. This is when and where Confederate General Joseph E. Johnston surrendered a large force (larger than the force earlier surrendered by General Robert E. Lee on April 9th at Appomattox) to Union General William Tecumseh Sherman.

Our church minutes should be able to give us a hint of what life was like during the war. Unfortunately, we have no surviving minutes for the period 1850-1863. We do not even know the name of the then church Clerk, but we do know that in 1863 charges were brought against him at a church business meeting and he was excluded. When the dust had settled, the minutes were gone.

Several members of our church served in the Confederate army and the church roll indicates the names of those who died in service. What the church record does not state is how its members felt about the war, how the local citizens suffered during the war, and the scars it left behind.

The primary issue that divided North and South was, of course, slavery. Slavery was critical for the agricultural economy in the eastern part of North Carolina but was not an institution of critical importance in Orange County. Indeed, in 1860, about 70% of the white male heads of household in Orange County owned no slaves. Most of the rest owned just one or two. Only a few wealthy planters had ten or more.

In the year 1831 there were two critical events that helped determine what was to happen over the next 30 years. One was the first publication of an abolitionist newspaper, _The Liberator_, which was to stir up the slavery issue constantly. The other was a slave revolt in Virginia led by Nat Turner that sent shockwaves throughout the south. It led to the passage of state laws that forbade teaching slaves to read and write and the assembly of slaves into groups unless there was a white person present.

The growing division between North and South regarding slavery can also be seen in the 1845 birth of the Southern Baptist Convention. Before then, Baptist churches, north and south, had formed a Triennial Convention (so named because it met every three years) to further home mission activities through an organization known as the American Baptist Home Mission Society.

In 1844 the Society passed a resolution stating, "... if anyone should offer himself as a missionary, having slaves, and insists on retaining them as his property, we cannot appoint him. One thing is certain, we can never be a party to any arrangement which would imply approbation of slavery."

In response, 293 delegates from southern churches (almost all from Virginia, South Carolina, and Georgia), state conventions, and Baptist seminaries met in Augusta Georgia and established the Southern Baptist Convention. It began with a total membership of 352,000 individuals enrolled in over 4,000 local Baptist churches across the south. There was no declaration of faith or principles. Instead, the issue concerned the appointment of slave owners to be missionaries.

As time went by after the North-South Baptist split, the division in the country grew worse. The issue was not so much whether the southern states had the constitutional right to keep slaves. Most Americans conceded that they did, the original Constitution having express provisions about slavery. The issue was over whether new territories admitted to the union should enter as slave states or as free states. The U.S. Constitution of 1789 stated, in Article I, Section 9, that Congress could not at any time before 1808 prohibit importation of slaves by states then permitting the importation of slaves.. This was not a big issue in the South because of the natural population increase of slaves, The political issue was the balance of power in Congress. This balance could be upset by the admission of new states to the country.

Whether new states would be admitted to the Union as slave or free states was important because there was then an even split in Congress between slave and free states: eleven each. The Missouri Compromise of 1820 resulted in the admission of Maine as "free state", Missouri as a "slave state", and the banning of slavery in the then western territory north of Missouri's southern border that was part of the "Louisiana Purchase" The compromise was updated in 1850 after the Mexican War extended the western border of U.S. to the Pacific Ocean.   The US map of 1850, when there were thirteen slave states and thirteen free states, then looked like this:

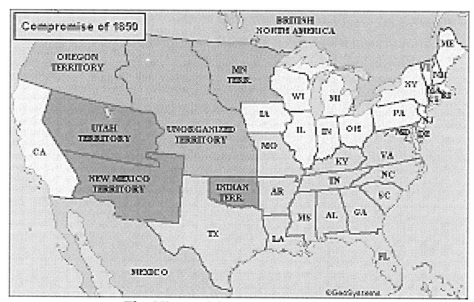

The Missouri Compromise of 1850

Besides slavery as a critical political issue, there was also a pressing moral issue. By the 1850s, slavery had become a national hot-button matter, Northern abolitionist groups were rapidly gaining strength, armed conflict was occurring in Kansas between pro- and anti-slavery contingents, and the Underground Railroad was helping runaway slaves get north to freedom. In our part of the state, the Underground Railroad was much abetted by Quakers, most of whom did not believe in slavery). Some brave abolitionists traveled through the South speaking out against slavery.

The *Hillsborough Recorder* (which published from 1820 to 1879) reported this incident in 1850:

> "A very large public meeting was held in Greensborough on Tuesday for the purpose of devising ways and means to clear the country of abolitionists who have for some time been in that section of the state disseminating their pernicious doctrines and poisoning the minds of such as came under their influence. Deep excitement pervaded the assemblage and prevails throughout the community to an extent never seen before. The following resolution was adopted by acclamation and evinces a resolute determination to free themselves from such pests –- peaceably if they can, but forcibly if they must:

> "Resolved: That a committee of five be appointed to notify Adam Crooks and Jesse McBride, persons who are said to be emissaries of Abolition Societies at the North, immediately to leave this country and that if they fail to do so, they must abide by the consequences."

In 1860, on the eve of the presidential election, secession was already in the air. During the campaign Lincoln had said he favored continuing the Missouri Compromise but wanted all new states to vote on the slavery issue. The fear throughout the South was that if he were to be elected, abolitionists would soon gain control of Congress because of the admission of non-slave states. Secessionist feelings were in the air. Those southerners who took a strong state's rights position argued that a state had a constitutional right to withdraw from the union and that the union had no right to use force to prevent withdrawal.

It was a time of political turmoil in the country. For years the national political contest had been between Democrats and Whigs. Now, several political parties vied with each other in the 1860 election in North Carolina. The old Democratic Party had split over the issue of slavery. The "Regular" Democrats were strongest in the North. They nominated Stephen A. Douglas for president. He was moderate on slavery and agreed with Lincoln that each new state should vote on slavery. This infuriated some Democrats. They formed the "breakaway Democrats" and nominated John Breckinridge, who advocated a strong pro-slavery stance.

The old Whig party was also much in disarray. Nationally, they had suffered a disastrous loss in the presidential election of 1852 and thereafter proceeded to tear themselves apart over the issue of slavery, splitting into Northern and Southern factions. At the national level they were virtually dead. They had no party organization to mount a presidential campaign. However, at the state level, a group of disgruntled North Carolinians tried to get the Whigs back together. They nominated a person for governor and put on a vigorous campaign even though they had no one to support at the national level.

A fourth party called itself the Constitutional Union party and its rallying point was the preservation of the union. They nominated John Bell of Tennessee for president.

Of course, there was another new political party nationally, the Republican Party, born in 1854 out of the ashes of the old Whig Party. It provided a home for anti-slavery sentiment. In the South it was virtually non-existent. In North Carolina it did not even have a slate of nominees for state office. The regular Democrats also had very little support in the state. So, the national race in North Carolina boiled down to a contest between Breckinridge of the breakaway Democrats and Bell of the Constitutional Union party.

In the November election, Orange County fell into the Whig camp in the state elections, voting for the Whig candidate for governor and all the Whig candidates for the legislature. In the national election the state went narrowly for the breakaway Democrat, Breckinridge, but in Orange County the vote went for Bell, the Constitution Union candidate. Nationally, Lincoln and the Republicans won office.

Southern reaction to Lincoln's victory varied. Sentiment throughout the country was to somehow preserve the union. In Orange County there was little alarm. Opinions expressed in the _Recorder_ reveal that, while few celebrated Lincoln's victory, still they viewed him as a man fairly elected and they expected him to uphold the Constitution and his oath of office. Senator Turner, stated in the _Recorder_ on January 16, 1861 that before the November election "I was often asked what the people of Orange would do if Lincoln was elected. I invariably said that ... you would continue to sow and to reap, to plow and to plant, until, under the constitution, you would have an opportunity to elect a better man..."

This calm reaction probably resulted from the fact that Orange County, like many other counties in the state, had a tradition of a strong two-party system (Whigs and Democrats). The losers in any given election could plainly see that their loss did not result in total disaster. Instead, things went along pretty much as usual, and one could always look forward to the next election.

This was not so in states further to the south, where there was more of a one-party system that, in the decades before 1860, had always been the Democratic Party. It is understandable that greater alarm was felt at the victory of an upstart Republican.

In South Carolina, things were even worse. Following the November election, the legislature met in December and voted to secede from the union. In short order most of the Gulf States followed suit. The secession of the deep South sent shock waves through the upper South.

In North Carolina, the Legislature asked the voters to express their opinion on whether the state should hold a convention to consider secession. The matter went to a vote in February 1861. Orange County overwhelmingly defeated the call for a convention by a four to one margin. In Cane Creek, at a polling station held at a country store run by Thomas Brewer, the vote to preserve the union was unanimous: 81-0. The state as a whole also narrowly defeated the call. The citizens of the state thought that the need to preserve the union was more important than a squabble over slavery and state's rights.

In April, the South Carolina militia fired on and then captured the federal garrison at Fort Sumter located on a small island in Charleston harbor. Three days later, President Lincoln issued a proclamation for all the other states to provide troops to march on Charleston and bring South Carolina to its senses.

WASHINGTON, April 14.—The following proclamation will be published to-morrow (to-day:)

" By the President of the United States, a Proclamation: Whereas, the laws of the United States have been for some time past, and now are opposed, and the execution thereof obstructed in the States of South-Carolina, Georgia, Florida, Alabama, Mississippi, Louisiana and Texas, by combinations too powerful to be suppressed by the ordinary course of judicial proceedings or by the powers vested in the marshals by law, now, therefore, I, Abraham Lincoln, President of the United States, in virtue of the power in me vested by the Constitution and the laws, have thought fit to call forth, and hereby do call forth the militia of the several States of the Union, to the aggregate number of 75,000, in order to suppress said combinations and to cause the laws to be duly executed. The details for this object will be immediately communicated to the several States by the War Department.

Lincoln's proclamation from Raleigh's *Semi-weekly State Journal,* April 17, 1861

Suddenly, the central issue had been transformed. No longer was it a matter of weighing preservation of the Union against a dispute over slavery; now, it was whether or not to raise arms against one's brothers to the south.

Governor Ellis immediately issued an indignant answer:

INSULT ADDED TO INJURY.

The Tyrant Lincoln calls upon North-Carolina for Troops to subjugate the South.

SPIRITED REPLY OF GOV. ELLIS.

WASHINGTON,
War Department, April 15, 1861.
To J. W. ELLIS : Call made on you by to-night's mail for two (2) Regiments of Military for immediate service.
SIMON CAMERON,
Secretary of War.

[GOV. ELLIS' REPLY.]

EXECUTIVE DEPARTMENT,
Raleigh, April 15, 1861.
To SIMON CAMERON, Secretary of War.
Sir : Your dispatch is received, and if genuine, which its extraordinary character leads me to doubt, I have to say in reply that I regard the levy of troops made by the Administration, for the purpose of subjugating the States of the South, as in violation of the Constitution, and as a gross usurpation of power. I can be no party to this wicked violation of the laws of the country, and to this war upon the liberties of a free people. *You can get no troops from North-Carlina.* I will reply more in detail when I receive your "call."
JOHN W. ELLIS,
Governor of North-Carolina.

Governor Ellis' Reply to Lincoln's Proclamation

At a public meeting in Hillsborough, a crowd thunderously approved a resolution containing these words:

> "Whereas the President, by a proclamation, has made requisition... for 75,000 soldiers for the subjugation of our sister states of the South... now we ... do hereby resolve that as citizens of a southern state, we are identified with our brethren of the Confederate States in sympathy, interest, and affection, and will not submit to their coercion..."

Money was also raised on the spot to support a company of volunteer militia to be known as the Orange Guard.

In May, the state legislature called for another vote on secession. Citizens of Orange County once again went to Hillsborough to debate the matter. There were two stark positions to choose between that might seem strange to modern ears. One was outright secession, and the other was continued membership in the Union but in a condition of open rebellion. Orange County voted to remain with the Union. In Cane Creek the vote went heavily for the Union candidates against the secessionist candidates: 76 to 4. But most counties, especially those to the east, voted to secede. On May 21st the state convention was held, and it voted to secede now that it was surrounded by states that had already seceded.

The County immediately prepared for war. The first soldiers came from the ranks of the militia. From times long past, every white male between the ages of 18 and 45 had been required to belong to a militia company and to drill and train periodically. Notices of such musters were regularly published in the _Recorder:_

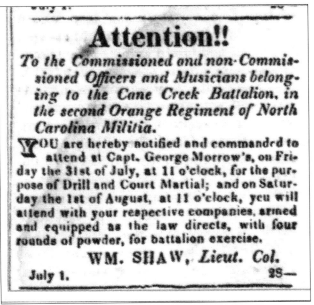

Attention!!

To the Commissioned and non-Commissioned Officers and Musicians belonging to the Cane Creek Battalion, in the second Orange Regiment of North Carolina Militia.

YOU are hereby notified and commanded to attend at Capt. George Morrow's, on Friday the 31st of July, at 11 o'clock, for the purpose of Drill and Court Martial; and on Saturday the 1st of August, at 11 o'clock, you will attend with your respective companies, armed and equipped as the law directs, with four rounds of powder, for battalion exercise.

WM. SHAW, Lieut. Col.

July 1. 28—

Muster call from the _Recorder,_ July 2, 1840

Small drills were held by individual companies of 36 men under the leadership of a resident Captain. Five companies comprised a Battalion and two battalions comprised a Regiment. Orange County had enough men to make up two Regiments or about 700 men in all. The drilling was probably not especially thorough, and it is extremely doubtful that any of the Orange County companies were anywhere close to military readiness. Indeed, charges at a church business meeting in 1845 were brought against Thomas

Sykes "for being intoxicated at muster at Crawford's." But at least the men were familiar with guns and knew a bit of close order drill.

In addition to the regular militia for which participation was required by law, there were several volunteer militia units that were better drilled, better uniformed, and in a higher state of preparedness. In Orange County the volunteer units were from Hillsborough, Chapel Hill, and Flat River (this was before the formation of Durham County from the eastern part of Orange County). The men of the Cane Creek area served in Company G of the 44th Regiment of the militia and went off to war together.

Very little happened at first. The soldiers of the regular militia trained for a while and then were sent off to the eastern part of the state where they were stationed at Fort Macon. The Flat River volunteers were not so fortunate. After five weeks of preparation, they left for the front in Virginia and fought at Manassas on July 21, 1861. In their Regiment, 16 were killed and 64 wounded.

On the home front, the women organized themselves into groups and made uniforms. Since the state had been totally unprepared for war, it had made no provisions for outfitting its soldiers. Thus, it fell to the women back home to do the outfitting, a job that occupied several months. Cornelia Phillips Spencer of Chapel Hill wrote about it as follows:

> "Few were the hearts in any part of the land that did not thrill at the thought that those that were doing the fighting for us were in want of food. From the humble cabin on the hillside where the old brown spinning wheel and the rude loom were the only breast-works against starvation, up through all grades of life there were none who did not feel a deep and tender, almost heartbreaking solicitude for our noble soldiers. For them the last barrel was divided, and the last luxury in homes that had once abounded, were cheerfully surrendered. Every available resource was taxed, every expedient of domestic economy was put into practice. ... I speak now of central North Carolina where many families of high respectability and refinement lived for months on cornbread, sorghum, and peas; where meat was seldom on the table, tea and coffee never; where dried apples and peaches were a luxury; where children went barefoot through the winter, and ladies made their own shoes, and wove their own home-spuns; where the carpets were cut up into blankets, and window curtains and sheets were torn up for hospital use; where soldier's socks were knit day and night, for home service clothes were twice turned and patches were patched again ; and all this continually, and with an energy and a cheerfulness that may well be called heroic."

We are fortunate to have a letter written by Sidney Whitted, a member of our church. He and his wife were baptized in the 1830s and by the 1840s Sidney was a respected member of the congregation who was called upon to represent the church at Association and State conventions. He composed the church's "Rules of Decorum" and investigated numerous cases of misbehavior within the congregation. The name, Whitted, by the way, is a version of the more standard "Whitehead."

Sidney had two sons who fought for the Confederate cause, Walter and Graham. In the fall of 1862, barely a year and a half into the war, Graham was recovering from a battle wound in a hospital in Wilmington. The battle of 2nd Manassas had just been won by Lee's Army of Northern Virginia, and Confederate troops were on the move in Maryland. It was a time of great Southern optimism. If Maryland could be taken, Washington DC would be entirely within rebel territory.

Sidney went to visit his wounded son, Graham, and a letter survives that he wrote to his other soldier-son, Walter, describing the event. It was sent from Chapel Hill on September 12, 1862 upon his return from visiting Graham. Sidney's handwriting is wonderfully clear, but his spelling and grammar betray a limited education. Here are some excerpts:

> "Graham was very sick when I got thear but was mending... He had all his things stole from him and had to come home in his shirt and pants barefooted and slept on the cold ground at night.
>
> The conscripts hav all left hear an gon. The trains are crowded every day with them. A good many war tied, having refused to go. They take every man whether subject to the law or not if he opposes the law. The opposition, as you know, is up the country...
>
> We are all well and hartey and could eate good things with a relish but aught not to complain when many of our soulders go 4 days without anything to eat, martch hard all day and sleep on the ground without tents at night....
>
> Unless we are unsuccessfull in Maryland, this state will not be troubled mutch moor. If defeated thear, you may look out for troublesum times... Your father, S. Whitted.

As the fall gave way to winter, Sidney returned to Wilmington and found his son shivering and cold because of a lack of clothing. Sidney, the loving and devoted father, gave Graham his coat and returned home by train, riding in an open box car in freezing weather. This brutal exposure led to pneumonia from which he never recovered. He died in January 1863. His son recovered from his wounds and lived until 1899.

Our preacher during the war was Stephen Gilmore. He is one of the few Cane Creek preachers for whom we have no picture. Gilmore wrote the following obituary that was published in the _Biblical Recorder_ in the January 28th issue.

"Died in Chapel Hill January 16, 1863: Sidney Whitted, in the 51st year of his age. A man faithful in every relation of life and beloved by all; having but few worldly advantages yet turning them to best account. His loss is irreparable to the community, the church, and his family. He seemed taken at a time when we could least spare his invaluable service; but God, we trust, has "has taken him from the evil to come." What a model he was as a Christian, mason, and a gentleman. Two Sabbath schools and a large helpless family must deeply deplore his loss...The Baptist church mourns his absence, and the community is sad at the remembrance of his death. Those who did not know him may think this is an exaggerated representation, but those who knew him know that the "half has not been told." Oh, that God may impel the living to follow in his footsteps and vouchsafe sustaining grace to those bereft by his departure from earth to heaven.   –Pastor"

The high-water mark of the Southern cause came at Gettysburg in July 1863. Here a fateful battle developed over control of a small town located at an important intersection of roads. The Confederate loss shattered Southern dreams of a quick and easy end to the war. Those who had been skeptical from the beginning now found their voice. Meetings were held throughout the countryside and many of them resulted in resolutions passed against continuing the struggle. One such meeting was held in our neighborhood and was recounted in _The North Carolina Standard_ (published in Raleigh) in its August 26, 1863, issue quoted in part below:

"At a meeting held at Thos. G. Dodson's muster ground in Orange County... on motion John C. Sykes was called to the chair and Anderson P. Cates was appointed secretary.

"A committee was appointed to draft resolutions (later passed by a vote of those present) consisting of Frederick Lloyd, Samuel Crawford, Samuel Stubbins, Thomas S. Cate, and Enoch Sykes. [Of the various men mentioned above, Anderson Cates, Samuel Stubbins, and Enoch Sykes were members of our church.]

"**Whereas** the time has arrived when the people of North Carolina should express ... their views in regard to the policy that the Confederate government has thought proper to pursue...

"**Resolved**: That enough blood and treasure has been sacrificed in this cruel war to prove that fighting will not accomplish the desired end.

"**Resolved**: we are in favor of negotiation... we will [vote] for no man to represent us in the Congress of the Confederate States who is opposed to negotiation..."

And for good measure:

> "**Resolved**: we do not think it proper in any man under 60 years to advocate secession who uses his influence to get other men into the Army and his money to keep himself out." [This latter referred to the practice of a conscripted man's opportunity, if he had the money, to hire another man to take his place.]

Although popular sentiment was beginning to question the wisdom of continuing the struggle, in the end North Carolina did persist with the war until the final surrender, after Appomattox, at Bennett Place near Durham. North Carolina, a reluctant participant from the start, lost more men than any other state.

The Battle at Fort Hamby

Before I leave discussion of the Civil War and how it affected our community, I would like to describe an end-of-the-war incident that few know about. It is worth describing because it involved a man, G. W. Gwaltney, who soon after became our pastor. Gwaltney studied at Wake Forest and served as a chaplain during the war. The incident now known as the battle of Fort Hamby occurred near Wilkesboro. There is now a Fort Hamby State Park just west of the town. In 1903 Gwaltney published an account of the taking of Fort Hamby.

G. W. Gwaltney

People who lived in North Carolina's high country long remembered with dismay the rampage through their towns of a federal army toward the end of the war. It is known as Stoneman's Raid, and it laid waste to Boone, Blowing Rock, Salisbury, Statesville, and Wilkesboro. In early April 1865 a Colonel Wade, serving under Union General Stoneman, deserted, and joined with other deserters, both Federal and Confederate. They began to raid and commit atrocities in Wilkes, Caldwell, Alexander, Watauga, and Iredell counties. Farmhouses were burnt, people murdered, and property stolen. They commandeered a large two-story log house on the Wilkesboro-Lenoir Road and used it as their homebase for weeks. The house was actually a brothel and had belonged to a widow named Hamby so it became known as Forth Hamby because it was almost impregnable. Local lore said that Daniel Boone had first picked this location for a campsite because of its unobstructed view on all sides and down to the Yadkin River.

Several attempts were made to dislodge Wade and his men, but they all failed, and the bloody raids continued. Wade would put on a Confederate uniform and pretend to be a southern soldier on his way home. So disguised, he could safely approach a farmhouse and be let inside. Then the shooting and looting would begin.

This was just after the middle of May 1865. Lee had surrendered his army at Appomattox in Virginia on April 9 and Johnston had surrendered his forces at Bennett Place in North Carolina on April 18. Confederate soldiers began their long treks home after the war only to find Wade and his group of "bushwhackers" terrorizing the countryside around Wilkesboro.

Finally, a few groups of local men came together and joined forces with Confederate Captain R. M. Sharpe, who provided the leadership. One of Sharpe's men was our future pastor, W. R. Gwaltney. One would suppose that his job would have been to save souls, comfort the wounded, administer last rites, and offer up a prayer before each battle. So, it is surprising to find that Gwaltney was actively engaged in the battle of Fort Hamby and to find that at a critical moment he was unable to offer a prayer.

Here are excerpts from Gwaltney's account. I have edited them for brevity.

> "The writer must speak as an eyewitness to all that follows … Col. R. M. Sharpe called together and held a consultation with a number of old soldiers, and it was soon decided that an effort should be made to dislodge Wade and his Alexander County men and put an end to the work of plunder and murder … The company numbered about twenty men. Having crossed the Brushy Mountains at Cove Gap … we met a man who told us that Wade was looking for us and he declared that he could whip a thousand of us and he hoped we would come on. We sent a man to notify federal troops camped at Lexington to send help and relieve the situation as soon as possible. We then met and joined forces with a company of men from Caldwell County. Now we had about forty men.

> "When we approached Fort Hamby, Col. Sharpe said to me, 'take five men and follow the path till you reach the hill yonder on the west side of the fort. I will take the company and station them on the north and east side of the fort and fire a shot to let you know when we have taken up our positions.'

> "When the shot was fired, such a yell was raised in the fort as we never heard before or since. It was more like the howling of devils, cursing us and daring us to come on. Then night came on and some said it would be the better part of wisdom to withdraw. Others said, 'Death is preferable to the miserable life they are causing us to lead and, live, or die, lets us stay till the work is done.'

> "At daybreak one of our Alexander County men crept up to the detached kitchen and set it afire. Soon the whole kitchen was ablaze, and sparks began to fall on the roof of the fort. Then the robbers raised a yell. They asked what we would do with them if they surrendered. 'We will kill the last one of you,' was the reply. They came out with Wade in front. Wade ran off toward the Yadkin River and escaped but the others were captured. Col. Sharpe told them they could have a little while to make any preparation for death should they so

desire. He turned to me and asked me to pray for them. I replied, 'Colonel, I cannot, for I never had such feelings as I have now.' I feared to approach the throne of grace just then lest I might come into his presence without sincere desires. We then moved to the place of execution and bound them to stakes. But before they were executed, I said, 'Colonel, I feel a desire to pray for them now.' I tried to pray for their forgiveness and salvation with all the earnestness of my soul. In a moment the command was given to fire, and they were in eternity.

"On our way back to Alexander County, I saw men on horseback. They had on blue uniforms. They asked me if I knew anything of a band of robbers at Fort Hamby. They were Federal troops from Lexington and were on their way to settle all the troubles. I told them what happened. It can be truthfully said that no men from whatever section ever came into our part of our State who were more cordially welcomed. This was the last of the troubles that followed the war in all that section of the State.

Two years after the events described above, Gwaltney graduated from Wake Forest. He was our pastor in 1870 and 1871. He was a key figure in the formation of the Mt. Zion Baptist Association.

With the end of the war, the South lay in ruins. Its economy was devastated. It would take decades for the South to regain any measure of prosperity.

I have tried to compile a list of all our members who fought in the war. My information comes from several sources. I began with Susan Trollinger's records of who is buried in our cemetery. I then found more names in our old minutes and our old membership rolls. There is a list dated about 1865 that is headed "people in the army" that gives quite a few names of people who do not show up on our official roll. These may have been local youth who were well loved but who had not yet joined the church. The names are shown on the last page of this chapter. The notation "NOR" means that the name is Not On our Roll, i.e., not officially a church member.

We are lucky to have one picture of a Cane Creek civil war veteran. Below are John W. Cheek (1847-1914) and his brother-in-law Sidney Durham. The picture dates to just after the war. John Cheek (on the left) was Margaret Cheek Miller's great grandfather.

John Cheek and Sidney Durham

CANE CREEK'S CIVIL WAR SOLDIERS

NAME		BORN	DIED	COMMENTS
Andrews NOR	Atlas		1863	"Died in the army"
Andrews	George A.			"Killed"
Cates	Archibald		after 1887	
Cates	Dennis M.		after 1886	
Cates NOR	Enoch		1864	"Died in battlefield"
Cates	G. W. P.	1841	1914	
Cates	Henry Mac	1838	1903	
Cates	John E. (of Sanders)			
Cates	Richard L.			
Cates	Sidney S.			"Dead"
Cates	Stephen P.			
Cates	William J.		1865	"Died "at Point Lookout" NOR
Cates	William S.			
Cheek	John Wesley	1847	1914	NOR

Clark	W. A.	1832	1920	NOR
Conklin	Cave			
Howard	John		1864	"Belongs to army. Died"
Howard	Thomas W.		1863	"Died at Gettysburg"
King	Nathaniel			
Minor	James F.	1822	1908	
Oldham	William P.			NOR
Pickard	Lafayette		after 1880	
Pickard	Thomas			
Roberts	Washington		after 1882	
Scott	Henry		1864	"Died "in battlefield" NOR
Sykes	Anderson		1864	"Hospital Raleigh; died" NOR
Sykes	David			
Sykes	John (of Henry)		1863	"Died at hospital" NOR
Sykes	Pleasant			
Sykes	Richard A.			"Died during war"
Sykes	Samuel Y.	1842	1862	NOR
Walker	Sidney			NOR
Whitted	Graham		1899	Wounded at Fort Fisher. NOR
Whitted	Walter			NOR
Workman	Henry			"Dead." NOR
Workman	S. H.	1840	1906	
Wynn	Charles H.			NOR

Now that we have discussed major national events that affected life in the Cane Creek community, it is time to take a closer look at how our church operated. We will focus on an aspect of church life in a rural community that, to modern ears, may seem strange and foreign.

12: THE CHURCH REGULATION OF BEHAVIOR

No denominations were better known for looking after personal behavior than Quakers and Baptists. Among Baptists, it was the Particulars who brought this oversight practice into church life in North Carolina. It makes perfect sense that early churches should have taken this obligation seriously. After all, the civil authorities were usually far away and, as the Regulator unrest shows, they were not trusted by common folks. But the church was interested in more than just enforcing civil law. It also wanted its members to adhere to accepted Christian beliefs and principles, particularly those that were especially dear to the individual church. Each case was recorded in the church Minute Book.

Our earliest records were destroyed by fire in 1829 so we do not know much about what went on in our church for the forty-year period 1789-1829. But it was standard Baptist practice to have a church clerk who recorded important events and decisions in the "church book." The first page or so would contain the church's organizing principles or covenant, as already discussed in Chapter 9. The next few pages would typically contain a list of members. After that, entries would be dedicated to recording each business meeting, which typically happened about once a month.

The mere fact that Baptists held regular business meetings reflects their view that they were the final authority in local church affairs. At the time of our founding we were not yet a Baptist church, but Thomas Cate had been trained under the care of Elnathen Davis at Haw River Baptist Church and therefore would have been familiar with Baptist practices. So, what were these early church meetings like?

Beginning in the early 19th century, a Baptist preacher would have a circuit of up to four churches and would hold a service at each once a month. He would appear in the community on horseback or in a buggy on Saturday around midday. The church members would gather and hear a short sermon. Then the business meeting would begin.

We can begin to learn something about these early meetings by starting at the Association level. The Sandy Creek Association was begun in 1758 and at the first few association meetings it was difficult to get anything done because no one was in charge. It was believed that a group discussion would soon arrive at a consensus that would please everybody. But within a few years they found it necessary to put someone in charge of the meeting and to adopt rules to regulate the proceedings. A set of twelve rules was adopted in 1816 (See Purefoy, p. 106). These Association-level rules were slow to trickle down to the church level.

Our rules date to 1841, when we called George Purefoy to be our pastor. Before Purefoy would accept the call, he asked for a set of "rules of decorum" to be drawn up. They were presented and adopted in February 1841. These rules appear in our Minute Book and are given in Appendix 3. They probably reflect informal practices that had been observed in our church for years.

Since this is a chapter on personal conduct, these are the relevant rules:

> 4th. First business that shall be entered into by the Church shall be an inquiry into the fellowship and orderly conduct of the members and if there be any disorder or cause of grief it shall be brought forward and acted upon.

> 17th. In all cases where it is deemed necessary to receive evidence from such as are not members of our Church, the Moderator may appoint a committee of three persons to hear such evidence and report it to the next conference.

According to Rule 4, the first order of business was an "an inquiry into the fellowship and orderly behavior of the members." At this point in the proceedings, anyone was free to stand and make a complaint against any other member. At later periods in the history of the church, a special group, first called the *Standing Committee*, and later known as the *Spiritual Committee*, had the responsibility of receiving complaints and allegations, investigating them, and reporting their findings at the conference meeting. Typically, the case would be thoroughly discussed by the congregation with the person involved present. An important issue was whether the person acknowledged his own guilt, begged forgiveness, and promised to offend no more. In such cases the church was very likely to forgive the offense and continue the member in good standing. But if the individual did not ask forgiveness and could give no assurance that the offense would not be repeated, then it was likely that he or she would be excluded from membership. In more serious cases, the individual was excommunicated.

Exclusion was a sort of social shunning. Churches and country stores were, in those older times, the focal point of rural life. People would meet at church and at the store to exchange gossip and discuss politics, weather, crops, and other important matters of the day. These were occasions for renewing acquaintances and finding out what was new in the community. Being cut off from one of these community focal points was a serious consequence for anyone.

The first disciplinary case recorded in our Minutes occurs with the very first entry:

> **May 1829**: A complaint was brought against Robert Cheek for fighting with John Workman.

The matter was discussed with no resolution and was postponed until the next meeting:

> **June 1829:** The case of Robert Cheek is considered but he is not present. Brothers Workman and Watson are appointed to labor with him.

This phrase, "labor with him," occurs frequently in the early Minutes. "Laboring" meant that the two brothers talked the matter over with Robert Cheek and through discussion, prayer, and exhortation attempted to bring about reconciliation. In this case, the process failed:

> **July 1829:** (a rare second meeting in the same month): Robert Cheek was excommunicated.

From this 1829 record, it is easy to conclude that such cases were brought up for many years before. If 1829 was typical of all the 40 years back to 1789, then there would be about 150 cases lost to history.

In many cases the excommunication or exclusion was permanent. The church never again had anything to do with the ex-member. But for others, the exclusion was temporary. In about a year the church might consider "restoring" the excluded member to full fellowship if he or she came to a conference meeting, expressed regret, and asked for forgiveness.

Between 1829 and 1917, when the last recorded exclusion took place, the minutes give us a total of 301 cases in which a member's behavior was called into question. Because of gaps in the minutes amounting to a total of about 20% of the monthly meetings, we can project about 360 cases in all. We can add to this the estimated 150 cases occurring before 1829 for a total of about 500 cases. Over the hundred-year period there is considerable year-to-year variation in the number of cases brought before the church. In some years there were none. The modal number of cases in any one year was three but there were a few years when there were a dozen or more cases.

One matter resulted in the disciplining of many Cane Creek members. It began toward the end of the Civil War in 1864 with the passage of a resolution: "we ... do not hold with the play frolics and the singing of carnal songs." Johnson (1937) gives this description:

> "In some communities 'dance frolicks' were held as often as twice a week, on Wednesday and Saturday nights. The young men would 'gallant the girls' to the frolic and dancing would last until midnight. The musician would be a local fiddler who would also call out the steps. Amid the sound of merry laughter and the cry of 'salute your partner,' 'cut the pigeon wing,' the dance would proceed. Mint-sling, blackberry acid and cider were served between dances and not infrequently the men also had their whiskey and brandy. But as the camp meeting movement became more popular, dancing came to be frowned upon. The fiddler became an instrument of the devil, and the pious looked upon the mere possession of one as an indication of an irreligious spirit."

In 1851 a committee reported on frolics at the annual meeting of the Beulah Association. The report said, among other things, that, "... dancing is injurious to Christian love, ... it is generally associated with other evils, ...it creates infidelity, and the best dancers are apt to be the worst scholars."

From this point onward many young boys and girls were charged with this offense and some of the older members were charged with allowing dancing to occur on their property. If the individuals repented and promised to "dance no more" they were forgiven, but if they were not repentant or if they did as Emoline Pickard did in 1878, "danced and said she would dance again," they were excluded.

So, what sorts of misbehaviors could lead to one's exclusion? Individual instances can be startling and sometimes amusing from the perspective of more than a hundred years later. Examples are:

> 1832: offering herself to the Methodists;
> 1840: advertised a beef to be shot for;
> 1841: being too intimate with certain young men;
> 1859: being intoxicated at muster;
> 1868: refusing to pay for pastor's salary (called "covetousness");
> 1877: living a disorderly life;
> 1885: firing his tobacco barn on Sunday;
> 1886: absconding with Joseph Stubbins.

The 1859 incident mentions "muster." All free white men aged 18 to 45 were enrolled in the militia and were required to report for a company muster at least twice a year. Regimental and battalion musters were less frequent. Johnson (1937) presents this description of what went on at musters:

> "The privates usually selected the place for holding the company musters. ...Muster day usually brought men together who otherwise would seldom have met. It was ordinarily looked upon as a holiday and celebrated as such by heavy drinking, betting, fighting, and sports. ... It was long a custom for the champion of one neighborhood to fight the champion of another. Candidates for election often provided liquor for the day and thus augmented the propensity for fighting."

If this behavior was common around Cane Creek, it is a wonder that more church members were not brough up on charges of "being intoxicated at muster."

The 301 recorded disciplinary cases may be divided into about a dozen categories. It is also interesting to divide the cases by sex because, first, many more charges are brought against men than women (81% overall despite there being a greater number of female members throughout the history of the church), and second, because men and women typically are charged with quite different offenses. The breakdown is as follows:

Number of cases Recorded

Offense	Males	Females
Absenteeism	20	0
Covetousness (nonpayment)	14	0
Fighting	13	0
Liquor: drinking, making, selling	51	0
Stealing	6	0
Exclusion at own request	6	2
Profane language	9	1
Spreading rumors	11	3
Sexual misconduct	17	6
Theological issues	11	5
Miscellaneous	23	4
Charges unspecified	35	8
Restoration (offense unknown)	17	7
Dancing and carnal songs	10	22
TOTALS	243	58

Of course, not every case resulted in the exclusion of the individual. Of the 223 cases where it is possible to determine what action the church took (usually either exclusion or forgiveness), 55% resulted in exclusion. Thus, the mere fact that a transgression was suspected often preordained the conclusion to the proceedings. But the nature of the offense also determined the likelihood of being excluded. Although dancing was an offense that was frequently heard after the Civil War, there was only a 20% chance of being excluded for it. One had to be especially stubborn, not ask for forgiveness, and refuse to promise to "dance no more" before one was excluded for this offense. At the other extreme, charges of sexual transgressions such as fornication, adultery, and bastardy were almost certain (91%) to result in exclusion. The few cases in which the case went unproved were, of course, males. Females would be left in an undeniable condition of pregnancy. The other offenses for which a charge was tantamount to exclusion (92%) were the theological matters that consisted of joining the Methodists (never any other denomination), heresy, allowing itinerant preachers in the home, and so forth.

One important issue concerned alcohol. Our early forefathers were hard drinking men and the consumption of all sorts of alcohol was routine. Recall that our first preacher's estate inventory listed two stills. But in the 1830s, during the debate over missions and benevolent institutions, several women's groups began to voice their concern about the extravagant use of alcohol. Eventually something had to be done.

Some of the cases came up because a call had gone out at the Convention or Association level against alcohol. In 1849, when Purefoy was our pastor, a motion was passed at a conference meeting saying that the church "will not hold in fellowship anyone who makes and sells ardent spirits." At the very next Cane Creek meeting a man was charged with this offense and, when he refused to desist, was excluded. From this time onward a small number of cases dealt with the manufacture and sale of liquor.

There is one case that made me curious because I didn't know what the words meant.

> **June 1899:** Lonnie Crawford was reported as a U. S. Storekeeper and Gauger. W. H. Lloyd, A. P. Cates, and B. T. Lloyd were appointed to see him.

> **September 1899**: The committee appointed to see Lonnie Crawford reported. On motion, the case was dropped.

> **April 1902:** James Lloyd was appointed to see Lonnie Crawford for Storekeeping at a Government Distillery in violation of the rules of the Church.

> **June 1902:** The committee appointed to see Lonnie Crawford reported and Lonnie Crawford was excluded.

I was initially stumped by the term "Storekeeper and Gauger." Research then revealed that the Office of the Commissioner of Internal revenue, the forerunner to today's Internal Revenue Service (IRS), began in the North in 1862 to help collect the first ever national income tax levied to help pay for the war effort. This IRS forerunner soon took over the collection of the whiskey tax that has been in effect since the 1790s. It would issue licenses to those who wished to sell whiskey. Presumably, the whiskey was in barrels and the storekeeper was required to measure out (to "gauge") any amount that he sold a customer. An excise tax had to be paid for each ounce sold. The whiskey had to be kept in a separate building under lock and key. A government official would inspect it from time to time.

The 1902 reference to a Government Distillery implies that the whiskey was made on-site by a licensed distiller. I wish I could uncover more about this. Maybe someone in the community has a recollection of hearing people talk about this long ago.

The last cases recorded in our minutes happened between 1915 and 1917. Here is the list of the final ones:

> **February 1915:** A committee appointed to investigate the trouble between Ed Snipes and W. T. Reynolds; the church voted the next month to drop the issue;

> **June 1915:** C. M. Roberson was forgiven for his wrong-doing (unspecified) by the Church;

> **August 1915:** Gaston McCauley asks the Church to dismiss him. In October "fellowship was dismissed for not cooperating with the church;"

> **September 1915:** Clyde Bradshaw was restored;

May 1916: Fellowship withdrawn from Wilbert Lloyd for joining the Methodists;

June 1916: Fellowship withdrawn from Archie Manniss for repeated absences;

April 1917: The Spiritual Committee recommends withdrawing fellowship from David M. Holmes, W. H. Stubbins, and Lillie Crawford.

By the 1930s the minutes of the Mt. Zion Association no longer listed the numbers of each church's exclusions. A new generation of Baptists had decided that other institutions such as the law enforcement system and the family were better places to exercise discipline and control. The church was left the duty of saving souls and removed from its role of identifying and punishing sinners.

Some of the church members who were disciplined by the church were black. In the next chapter we will look at the role slavery played in our church and see how after the Civil War freed slaves remained in the church.

13: CANE CREEK'S BLACK MEMBERS

In this day and time, when many rural Baptist churches are virtually all-white, it is difficult to imagine that there ever were Black members whose presence was routine at Sunday services. Since our earliest records are missing, we do not know exactly when the first slaves were taken into the Church. But it must have occurred from the outset, for slaves were present in the area well before the church's establishment in 1789. Indeed, our first preacher, Thomas Cate, was a slave holder.

Slavery in America dates to 1619 when slaves were first brought to Virginia. Before that there were plantations in Barbados and the Bahamas that used slave labor to grow sugarcane. The first mainland plantations specialized in rice, tobacco and indigo.

In North Carolina slavery was endemic to the eastern counties and formed the basis for a small but elite planter society (the term "planter" was reserved for anyone owning 20 or more slaves). Planters owned vast plantations, huge numbers of slaves, and controlled the political and cultural life of the state. In 1755 Halifax County, for example, had a slave population that outnumbered the white population four to one.

These eastern planters regarded the interior of the state as a frontier peopled by a rough and ignorant breed who lived a hard-scrabble existence. One observer of the time noted that the inhabitants of these two regions were as different as if they composed two separate and opposing states. Indeed, later when the interior population swelled to surpass that of the prosperous agricultural east, the two regions came into conflict over numerous issues ranging from the Regulator movement to the building of a State railroad in the 1850s.

In colonial times, as one traveled west in the state, one encountered fewer and fewer slaves. This was partly due to the nature of the land and the poor state of transportation, which made it difficult to operate a large plantation much west of about Fayetteville. Further, there was the rugged individualist nature of the frontier settlers who had come from places where slavery was almost non-existent.

A serious issue concerned how representation in the State legislature would be determined. Like most states, the North Carolina constitution apportioned seats in the House of Commons by population. The State Constitution allowed the eastern counties to bolster their population numbers by including slaves in the count. As expected, this matter stuck in the craw of those in the central and western parts of the state, where the number of slaves was relatively small.

In 1755, when Orange County had a population of about 4,000, only 8% of the families owned a slave and the largest slave owner, Mark Morgan, who settled along Morgan Creek, owned only six. A hundred years later, on the eve of the Civil War, the slave population of Orange County amounted to 31% of the total population, about average for a central North Carolina county and much lower than the eastern counties. Just under half of the county's landowners had slaves and the vast majority of them had just one or two slave families. Slaves were, of course, counted as property and, as such, had a value placed on them. The 1860 average value of a slave in Orange County was about $300, which was about what 100 acres of farmland would have been worth.

The basis of slavery was, of course, a matter of economics. One could be more prosperous with slaves than without, if one's livelihood depended on the use of relatively unskilled labor. But if a southern slave owner had been asked his justification for owning slaves, he would not have made an economic argument. He probably would have justified slavery with a religious argument. Most of the antebellum books written to justify slavery used religious arguments and, unfortunately, were written by Southern ministers.

These arguments often begin by citing Genesis 9,18-27:

> "And the sons of Noah that went forth from the ark were Shem, Ham, and Japheth, and Ham is the father of Canaan. These are the three sons of Noah and of them the whole world overspread. And Noah began to be a husbandman, and he planted a vineyard, and he drank of the wine and was drunken; and he was uncovered within his tent. And Ham, the father of Canaan saw the nakedness of his father and told his two brothers outside. And Shem and Japheth took a garment and laid it upon both their shoulders and went backward and covered the nakedness of their father; and their faces were backward, and they saw not their father's nakedness. And Noah awoke from his wine and knew what his younger son had done to him. And he said, cursed be Canaan: a servant shall he be unto his brethren. And he said, blessed be the Lord God of Shem; and Canaan shall be his servant. God shall enlarge Japheth, and he shall dwell in the tents of Shem; and Canaan shall be his servant. "

This passage eventually became the foundational text for justifying slavery. In its most common version, nicknamed, "the curse of Ham," Canaan was dropped from the story, Ham was made black, and his descendants were made Africans.

The favorite New Testament text was Ephesians, 6, 5-7:

> "Servants, be obedient to them that are your masters according to the flesh, with fear and trembling, in singleness of your heart, as unto Christ, doing the will of God from the heart; with good will doing service, as to the Lord, and not to men: knowing that whatsoever good any man doith, the same shall be received of the Lord, whether he be bound or free."

Another typical justification for slavery was the idea that slavery actually benefitted African slaves and that they should be happy and contented. Bishop Stephen Elliot of Georgia put it like this:

"Critics of slavery should consider, by their interference with this institution, they may be checking and impeding a work which is manifestly providential. For nearly a hundred years the English and American churches have been striving to civilize and Christianize Western Africa and with what result? ... A few natives have been made Christians ... but what a small number in comparison with the thousands, nay, I may say millions, who have learned the way to Heaven and who have been made to know their savior through the means of African slavery. At this very moment there are from three to four millions of Africans, educating for earth and for Heaven in the so vilified Southern States – learning the very best lessons for a semi-barbarous people – lessons of self-control, of obedience, of perseverance, of adaptation of means to ends; learning, above all, where their weakness lies, and how they may acquire strength for the battle of life. These considerations satisfy me with their condition and assure me that it is the best relation they can, for the present, be made to occupy."

The abolitionist movement in the North began as early as 1688 in Pennsylvania with the *Quaker Petition Against Slavery*. It took a while, but slavery among Quakers was almost gone by the Revolutionary War. All northern states had laws against slavery by 1804.

Throughout the North the attitude toward slavery was that it should gradually be abolished, with return to Africa as a favored option for former slaves. This gradualist attitude shifted slowly toward immediate emancipation and became more pronounced when William Lloyd Garrison began to publish a newspaper, *The Liberator,* in 1830.

By 1850, the "underground railroad" was in full swing in spite of The Fugitive Slave Law, which made the smuggling of slaves into free states illegal. That same year Harriet Beecher Stowe published *Uncle Tom's Cabin*, which was widely read and aroused popular opinion against slavery.

When Congress passed the *Kansas-Nebraska Act* in 1854, many people were outraged because it allowed these two territories to enter the union as slave states if the citizens so voted even though as part of the "Missouri Compromise" it had been agreed that new states in the Louisiana Purchase territory would be free states). This outrage was a large contributing factor in the formation of the Republican Party. In 1860 , the party nominated Abraham Lincoln for president.

At Cane Creek as well as most other southern churches, slaves could join, and many did. Their names appear in our church minutes from time to time with their last names given as the name of their owners. Our rolls indicate the names of our early slave members and among these we find the following family names (and numbers of slave members from each family in our church). These forty slaves include 31 females and only nine males. Obviously, there were slaves in the community that did not belong to the church.

Andrews (1)	Kerr (1)	Reeves (1)
Bailey (1)	Lashlay (1)	Roach (1)
Brewer (3)	Lloyd (1)	Strother (1)
Burnett (1)	Minnis (1)	Thompson (6)
Croker (2)	Moore (1)	Walker (1)
Crutchfield (1)	Morrow (2)	Watson (1)
Esterse (2)	O'Daniel (1)	Westen (1)
Hopson (2)	Oldham (4)	Whitted (1)
Jones (2)		

There were a few lonely anti-slavery voices of dissent in the south. The (Presbyterian) Reverend Minister from Alamance County, Eli Caruthers, was known widely to be against slavery but his congregation tolerated it because he made little of it when preaching and because he was such an effective preacher. But the congregation had had enough when he closed a Sunday service at the beginning of the Civil War by praying for the young soldiers just going off to war by saying, "May they be blessed of the Lord and returned in safety, though engaged in a lost cause." Their congregation, enthusiastic and hopeful about the upcoming war, was outraged and asked for his resignation.

When Caruthers died in 1865, a manuscript was found among his belongings. It was entitled *American slavery and the immediate duty of southern slaveholders* and had never been published. Scholars of American slavery have called it a better critique of slavery than anything the Northern press produced. Caruthers deduces from the creation story in Genesis, quoted above, that we have no right to hold anything as property without an express grant from the Creator. He cites Genesis 90, 2-3, which speaks of a new beginning for the human race following Noah's flood:

> "The fear of you and the dread of you shall be upon every beast of the earth, and upon every bird in the air, upon everything that creeps on the ground, and all the fish of the sea; into your hand they are delivered. Every moving thing that lives shall be food for you; and as I gave you the green plants, I give you everything."

Caruthers concludes that no allowance is made at creation for human beings to possess other human beings. God is saying, in essence, "you may have the earth and all its products but on your fellow man you must not lay your hand."

Caruthers agrees that all the non-Hebrew races were descendants of Ham. These races spread throughout the world, and all had their ups and downs. Magnificent cities were built only to be destroyed. Some races have sunk into savagery. Africans (at least those of northern Africa) built the pyramids but have since sunk from their heights. The Angles and the Saxons, now at an apex, were once despised as savages by the Romans.

Caruthers then cites Exodus 10.3:

"So, Moses and Aaron went in to Pharaoh and said to him, "Thus says the Lord, the God of the Hebrews, 'how long will you refuse to humble yourself before me? Let my people go that they may serve me.'"

The statement, "let my people go," Caruthers says, now applies to African slaves. Slavery anywhere is a violation of God's will because, "slaves cannot make the entire surrender of themselves to the Lord which the gospel required, and to which renewed nature prompts them." They cannot do this because they do not possess even themselves.

Returning to our local black population, I would like to add a few memories recorded by James Cheek. He was born in 1874 and was baptized in our church in 1886. After his days as a logger and homesteader, he went west, found religion, and ministered to people of all races for the rest of his life. He recorded his recollections in a 1949 autobiography, _Footprints of a Human Life._ In his childhood the Civil War was fresh in people's memory, but by then Reconstruction was at an end and the state and county were back under local control. We have a copy of his book in our library courtesy of Virginia Perry.

"Uncle Sandy Cheek was a "slave drover," buying up Negro men and women and taking them through the country to sell as a horse trader would sell mules and horses. (p,. 17).

James Cheek

"I recall Grandpa Cheek tell about a peculiar old man who had a slave called 'Basket.' The old gentleman would lie in bed in the morning until Basket got up and built a fire in the fireplace 'Basket, Basket, is it cloudy?' The master would call to him. 'I dunno, it's raining,' Basket would answer. (p. 37).

"I heard mother say that when the war was over, Grandpap came home and told the family that the slaves were free. George, a slave whom Grandmother Bradshaw Moore brought with her when she and Grandpap were married, was working in the cornfield. 'Well, George, you are free,' said grandfather, who was quiet-spoken and brief. 'Ah'm gonna give my Marse Dave one mo' day's wuk,' George replied. But George got to thinking about his wife, who was in the little town of Durham, and it was not long before he laid down his hoe and started for Durham. (p. 31).

"In our immediate neighborhood were Grandfather Cheek's place, the Hooker Nix farm, and the Woods estate. This estate of several hundred acres was bought by Caswell county Negroes, Haywood and Bob Jones and others. Caswell County was a noted tobacco raising district and when they moved into the neighborhood their main crop was tobacco. We noticed how well they worked in building their houses, clearing land, and cultivating their fields.

"Haywood Jones was one of the solid citizens of the neighborhood. By his industry and good management, he was able to live better than many white folks in the community. Bob Jones was one of the finest specimens of manhood I ever saw, tall straight, and strong. He came to help us one day along with other neighbors, in putting up a log house for our family on Grandfather Cheek's place. To raise a log, it was placed on the skid poles and a rope put around it, by which it was pulled into place on the wall with the help of some pushing from below. Bob could pull a log up with one hand as though it were a light stick of wood. (p. 36).

"Aunt Charlotte Walker was another outstanding Negro character whom the white folks loved. She did not live in our neighborhood, but I learned about her at election time. I could not help but see the love and respect which people had for her. She made chicken pies and took them to our election ground near Cane Creek Church. She charged twenty-five cents apiece for a small pie. People who could afford to buy a pie did so, but some of us who did not have the price, had to satisfy ourselves with a look at the nice brown crust. One meeting day she came out to the old Cane Creek Church. I heard her talking to some white men and these men seemed to regard her as equal in judgment and character with themselves. Those who know God may 'sit with princes.' (p. 37)

In the typical Baptist church before the Civil War, a separate section of seats would have been reserved for use by slaves. They would undoubtedly have participated in the singing and "amening" but otherwise would have been expected to keep quiet. Just like white folks, they would be brought before the church for such offences as drunkenness, fighting and stealing.

We know from our own minutes that there was some sort of physical barrier in the church building between the races for, in September 1835, a Brother Cates has the temerity to suggest the "removal of the barrier between the blacks and the whites." This caused an uproar and disciplinary charges were brought against Cates for suggesting it. At the next meeting Brother Cates asked for and received forgiveness for having made such a reckless suggestion. We do not know Brother Cates' first name.

Despite many Southern Baptists owning slaves, they must have felt a degree of moral conflict. In Purefoy's history of the Sandy Creek Association, we find that in the very first Associational meeting for which he could find records, the 1805 meeting (Purefoy, p. 75), a local church asked for guidance on the validity of marriages between slaves. The question was a hard one because the laws of the state recognized no such thing and yet it was common for slaves to live together in an arrangement that they and their masters regarded as marriage. The Association pondered the matter for several years before giving its answer in 1808: slaves could be considered married "when they come together in their former custom having no other companion." Owners were also encouraged to prevent such couples from ever being separated, "putting themselves at some inconvenience" if necessary, in buying, selling, or exchanging since "both moral obligation and humanity demand it."

It is interesting to note that at the 1809 Associational meeting, the throng was addressed by the usual number of ministers, but also "Ralph, a colored minister."

July 1832: Received for baptism, a colored woman belonging to James Thompson.

May 1835: Received by letter, a black woman, Lucy, belonging to John Crutchfield and a colored woman, the property of John Kerr, from Lynch's Creek.

May 1838: Received for baptism, Alford, a servant of Mrs. James Thompson.

June 1838: There is a report in circulation against Abram, a servant of James Morrow. A committee is appointed to investigate. In August: The case of Abram is taken up. The committee reports that he is guilty of conduct unbecoming a church member and is excluded.

September 1838: Received for baptism, Hettie, a servant of Mrs. William Thompson, and Rhoda, a servant of William Hopson.

November 1838: Received for Baptism, Charles, a servant of Ezekiel Brewer.

February 1840: Letters of dismissal granted to James Crutchfield and wife and a black woman, Rhoda.

June 1840: A charge is brought against Bethlehem [Thompson] a colored sister.

August 1840: Received for baptism, Joe, a servant of William Thompson

September 1840: The case of Bethlehem is considered. She is guilty of adultery and is excommunicated.

May 1841: Received for baptism, January, a servant of Thomas Brewer.

************** (Minutes from 1849-'64 are missing) ************

May 1864: A colored woman, Julia, a servant of William Jones, relates her Christian experience and is received. Received, William, a slave of T. D. Oldham, George, a slave of J. Watkins; Brooks and Jordan, slaves of T. D. Oldham.

October 1864: The Standing Committee recommends that Lucinda , a servant of David Roach be retained in fellowship.

November 1865: Received: Channa, a servant of T. D. Oldham, Venus and Violet, servants of J. F. Morrow, Cammelia, a servant of T. D. Oldham.

December. 1865: The Standing Committee reports the exclusion of Jordan, a former servant of T. D. Oldham. The charge is stealing.

November 1867: Received: Elisabeth Jones, colored

February 1868: A letter of dismissal is granted to H. Brooks Oldham, colored.

September 1869: Martha Hopson (colored) received for baptism.

November 1871: Received for baptism, Berthemus Alston, colored.

African-Americans Mentioned in Our Minutes 1829 - 1871

In 1835, the Association addressed the issue of slavery more directly and passed the following resolution:

"Whereas we believe it inconsistent with the spirit of the Gospel of Christ, for a Christian to buy and sell negroes, for the purpose of speculation or merchandise, for gain. Resolved, therefore that this Association advise the churches of which it is composed, to exclude members who will not abandon the practice, after the first and second admonition."

A close reading of this resolution reveals that it does not call upon Baptists to give up the buying and selling of slaves. It does call upon the professional slave trader who bases his livelihood on such buying and selling to give up the practice. Presumably, it remained proper to buy and sell slaves for the purpose of carrying on other professions, which in most cases would have been farming. No one at Cane Creek was ever accused of this offense.

Although there were few slave traders in Orange County, slaves were still bought and sold. Below is an ad from the Hillsborough Recorder for June 22, 1859, advertising the sale of the estate of Ann Thompson, who lived just to the west in Alamance County. The estate included several slaves.

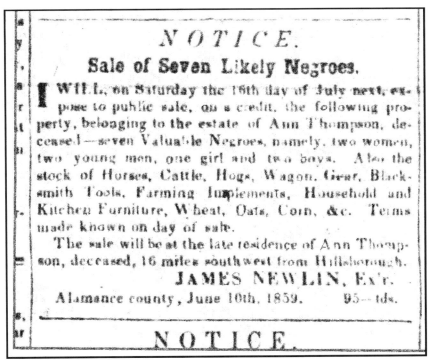

Slave sale in 1859

One would think that the slavery issue, which began to boil on the political front in the 1830s, would have become a topic for constant debate within churches of all denominations. This does not appear to have been the case, at least for Baptists. (Recall that Quakers had long since been opposed to slavery.) There is no record in our own minutes of the matter ever being discussed and Purefoy's history of the Sandy Creek Association fails to note any such discussion beyond the little mentioned above. The primary moral issue of the day was not slavery but the use of "ardent spirits" and much time was spent in debating whether and how Baptists should use whiskey.

In both our own minutes and in Purefoy's history, the year 1845 goes by without special note. Yet this was the year when the nationwide convention of Baptists fragmented over the slavery issue and the southerners withdrew to Georgia to form the Southern Baptist Convention.

While many Southern whites considered slavery to be an acceptable practice, they were concerned for the spiritual welfare of their slaves. Indeed, part of the rationalization for slavery was that slaves could gradually improve themselves through contact with white institutions. The foremost institution was, of course, the church. Thus, whites had no problem with the fact that their church should include black members.

In 1869 Martha Hopson, "colored," joined the church. This is probably the woman actually known as Cammie Hopson who, along with her husband, Jessie, instituted the move to withdraw from the congregation and build a separate black church. It began in September 1873 when "the colored brethren asked the Church to advise them on putting up a house of worship." The Church advised them to complete the building before asking for letters of dismissal.

These two members together with Franklin Lloyd, a member at Bethel Church, began the difficult task of raising money and rallying their friends and relatives in the neighborhood. Cane Creek admitted its last black member, Barthemus Alston, in 1871 and in 1875 Jessie Lloyd (but probably actually named Jessie Hopson) asked for and was granted a letter of dismissal. In 1877 the little congregation purchased two acres for $10 and had soon built the first Hickory Grove church building – a log church with one door, one window, and no floor – a building that was probably little different from the original Cane Creek meeting house. As the black members ceased worshiping at Cane Creek, we find the last mention of the matter in the minutes for July 1876, when the Church voted "to stop the colored people from burying their dead in the graveyard." By now, they had a graveyard of their own.

In 1989 at the two hundredth celebration of the founding of Cane Creek, the Church was honored by the presence of the grandson of Jessie and Cammie Hopson. The congregation went out to our graveyard and dedicated a new monument honoring our black members. That we have a monument at all is due to the efforts of Rebecca Crawford.

IN SACRED MEMORY TO OUR
AFRICAN — AMERICAN MEMBERS
1789 — C. 1880

14: AGRICULTURE AT CANE CREEK

Agriculture has been the backbone of life at Cane Creek for most of its 250 year's existence. It would be interesting to know something about how it was done by the first settlers and how it evolved over the years. Did farmers have oxen, horses, cows, sheep, mules, pigs, and such? What crops were planted? How much land was tilled? How did they get their harvest to market so that they could buy the things they needed to maintain life in the back country?

Our earliest settlers would identify the best patch of unoccupied land that they could find. The trees would be cut and crops, mostly corn or wheat, would be planted among the stumps. These early farms were on large tracts, often hundreds of acres. If the original patch of land became exhausted after years of cultivation (called an "old field" in times past) and grown up in broom straw, the farmer cleared another patch of land. None of the fields were large.

One reason that fields had small acreage was that early plows were made completely of wood and tilling was extremely difficult. Plows could be made by the farmer from local hardwood trees. There would be a plowshare, the part that actually dug into the earth. Above and behind, it was a moldboard that turned the plowed soil to the right. The idea was that it brought deep soil to the surface; soil that might be richer than that on the surface. Turning over the plowed soil also buried weed seeds. Handles were attached so that the farmer could control the plow, which was pulled by a horse. Planted fields were small, containing only a few acres.

In England, the "acre" was determined by what a man and a team of oxen could plow in one day. Since the moldboard tossed the earth in one direction, usually the right, a field would be plowed in clockwise direction. The plowman would drive his team until the oxen needed a break. This distance was standardized to 220 yards, called a furlong (or "furrow's length"). Then the plowman would turn his team to the right, lift the plow out of the ground, and carry it to the far side of the plot. The distance he could conveniently carry the plow across to the other side was standardized at one "chain" or 22 yards. This would yield a field 220 yards long by 22 yards across. Doing the math, this figures out to be 43,560 square feet or one acre.

Plowing was so laborious that only a small field could be planted. If done well, and if the weather cooperated, a field could keep a family supplied with food for the year. There might also be a small "kitchen garden" for vegetables that needed close attention throughout their growth. Crop fields were fenced in to keep the livestock, which roamed at will, from eating what was being grown. These days, most fences are less for keeping animals out than for keeping them in.

In 1789, the year of our church's founding, Thomas Jefferson, after inspecting farming methods in Europe and consulting with mathematicians, designed a superior wooden plow and attached mould board. The moldboard was not just a flat wooden "wing" behind the plowshare. It was a precisely curved shape that would turn the plowed soil exactly upside down. It was not widely used but, a decade or so later, the basic shape was used in the first plow to have iron parts. This made plowing much easier and allowed for larger fields. It was not until the 1830s that the first workable metal plow with a steel moldboard was developed by a Midwestern blacksmith named John Deere. By 1849, he was selling 2,000 plows a year.

The Jefferson Plow

John Deere's Plow

Farming, in the early years, was not at all up to modern standards. A field would be plowed several times a year and the same crop planted year after year. There was no fertilization, crop rotation, or contour plowing. The practices of the time could wear out a field in several years, and then more land would have to be cleared for a new field.

An examination of Orange County's first newspaper, the _Hillsborough Recorder_, begun in 1820, shows the concerns about the state of agriculture locally. The primary one was that the best land, farmed by the first settlers, was worn out. This meant that inferior land that was hilly had to be cleared and plowed to plant more crops. So, the question these farmers wanted to answer was, "can worn-out fields be reclaimed?"

We can gain a better understanding of the problem from Elijah Mitchell, the UNC professor who later died while exploring our state's and the Eastern seaboard's highest mountain, which now bears his name. In an address to the North Carolina Board of Agriculture in 1824 he said:

> "The clearing system by which the planter divested a track of its wood and continued to cultivate it till it was exhausted and then resorted to a new one was good so long as he had the whole country lying in wilderness before him. ... In the process of time the planter will look down from the barren ridges he is tilling, upon the grounds from which his fathers reaped their rich harvests but which are desolate and abandoned, and inquire whether he cannot restore to them their ancient fertility at a less expense than he can cultivate those lands of an inferior quality with which he is now engaged. Until he is driven by necessity to make this inquiry, we can hardly hope that agriculture will be studied as a science."

As another writer put it in 1853:

> "It is only necessary to visit one of the frontier states and look over the immense fields, where crops grow amidst deadened stumps, standing almost as thick as the original forests – where the exuberant fertility of the soil makes up for the imperfect cultivation, and you have a picture of many portions of North Carolina ... He who removed the trees and gave space for the production of bread was a great benefactor and the necessity of improving soils never occurred to those to whom a boundless and fertile country spread its inducements to advance still farther. ... The sin of exhausting the land and bringing it to its present state rests not upon them but upon the generations who succeeded them."

Several solutions were proposed and re-proposed for decades in the _Recorder_. The first was crop rotation. It was well known in those days that constantly growing the same crop on the same field would result in ever decreasing yields. Tobacco, especially, had this reputation. A second suggestion involved deep plowing – not to a depth of three or four inches, but to seven or eight. And a third suggestion was the use of additives such as manure, salt-peter, and plaster of Paris. This is what a Northampton County farmer proposed in 1850 (I have slightly edited it):

> "There are large bodies of land lying in middle North Carolina which have been so much reduced by continual cropping, planting tobacco, cotton, and sewing oats as no longer to pay the cost of cultivation and are turned out as waste land. ...These lands may be reclaimed and have their productiveness increased from 100 to 150 percent. This is the method I have adopted, and by which I have increased the products of such lands from one and a half barrels of corn to four barrels per acre. In the broom straw to which these waste lands always grow up, let the land be plowed with the largest size

plow drawn by three or four horses, running as deeply as possible, say, nothing less than ten inches, and turning everything under. If possible, follow with a subsoiler and go six or eight inched deeper. About the middle of June, when the weeds are about half grown, sow the land broadcast at the rate of a bushel an acre with any of the numerous varieties of peas. As it is important to give the peas a start over the weeds and grass, I soak them six hours in water and rub them in plaster of Paris. When 12 inches high, sow plaster of Paris at the rate of a bushel an acre. When the peas are half ripe, hogs should be let in to trample and cut up the vines. When this is done the hogs should be taken off. Turn this mass of vines under over which sow a bushel and a half of wheat per acre and six quarts of clover seed. Harrow both in thoroughly and let the work be finished by the middle of October. I venture to affirm that it will amply repay all labor and outlay and astonish by the great results apparently from so trivial a cause."

We can get an idea of what was happening on Orange County farms by taking a look at the forerunner of the county fair. In 1824 there was an Orange County Agricultural Society. They decided to hold a competition and award prizes for the best in several categories.

- The best stud horse
- The best bull calf
- The best yoke of oxen
- The largest and fattest ox
- The best boar
- The best sow
- The greatest quantity of corn from one acre
- The greatest quantity of cotton on one acre
- The largest quantity of Irish potatoes form one quarter acre
- The largest quantity of carrots from one quarter acre
- The best piece of woolen fulled cloth at least ten yards long
- The best piece of cotton and woolen cloth at least ten yards long
- The best piece of flannel at least ten yards long
- The best piece of blanketing at least ten yards long
- The best piece of flax linen at least ten yards long
- The best vest pattern
- The best pair of woolen stockings
- The best pair of cotton stockings
- The best pair of flax thread stockings
- The best two-horse plow
- The best one-horse plow

Agriculture in the back country was a difficult enterprise. Farmers could sell a few of their products locally but to get cash crops to market involved shipping them by horse-drawn wagons to Fayetteville, where they could be loaded onto barges and taken to

Wilmington. The cost of shipping was high, so that the so-called cash crops did not yield much cash. This was the state of things during the gloomy times of the early 19th century. The Piedmont of North Carolina was the joke of the south, backward in many ways. But a change was coming that would revolutionize and invigorate western North Carolina: a railroad.

The first railroad in American began operation in Massachusetts in 1827. Within five years there were almost a hundred miles of tracks in use in the country. By 1843 there were about 4,500 miles in use and by 1851 this had doubled.

South Carolina put its first railroad into service in 1830. It connected Charleston and Hamburg and ran for 136 miles, the longest railroad in the world at that time. The first Virginia railroads were in operation in the same decade. North Carolina built its first railroad, connecting Wilmington and Raleigh, in 1840, but its construction was so poorly done that it became a laughingstock. As the _Recorder_ wrote, "the railroad was the subject of jest and sneer by all who were so unfortunate as to be compelled to ride over it."

The idea of a state-wide railroad in North Carolina was first floated in the 1830s, when some wealthy easterners began to think that perhaps a railroad into the back country would allow them to sell more goods to western citizens. This was a radical, not to say expensive, proposition, and it took several years for the proposal to bear fruit. In 1848, after much debate, the legislature finally authorized the formation of a public-private corporation, The North Carolina Railroad.

Even after this approval by the legislature there was still opposition to the state's involvement in more railroad construction because of the poor reputation of the Raleigh & Wilmington line,   ut in 1849 the North Carolina Railroad Company was formed with an investment of two million dollars, equally shared by the state and private investors. Construction began in Raleigh and in Charlotte in January 1852. Much money was also spent on rehabilitating the line that went to Wilmington.

As construction started, the _Recorder_ wrote:

> "It was scarcely to be credited that the state which was the first to throw off the galling yoke of British bondage [i.e., the Mecklenburg Declaration of Independence celebrated on our State flag], the first to seize the torch of liberty should have long been satisfied to remain in a condition of commercial vassalage – a mere tributary to Virginia on one side and South Carolina on the other. States which, after draining us of our strength to build up our towns and villages, have lost no occasion to sneer at and insult us. ... But we rejoice that a brighter day has at length dawned upon us. "

Looking forward to having a rail connection to the coast, the _Recorder_, in 1853, noted that the cost of transporting a ton of farm produce a hundred miles by wagon is twenty dollars. By rail, it should only cost a dollar and a half.

The first train made its run from Raleigh to Charlotte in January 1855. The effect was electric. Land values went up along the track. Companies formed to take crops to the coast. Indeed, the _Recorder_ of May 1855 carries an ad saying that:

> "J. P. Turner & Co. announce that they have opened a Commission House in the Town of Hillsborough and will promptly attend to forwarding produce and receiving goods at the Rail Road Station. They have provided facilities for getting goods and produce to and from the Station, and ample room for storage. They solicit consignments and will endeavor to please in every respect."

This was the beginning of the shaking off our state's "Rip Van Winkle" reputation. The railroad was a tremendous success. The first train probably looked very much like the etching below that appeared at the top of every railroad bond the state sold.

I have belabored the point of the early agriculture problems because they were so important to rural farmers all over the state. However, I suspect that the good advice published in the _Recorder_ about reinvigorating tired fields fell on deaf ears. The ones who did listen were probably the wealthier farmers close to Hillsborough who had slave labor to get the job done. And it is likely that ordinary farmers never read the new agricultural journals that had begun to advise farmers on the latest best practices. Below is the masthead of the _Farmers Journal_, which contrasts the new way of getting produce to market by train with the old method of using wagons.

We have little direct knowledge of what farming was like in the middle of the 19th century. We can get a glimpse from just before the railroad from the following two notices published in the *Recorder.* From 1845:

"Public Sale

Will be sold to the highest bidder on the 23rd of October, at the plantation of William Hopson, deceased on North East Creek in the lower part of this county all the perishable property of the deceased on said plantation consisting of corn and fodder, cattle, hogs and farming tools.

"And on the 28th, at the late residence of the deceased, on Cane Creek [where Cecil and Mae Crawford lived], will be sold his household and kitchen furniture, crops of corn, fodder, etc., farming utensils, horses, cattle and hogs, wagon, and other articles too tedious to mention. Also, nine likely negroes. William Thompson, executor."

And from 1850:

"Valuable Plantation for Sale

The subscriber offers for sale the valuable tract of land on which he now lives, containing about 340 acres. It is the place where his father, Ezekiel Brewer, deceased, formerly resided, near Cane Creek Meeting House. It has on it an excellent dwelling house and convenient out houses; has a good orchard, is well watered, has a good proportion of excellent wood land, and a part of it is first rate tobacco land, and altogether it is as desirable a plantation as any in that section of the county. Terms of sale will be liberal. Saxfield Brewer [grandson of the original settler, Sackfield Brewer.]

Another clue to 19th century agriculture comes from a 1850 letter to the *Recorder* from William Bingham, who ran Bingham Academy. He had been asked to describe agriculture in Orange County. [I have edited it for brevity.]

"I have this day received your agricultural circular and proceed to answer:

Wheat: Varieties in use include golden chaff and Black Sea, white bearded. Time of planting is October with a harvest about June 20. The yield per acre has been diminishing for many years, falling to an average of five bushels per acre. By gradually improving the soil, a few of us have brought old broom-straw fields up to eight to ten bushels per acre.

Corn: Common gourd seed and Collins. Average harvest is fifteen to twenty bushels per acre. Others do worse.

Oats: Generally sown on the worst land; regarded as an exhausting crop. In good ground, produces thirty to forty bushels per acre. Common average is about ten bushels.

Barley and rye: Not cultivated.

Beans and peas: Not much cultivated except for the table.

Clover: Found valuable by the few who have adopted it.

Timothy grass: Sown mostly in meadows though most meadows grow up in course native grasses.

Cattle: Neat cattle receive little attention here, cost little and are worth little.

Dairy cows: Sell at from ten to fourteen dollars each. A few Durhams were introduced a few years ago, without profit. The Devons will probably succeed well.

Sheep: Very little attended to, and sadly are annoyed by dogs."

And toward the end of Reconstruction in July 1877:

"Abundant rain last week; in some sections somewhat too much. Tobacco and corn rejoice in the prospect. The harvest is all over except a few remaining fields of oats, and everybody is satisfied as a general thing. With a good small grain crop, a fair fruit crop, a promising tobacco and corn crop and, in most parts of the county, a promising crop of hogs, the dawn of prosperity, ought to be about to break upon a county so long under the blight of poverty and disaster."

Another glimpse of farm life can be gathered from James Cheek's book, *Footprints of a Human Life.* He was born in 1874 so his memories are most vivid for the 1880s, but he also reports on the stories he heard his father and grandfather tell.

"In my childhood, all through our part of the country, ... there was a spirit of all things common in the work on the farms.

"When we killed hogs, which took place when the weather began to turn cold, we would invite several of the neighbors to come help us, and then everyone would be given fresh meat if they had none at home. The same rule was caried out in wheat threshing, the people of the neighborhood helping each other. In those days the threshing was done by horsepower, but about the time I was grown, they began to use the stream engine. We also had corn shuckings. Before inviting the neighbors, we would haul up our corn and put it in long piles. All would gather around the pile and have a great time talking while they worked. Sometimes when we wanted to clear land, we would invite the neighbors to bring their axes and saws and come to help us cut down trees which we called clearing up a new ground.

"In those days we did not pay much attention to fertilizing the land as people do today, nor planting cover crops. We kept right on raising the same crop year after year, until the land was worn out, then it naturally grew up in broom sage, scrub pine and red cedar.

"They had what they called coulter plows, which they made from a bent tree, on which handles were bolted and to which was attached a long piece of iron about one by two by twenty inches. They were used in breaking new land.

"Grandpa said that in the early days, after coming from Virginia, they would let their horses run through the woods at night to graze, then go after them in the morning for farm work. They did not have threshing machines, but would flail the wheat and also have the horses tramp upon it... It was winnowed by pouring it on a big cloth on a windy day, or some similar way. Later, fans were invented, through which they could run the wheat to separate it from the chaff. Still later they improved the threshing process until they had what they called the 'ground hog' threshing machine. "

So, we have a picture of the typical Cane Creek farm consisting of fields of wheat, barley, tobacco, corn, some cotton, and other crops in lesser quantity. There were also horses and cows, pigs, and chickens. Kitchen gardens included a variety of vegetables including turnips and potatoes. Many farmhouses had spinning wheels and looms for the making of clothes, curtains, sheets, and blankets.

More recently, Cane Creek became known as a rich dairying section and the road from Chapel Hill was renamed Dairyland Road. Local lore is that this began in the early twentieth century before the advent of electricity. Fresh milk was stored in a spring house to keep it cool and was carried daily to the nearest processing plant (such as Durham's Long Meadow Dairy) for processing and bottling.

Later, a few farms had a generator to power a refrigerator to keep the raw milk cool. Electricity reached our community in 1937, allowing dairying to flourish. Now, there were no more horses and hogs. Fields were planted in food crops for the cows. The introduction of tractors, harvesters, and such greatly increased the land that could be cultivated and so too the size of the fields and the herds. Local dairies run by the Kirks, Snipes, Stanfords and Teers were prosperous.

Below are some pictures taken by Quentin Patterson (a member of our church) when he was stationed in Hillsborough as an Agricultural Extension agent. They show agricultural practices across several decades of the twentieth century.

1948: Bringing in pitch-forked hay

1930s: Virginia Perry milking

1950s: Ed Snipes with a farm hand on a Ford 8N tractor

1950s: Cutting hay with mule drawn and a tractor drawn cycle cutters

1920s: A. A. Perry with his mules

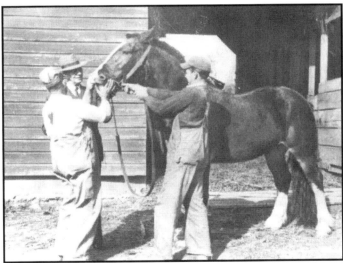

1930s: The Snipes inspect a new horse

Today, Cane Creek is mostly a bedroom community for people who work in nearby towns, but we are blessed to still have a few farmers, such as Kenny Kirk, who still tends hundreds of acres with modern machinery and a crew of farm hands. In 1850, William Bingham reported that a good corn harvest was 20 bushels an acre. Today, Kenny Kirk can harvest 200 bushels an acre in a good year.

15: OUR CHURCH BUILDINGS AND CEMETARY

The First Church Building - 1789

When we celebrated our 200th anniversary in 1989, Cecil Crawford led a small group of celebrants into the woods to a location that he said had been shown to him long ago by "Mr. Tommy" Lloyd. It was, Mr. Tommy had said, the location of Cane Creek's first church.

Cecil Crawford in the 1980s   **Mr. Tommy Lloyd in the 1940s**

Below is a rough map Showing Mr. Tommy's location of our first church. It is marked with an "X." The current landowners are indicated. Our present church lies a half mile to the east.

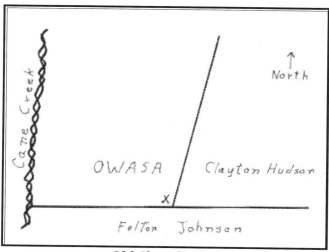

Old Church Site

There used to be some doubt as to how many buildings have housed Cane Creek Church since 1789. The short history compiled by A. G. Crawford (*see* Appendix 1) written in 1933, before our current church was built, contains the following:

"From history handed down by former generations and given by Brother Jas. H. Lloyd (now deceased) we get this history given below. The present building is the fourth, the first two being located about one half mile west of the present building. The only thing remaining at [the] first site is what former generations designated 'The Meeting House Spring'."

We have no better record than this from the mouth of a man born in 1881 who cites a man born in 1855. If these recollections are correct, then the present building, erected in 1949, is Cane Creek's fifth building.

Tradition, then, locates the original meeting house on a rise about a half-mile west of the present church and a half mile south of Buckhorn Road overlooking Cane Creek. We know where our previous church was located (about where the paved basketball court now is). And we know where our current church is. That makes three churches. If our tradition is correct, there are two more church sites to uncover.

In 1992 OWASA (the Orange Water and Sewer Authority that operates the Cane Creek Reservoir; *see* Chapter 19) gave me permission to search for remains on the spot that Mr. Tommy Lloyd had showed Cecil Crawford. I was looking for nails and other metal artefacts, so I used a metal detector. Altogether, I found over 650 artefacts, mostly old nails that an expert dated to late 18th-early 19th century. The "X" on the previous page's map corresponds with the greatest cluster of nails in the scatter plot. The area of concentrated findings is about a 40 by 40-foot square.

Next, I went to the Register of Deed's office in Hillsborough to locate the original deed. It was a deed from Thomas Durham to "The Cane Creek Meeting House." The actual wording of the deed was given in Chapter 8. The "meat" of the deed reads as follows:

"Beginning at a black oak in the old path joining John Strother's line, along the old path to a hickory adjoining John Strother's line, thence east with Strother to a post oak, thence a direct line to the beginning."

This describes a one-acre tract in the shape of a triangle. Old deeds and land grants in Hillsborough and at the Department of History and Archives in Raleigh revealed exactly where the Durham and the Strother tracts were in 1789. The original property lines are in the same location as they are now; only the owners have changed over the years. The church tract, as described in the deed shown above, is marked with an "X" in the diagram below. The tract noted as belonging to the State was likely one that had been granted to a Tory. The State took possession of such land. Later, one of our largest landowners, Sackfield Brewer (who originally owned the large Snipes tract known now as Analoric Farm) bought the land in 1795. The Brewer deed contains the language, "near the meeting house." There is no record that the church ever officially bought the land from Sackfield Bewer.

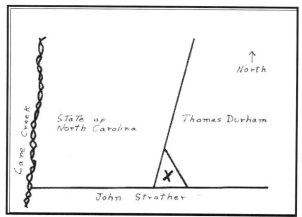

Site of First Church

Thus, the original church tract sat in the southwest corner of a tract owned by Thomas Durham. A comparison of this map with the one shown on the previous page shows the "Xs" in different locations. We will have to resolve this contradiction.

But first, let's look at what the first meeting house might have looked like. Almost certainly it would have been like other meeting houses that have been described by early travelers. It would have been a rough log building perhaps 20 by 30 feet with a split shingle roof, windows (without glass) cut into the two long sides, and a doorway at the end. There would have been no floor other than the bare ground. The congregation would sit on logs or rough plank boards stretched between two logs lying on the ground. A pulpit would occupy the front of the building and be constructed so as to elevate the preacher above his congregation. At first, the walls may not have been chinked against the wind and cold. There was no source of heat to ward off the winter chill. So, it would have taken a stern and determined Christian to endure a meeting in the dead of winter or in the heat of summer. Here is one person's idea of what an old meeting house may have looked like (although it is probably larger than ours was).

An Early Meeting House

Early meeting houses were often not dedicated to a single denomination. That is why they were called a "meeting house" and not "the Presbyterian or Baptist meeting house." Preachers of various denominations could preach there. There are many cases when Baptists and Presbyterians shared the same meeting house for years.

Although the site of these first two buildings is now remote and quite a walk through the woods, it was not remote when it was built. The site was selected in the first place for its proximity to three important things: a road to get there, a spring to drink from, and a creek for baptizing. Little trace of the road now remains. It probably paralleled the creek high up on the ridge. To the north it would have joined in to the so-called "Great Road" that connected Hillsborough with a crossing point on the Haw River at Woody's Ferry (in Alamance County). To the south the road would have kept on south, crossed present Teer Road and would have been the "Meeting House Road" mentioned in several old land grants dating from the 1790s that were located between Teer Road and NC 54. The land around the Meeting House was more open than it is now and there were probably houses and barns nearby. One old deed refers to "a barn just north of the Meeting House."

The Second Church Building – About 1806-1813

Because of the roughness of the meeting house, it was probably the case that the congregation saw to it that a move would soon be taken toward constructing a more church-like building, one with a floor, glass in the windows, a door, and more comfortable seating. We can make a good guess about when the second church was built.

It is highly likely that it was erected just after the turn of the nineteenth century in anticipation of joining the Sandy Creek Baptist Association in 1807. We also know that the Sandy Creek Baptist Association held its annual meeting in our church in 1813. Certainly, the second church would have been in existence by then. So, it is likely that we can date the second church's construction to 1806-1813.

The size of the congregation then was probably around 40 or 50. The earliest membership records we have from the Sandy Creek Association indicate an average size for Cane Creek of 55 members between 1815 and 1825. If the church had a central aisle and if four people could sit on either side, then only eight rows would be needed to accommodate the entire congregation, with room to spare.

We can also make a good guess of what the church looked like because a good example of an early 19th century rural church is located near Liberty. Sandy Creek, which was founded in 1751, built itself a new meeting house in 1802. They used it for many years and as time went by, they decided to modernize it by putting on weatherboard siding in 1870 and then asphalt siding in 1953. Eventually they outgrew the church and built a new one. Recently, they have restored the old church to its original appearance, both inside and out. Since Sandy Creek's church was built at almost the same time as our second church, it is the best example we have of what our second church may have looked like. It is worth taking a short trip down to Liberty to see it. They never lock the doors.

Sandy Creek's 1802 Meeting House

The building is about 20 feet by 25 feet. It has two doors, which probably means that there was one for each sex. Inside there is seating for about two dozen people. There is some balcony seating that very likely was intended for the slave members.

Sandy Creek from the Front Door Looking in

From the Pulpit Looking Outward.

Soon after we built our second church, a new road came through the community. It connected Raleigh with Greensboro. It roughly followed the current route of Dairyland Road and continued westward past Cecil and Mae Crawford's house, crossed Cane Creek below the Hopson mill dam, and climbed Thunder Mountain (known earlier as Thompson's Mountain.) It had various names including "the Chapel Hill-Greensboro highway " and "the Greensboro Stage Road."

The Third Church Building – c1852

Gradually, the center of gravity of the community shifted to the southeast because of the construction of this new stage road. In 1852 the congregation decided to move to a new location. It bought a ten-acre tract from Thomas Brewer (a son of Sackfield Brewer) and soon built a new church. Unfortunately, our minutes for this period are lost so we do not know any of the details. This ten-acre tract is the one we currently own but no one has had a clue as to where our third church building was located. A little sleuthing, though, can help us pin down its location.

There is a petition made by local people in 1855 to the court in Hillsborough. The petition calls for the construction of an official "public" road that we now call Buckhorn Road. Part of the petition reads as follows:

> ."... so as to cross Cane Creek at the old ford above the mouth of Turkey Hill Creek where it enters into Cane Creek and then the best direction to the Chapel Hill Road by Cane Creek Meeting House ... We, the undersigned, desire the above-mentioned road for the convenient way and course of getting to Mill (i.e., Thompson's Mill where I live) and to Meeting."

This route brought the road up to the Thomas S. Cate's house (where Hight and Virginia Perry lived), then on by the pasture that Denise Hudson now owns, and then turned sharply south where the driveway now is. It then connected to the Greensboro Stage Road) "by the Cane Creek Meeting House."

In the 1890s, George W. Tate published his map of Orange County. He probably relied a lot on his own memory for he shows our church in its 1852 location, not its 1890 location. But it tells us where the third church was located. Here is the part of the map showing our neighborhood:

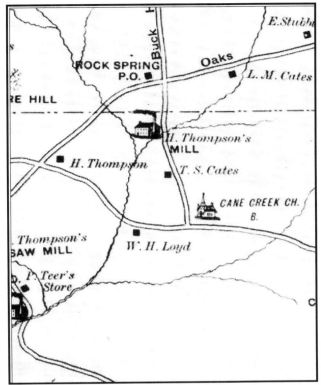

Location of Our Third Church

The road running east to west in the center is the Greensboro Stage Road. The road labeled "Oaks" is Bradshaw Quarry Road, and the one crossing it vertically is Buckhorn Road. Orange Grove Road did not yet exist. So, we now know where our third church was: very near the large oak tree at the far southwest corner of our cemetery.

It would be nice if we had a picture of the church. Undoubtedly, it was a larger, finer building befitting the largest congregation in the Beulah Association. We have only this description of our third church from James Cheek's _Footprints of a Human Life:_

> "Cane Creek Church had the old-fashioned high pulpit, about three feet high with four or five steps leading up to it. The front seats were reserved for those who responded to the altar call. A space was partitioned off in the back for the slaves."

We also know that, as originally built, the church had no heat. We know this because we have an old list of members who gave money to have wood stoves installed. The list has been framed and is in the history display room off the sanctuary. By comparing names on the list with known death dates, we can date the list to 1872. In the lower righthand corner of the list is a tiny sketch of how the stoves would be placed in the church. This sketch is the only one we have for our third church. The pulpit is at the left. The two horizontal lines within the church show where the two stoves would have been vented to the outside.

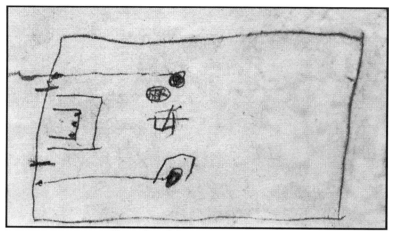

Sketch of the 1852 Church

The two stoves seem to have cost about $15 each. This was during Reconstruction when money was scarce. There are 61 names on the list. Most people (38) pledged 25¢. Fifteen were able to pledge 50¢. Anderson Cates pledged 75¢ and John Moore pledged $2.

The Fourth Church Building — 1888

In 1883, with membership standing at just above 200 (it had been as high as 300 in 1876), the Trustees formed themselves into a Building Committee to decide whether to repair the old church or to build another one. This was after the official end of Reconstruction but still at a time when the South's fortunes were at low ebb. It was rather a courageous recommendation, then, when the Committee, in November 1883, said:

> "We, the undersigned, do hereby recommend that the Church at Cane Creek take steps to build a new church."

If they had known how troublesome it was going to be, they probably would have just repaired the old building.

Things began optimistically enough. T. J. Cates, the chairman of the building committee, announced at the January meeting in 1884 that the congregation would come together on the 16th for the purpose of cutting timber for the new building. During the spring there was no mention of work in the church minutes, but we can infer that beams were cut and joined and that the main frame of the new building was raised and set into place. It was very likely post-and-beam construction.

At the June meeting the Chairman asked the Church for $25 to purchase 23 thousand shingles to weather-in the new structure, this being half the actual cost. The money was raised on the spot. Contrast this instant raising of $25 with the painful process of raising money, a quarter at a time, in 1872 for two wood stoves. Times were getting better.

With the roof on, A. T. Cates, at the July 1884 meeting, was authorized to make arrangements with a Brother Jeffries for the lumber, presumably for the siding. Work was to begin in August on this phase of construction.

It was not until February 1885 that the minutes record another call for the membership to come to work on the new building. Still another call was made for March 4th. In May, the Building Committee reported the hiring of John Dodson to put some timbers together "to raise the [illegible]."

In the June 1885 minutes it became apparent that there had been trouble with Mr. Jeffries, who was supposed to supply lumber for the church. He had apparently been unable to supply satisfactory lumber and had also refused to return the $35 advanced to him. He said he would furnish lumber, not money. The Building Committee then turned to Yancy & Cates to supply the weather board for the outside walls of the building. There was need, then, for $50 to buy the lumber at $1.45 per hundred feet. Most of the money was raised at the meeting.

At the next meeting in July, T. J. Cates made the sad announcement that, although the lumber had arrived in Mebanesville by train, it had turned out to be so damaged that they had refused to accept it. A special committee was created to place an order with White Company, not only for the lumber, but also for the doors, door frames, windows, window frames, and sashes.

In November, T. J. Cates announced that the order of lumber and materials was ready to be picked up, that the money has been raised to pay for it, and that he was resigning as Chairman of the Building Committee and would not even serve as a committee member. His replacement seems to have been John Dodson, who was absent from the next meeting and so could not make a progress report.

At the January 1886 meeting, two years after the first timber had been cut, the Building Committee announced the hiring of two men to superintend the remaining work on the church and that it would begin the next Monday. In the absence of a pastor, someone made a motion to name Thomas J. Cates permanent Moderator until a pastor could be found. The motion failed. There was apparently dissension in the congregation over the problems and aggravation of building a new church.

For over a year we are told nothing in the minutes about the new church. Finally, at the March 1888 meeting: "The Chairman of the Building Committee wishes to make arrangements for the completion of the church." Pledges amounting to $150 were taken and a committee of four men was formed to solicit further funds. In June it was announced that Mr. Jeffries, with whom the Building Committee had had a falling out three years earlier, would supply the wood for the floor of the new church. Several members agreed to go and haul it back. John Dodson announced that he would begin laying the flooring on July 25th. The final mention of the new church is at the August 1888 meeting, when John Dodson reported that $30 was still owed on the lumber. It is possible that this announcement was made to a congregation sitting in a new building thanking God that what had begun on a cold January day in 1884 had finally come to an end after four and a half years.

The final chapter in this episode was written in 1890. The Chairman of the Building Committee announced that the old church building had been sold for $58.50 and that the proceeds had been used to pay off what was owed Mr. Jeffries. We are not told the fate of the old church. Most likely it was dismantled for the lumber, windows, and other salvageable materials. Perhaps traces of this old church remain as parts of houses or old barns in the community.

This 1888 church building was magnificent. Surviving photographs show a large wooden structure about 30 by 100 feet with a seating capacity of over three hundred. The south end of the building faced the Greensboro-Chapel Hill stage road and contained two front doors, one for men, and the other for women. There were several large windows with the panes painted white to let in light but to discourage aimless gazing during the sermon. This is the oldest surviving photograph we can find. It is dated around 1900. The man standing in the lower right corner is J. F. McDuffie, our preacher.

Our Church about 1900

Here is a more recent view.

Our Church in 1948

As the church was originally built, the pulpit was probably at the north end of the building. Early in the 20th century the building was drastically remodeled. The two doors at the south end were permanently closed and a new entrance on the east side was constructed along with a vestibule and a small steeple over it for the church bell. A small jut-out addition was added to the west wall and the pulpit was moved into it. The pews were arranged in three sections facing it. There was an aisle running the long way through the center of the building with a wood stove midway toward each end. The stove pipes ran to the center of the building and out the roof. Below, the first picture is the jut-out in the west wall and the second picture is the altar decked out for a wedding in 1947.

The Rear Jut-out for the Pulpit

The Pulpit Decorated for a Wedding

This building served the congregation for sixty years, longer than had any previous building. At the close of World War II, a familiar issue arose once more: shall we repair the old building or build a new one? Times were changing rapidly. The community was now served with electricity and Orange Grove Road was about to be paved. The end of war shortages and the prospects of prosperity and development made some members of the congregation wish for a modern building in keeping with a modern community. Others looked back on a long and glorious tradition and hated to see a perfectly respectable old church building pulled down.

The Fifth & Current Church Building - 1950

At the May 1945 business meeting (we had just defeated Germany in World War II but were still fighting Japan in the Pacific), a committee was appointed to "submit plans for a new church." Nothing happened for two years. Then in May 1947 our preacher, J. M. Wright, moved that we set aside one collection a month for a building fund. The motion failed but was replaced by a successful motion to put $100 into the building fund.

Another two years went by and in May 1949 (James Rittenhouse was now our preacher) the minutes state that, "The building program was discussed. The question arose whether to build a new building or remodel the old one." Two committees were appointed, one to investigate each possibility.

Church minutes are bare bone records. There is rarely any meat on the bones to suggest what actually went on. We know from the recollections of the church's oldest members, however, that much more happened at this May meeting than was recorded. A pillar of the church made an impassioned plea for a new building. A member of an old Orange Grove family stood up and challenged what had been said and was followed by an elder from another old Orange Grove family who challenged the challenge. Fingers were pointed and much was said that was later regretted.

James Snipes, before his untimely death in 1993, told me of his recollection of the discussions about the new church. His father, Jim, had spoken with fervor on the issues and had returned home with such hurt feelings that his family strongly suggested that he would be wise to keep his mouth shut at future church meetings. Harry Byrd (our preacher from 1953 until 1957) visited us at homecoming in 2007 and told me that he had been told that one of his missions here at Cane Creek would be to assist in the healing from the strife of building our new church. The controversy was long remembered and it had a lasting effect on the congregation: afterwards, we have settled any differences of opinion in a calm and gracious manner.

At the June meeting it was reported that the cost of renovating the old building (installing a new floor and adding brick veneer to the outside) would be at least $20,000. The other committee said that a new brick and block building measuring 50' x 28' with four Sunday School rooms would cost $7,026. This was at a time when the annual budget of the church was much less than $10,000. The congregation voted on the spot to build a new church.

Below is what our church tract looked like on the eve of construction. It is a plat from a survey done in September 1948. It shows the old Greensboro Road as now a driveway that went to the Crawford farm. A small chunk of land in the southeast corner had already been cut out for the Manley Snipes General Store. The new Orange Grove Road runs north and south but has not yet been named. It sliced through the old church tract and cut off about two acres on the east side from the main tracts. The cutoff land was split in two and sold to Jim Snipes and Banks Lloyd. A spring on the Lloyd portion had once been the sole source of water for church goers. Also shown is the old Orange Grove Academy Building and our old church shown above. And note the "old road" that connected the Orange Grove community to Buckhorn Road.

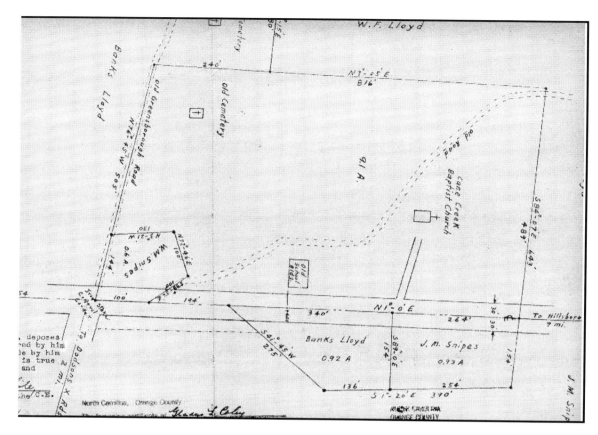

A Plat of the Church Property in 1948

Groundbreaking for the new church was held on September 18, 1949. Below is a picture from the groundbreaking ceremony in 1949. The man with the shovel is Mr. Tommy Lloyd, the chair of the Deacon Board. Next to him is our then new preacher, James Rittenhouse.

Groundbreaking for the New Church

Below is an early picture of the completed church. The grass has not yet come up. The old church is at the right and was soon to be demolished. The seating capacity was just over 200. The new sanctuary was first used for a Sunday service in the fall of 1950. To save money, the pews from the old church were installed in the new church. They were used into the 1970s.

The New and the Old Church in 1950

Here are two early views of the inside of the new church.

The Interior in 1959

... and about 1975

The altar in the new church was backed by a painting of Christ, the good shepherd. It remained with us until we added better choir seats behind the pulpit. We donated the painting to a church in the north of the county,

The Altar

A prominent feature of our new church was its sixteen stained glass windows. We know nothing of the discussions that led to stained glass instead of clear glass. The extra cost of the windows was borne by families in the congregation who dedicated their window to someone recently deceased within their family. Each window is accompanied by a plaque naming the person honored by the window. The ones honored are shown below.

Two Windows

Individuals honored by our stained-glass windows

- Zalph Andrews July 9, 1921 – July 5, 1944
- J. Talmage Andrews July 15, 1907 – January 10, 1943
- James W. Aldridge and family
- Nerius A. Cates and family
- June L. Cheek and wife Bessie Durham Cheek
- Cad Wallendar Lloyd
- Manuel C, Garrett and wife Addie Dodson Garrett
- George S. Howard and wife Nany Ann Howard
- Arthur and Dwight Glosson
- James I. Andrews
- John T. Lloyd 1883 – 1948
- J. Graham Kirk and wife Martha Frances Kirk
- Alphonzo A. Perry 1856- 1935
- Jesse B. Dodson family
- Dr. Frank Crawford and wife Martha Cates Crawford
- Luther Madison Cates and wife Nancy Crawford Cates

In 1958 the congregation was ready to add to the church building and had to decide between building a parsonage for a full-time pastor, or an adjoining building with Sunday School rooms and a church office. The new preacher was James Ballard and the church had already rented a house in the community for him to use, so he became our first full-time resident pastor. With the housing issue settled for a while, the church voted to construct our Educational Building. Rev. Ballard described the construction as follows.

"Floor plans had been secured earlier by our Building Committee from our Convention architects. Having already begun a building fund drive to raise the needed money, the church secured the services of the Van Thomas Construction Company in Siler City to build the exterior of the 2210 square foot educational building plus a pump house, for the sum of $4700. Various members of the church contributed timber, a group of our members cut, sawed, and planed 23,000 feet of lumber for the new building. The ground was broken in September 1958, members of the church dug and poured the foundation, and construction was begun by the contractor in November. The contractor met his terms of the contract in late February 1959 and was paid in full for his services in March. Since that time, work around the outside of the building has progressed and the building has been wired electrically. All the work done thus far on the building has amounted to $5700. The building which would have cost around $22,000, had been done entirely by a contractor with his purchasing all the material, will be completed on the inside by members of the church at approximately half the estimated contract cost ... All total there will be twelve rooms which will give our educational program a great boost."

In 1969 we built a parsonage for about $18,000 so that, for the first time, we could have a full-time preacher who lived on the premises. The first resident was James McBride. Our pastors lived here until the late 1990s. The parsonage began to show its age compared to new houses being built nearby. Thereafter, we have given our pastors a housing allowance so that they could find their own housing and the parsonage has served as our church office with a pastor's study and storage space.

The Education Building built in 1959

The parsonage built in 1969

The new steeple in 1979

The Activity Center

Our Activity Center, just up the road from our church, has an interesting history. The tract was originally part of Sackfield Brewer's large land grant (from 1752) that evolved into the Anilorac Dairy Farm run by Charles and James Snipes. In 1922 five acres of the farm were split off and sold to the Orange County Board of Education for the construction of a new school.

When the school burned in 1944, the land sat idle for a few years until the church got word that the Orange County Board of Education had decided to sell the land to the highest bidder. In 1947 the church authorized Mr. Tommy Lloyd to go to Hillsborough and bid as much as $25 for the five-acre tract. He was the highest bidder. The land then sat idle for almost 20 years and grew up in vines and saplings. In 1963 the church gave the land to a new group of Orange Grove citizens who called themselves the Orange Grove Community Center. They were motivated to make a place for the Grange to meet following the demolition of the old Cane Creek Academy building in 1950. In 1964 they built what was then known as the Community Building and ran it for years. But eventually the building became too much of a burden to care for and it was donated back to the church in 1989. Since then, the church has vastly improved the facility, adding air conditioning, a new roof, and storage rooms. It is used now for such events as our annual homecoming celebration, our Wednesday night suppers, and many special events such as serving as the voting place for the Orange Grove Precinct. It can also be rented out for private parties.

The Activity Center in 2021

Most Recent Expansion of the Current Church Building

Finally, in 2005, we decided to expand the rear of the sanctuary of our church to install an indoor baptistry. This enlarged the choir area, added two rest rooms, a choir changing room and an historical display room. The groundbreaking in 2006 featured some of our oldest members. Left to right below are Jewel Lloyd Crawford, Decie Kenyon, Ethel Cheek, Priscilla Lloyd, and Charles Snipes.

Groundbreaking Ceremony in 2006

Here are two pictures of the sanctuary altar: before and after construction.

Before the new construction

After the new construction

Everyone is thrilled with our church. For a while, we are comfortably equipped.

Our Cemetery

Our church moved away from the banks of Cane Creek in 1852 when we bought our present tract of land on Orange Grove Road. We built our third church at the southwest corner of the property beside the old Chapel Hill-Greensboro stage road that went westward by the Crawford house and on across the creek. Up until this time, it was the custom to bury the deceased in family plots near the home place. The nearest family plot is beside the barn at the old Crawford home place and contains several graves of Hopsons. The only legible inscription reads "Rebecca Hopson, died Dec. 1834, aged 73."

The oldest grave marker in our cemetery belongs to Nancy Brewer who died in 1844, so it is necessary to figure out how someone could come to be buried in our cemetery eight years before we owned it. This is the story.

Sackfield Brewer was a prominent early landowner in our community. As far as we can tell, he was not a member of our little church. Early in the 19th century one of Sackfield's sons, Thomas, married Nancy Lloyd (who soon died) and later married Nancy Petty and built a house beside the old stage road on Brewer land (behind where Watson's shop now is). By the 1840s, Thomas owned all the old Brewer family land where the "Anilorac Dairy" would later be located. Thomas never joined our church, but his first wife, Nancy, did in 1835 at the age of 64. Nine years later, in 1844, Thomas and his second wife both died and were buried near the house in a family burial plot. Thomas, Jr. inherited the family land and sold ten acres to "the Regular Missionary Baptist Church of Christ," as we called ourselves in those days. In 1852 we built our third church and decided to install a cemetery beside it, as was becoming the custom in rural churches. Since the Brewer family cemetery was already present, the church simply continued to use it as the church cemetery. Thus, our church cemetery began as a Brewer family cemetery.

I want to comment about the neat appearance of our cemetery and the several hundred blank grave markers all laid out in nice rows. Both Mae Crawford and Sam Crawford have told me that originally there were many individual family plots lined with iron fences and stone walls. The graves were laid out in a helter-skelter fashion, which made it difficult to keep the cemetery looking nice. In the late 1940s Manley Snipes was responsible for clearing out the old fences and stones and for straightening the rows of headstones. H. B. Dodson told me that this began in 1949 when Manley Snipes asked the 17-year-old Dodson to plow between the tombstones so that grass could be seeded. Sam Crawford remembers helping with the neatening up in the early 1960s, so it was an on-going process. This was when the blank concrete stones were installed. Presumably, they were to indicate graves originally marked only by fieldstones. It is probable that not all the blank stones indicate that someone lies beneath. If we knew which ones marked true graves, we could use the others for new burials.

Finally, I need to comment on the Charlie Crutchfield monument. Located toward the front of our cemetery next to the broken Elisabeth Crutchfield marker, it is not a real grave marker. It says "Charlie Crutchfield: First person to be buried in Cane Creek cemetery during 18th century."

The Charlie Crutchfield Memorial

This little monument presents us with four mysteries: 1) Why does it say "18th century" when the cemetery did not come into existence until about 1844; 2) Why would a Crutchfield be the first person buried in a Brewer family plot? 3) Why is the name given as "Charlie" and not the more formal "Charles?" and 4) Why is there no Charlie Crutchfield headstone to be found anywhere in the cemetery. Here is the story.

Not long ago a woman now living in Texas, Janel Crutchfield Howell, called me and said that she had read the Historical Sketch posted on our website entitled, "Who was Charlie Crutchfield?" She said, "I know who Charlie Crutchfield is!" What follows is derived from what she told me and family trees she has shared.

Charles Chambers Crutchfield was the first child of John H. Crutchfield (1803-1877) and Elisabeth Workman Crutchfield (1810-1858). Both are buried in our cemetery. Charlie died in 1837 at the age of one year. This solves one mystery. He was a baby, so the tombstone records a nickname. His parents went on to have five more children.

Janel Howell's husband was once stationed at a North Carolina military base and while there, they visited our cemetery to look for Crutchfield ancestors. She found the monument shown above. Then, scratching around in the dirt, she found part of a shale headstone with Charlie's name on it. Alas, she took it to Texas with her! This solves the mystery of the missing headstone.

Three of the four mysteries are now solved. We have located Charlie's headstone and we know why he is called "Charlie." We also know that the memorial plaque should read "19th century" instead of "18th century." But since he died in 1837, how is it that he is buried in our cemetery, which was not established until 1852? The most plausible answer was suggested by David John Hailey, our pastor at the time. Little Charlie's grave must have been transferred from a Crutchfield family plot (they owned land west of Cane Creek) to our cemetery when his mother died in 1858. The two graves are side-by-side, so it makes good sense.

So now we have solved the four mysteries and debunked the mis-dated monument shown above. But debunking can be sad. Is there anything left that makes Charlie special? Yes, there is! Having died in 1837, we can safely say that no one in our cemetery has an earlier death date than Charlie. And Charlie's headstone is our oldest one even though it started out in some other burial plot.

A remaining mystery is that neither John nor Elisabeth Crutchfield is listed on any of our church membership rolls, nor are any of their other children. I have found Charlie's father, John, in several places in our minutes, so he must have been a member whose name never got on the official roll. Perhaps Charlie's mother's name, by mistake, never got on a roll either.

Furthermore, all the other Crutchfields mentioned in our old roles (with one exception) remain unidentified even to Crutchfield genealogists. The one exception is Enoch Crutchfield, who was Charlie's uncle. He was our clerk in 1829 when his house burned down and all our old records were lost. He became a prominent minister but there is no record that he ever preached at Cane Creek. He married four times and had 18 children.

The headstone that Janel Howell sent us is only a fragment of the original headstone, and the inscription is a simple carving probably done by his grieving father, John. The words, "Charlie Crutchfield" are hard to make out. You would not know what is says without the clue that it was found buried next to his mother's grave and next to the monument shown above. The birth and death dates, if they were ever on the stone, are now obliterated. The stone is made from local shale and is very fragile. We have had it mounted behind museum-grade glass and it is now in the History Display Room just off the sanctuary.

Charlie Crutchfield's headstone

16: EDUCATION IN THE CANE CREEK COMMUNITY

The Orange Grove community has long been associated with education. Even before Reverend MacDuffie led Cane Creek Baptist Church into the education of young men and women in the 1890s, there were schools and academies in the neighborhood. But this had not always been the case. In the beginning, the area around Cane Creek was destitute of learning.

Most of our ancestors who settled in Orange County in the eighteenth century had little or no education. If they could read or write at all, they owed it to the instruction of their parents or, if their parents were well-to-do, to a hired tutor. The ability to read, write, and to calculate was not widespread.

However, once the county began to be settled, and once houses were built, fields cleared, and roads located, some families banded together to see to the education of their children. They might combine forces to hire a teacher, or they might prevail on a literate member of the community, sometimes a preacher, to undertake the education of a few children in his home or in what was known as an "old field" school because so many of these small neighborhood schools were located in old worn-out fields.

The history of education in Orange County involves both public and private schools. The story of these two types of schools is deeply intertwined but I will describe them separately, beginning with private schools.

Private Schools

The University of North Carolina, which opened its doors in Chapel Hill in 1795, offered a boost to education locally. When it became apparent that many of the young men who wished to enter the University were unqualified, there grew up a number of academies in Orange County whose function was to prepare young men for college. These Orange County academies sprang up several decades before the establishment of public schools.

The first of these, according to Lefler and Wager (1953), was the Hillsborough Academy, which opened at least as early as 1801 "for youth of both sexes" and with a curriculum including Latin, Greek, English, reading, writing, arithmetic, geography, bookkeeping, "and the plainer branches of mathematics."

In 1812 the name of William Bingham appears as principle of the Hillsborough Academy, beginning the reign of the Bingham family in Orange County education that was to span three generations and leave a lasting impression, not to mention the name of our township. William Bingham was a 1778 graduate of the University of Glasgow. He came to this country, taught in Wilmington in the early 1790s, opened a school in Pittsboro in 1800, and later moved to Hillsborough. After his tenure at the Hillsborough Academy, he opened his own school at Mt. Repose five miles from Mebane. He died in 1826 and his son, also named William, took over and soon moved the school south to the Oaks community in 1844. He ran the school until it moved, during the Civil War, to Mebane and changed its mission temporarily to military education under the leadership of a third generation Bingham also named William. The Mebane school was large, wildly successful, and lasted into the 1890s. The three William Bingham's reputation as educators was unexcelled. Below is an ad in the _Hillsborough Recorder_ for the school at Oaks.

SELECT
Classical and Mathematical
SCHOOL.

THE subscriber, having resigned the charge of the Hillsborough Academy, contemplates opening a _Select School_, twelve miles south west of Hillsborough, and the same distance, — west nearly, — from Chapel Hill. His leading motive is to _educate his own sons in the country;_ and his selection has been made with special reference to this object.

For details apply to him — post paid — at Hillsborough, till November next, when the school is to begin.

W. J. BINGHAM.

Hillsborough, May 8.   95 —

☞ Raleigh Register, Standard, Fayetteville Observer, Wilmington Chronicle, Edenton Gazette, Newbernian, Halifax Republican, and Carolina Watchman — insert twice a month for five months, and forward accounts to this office for payment.

Opening of Bingham Academy.
Hillsborough Recorder May 16, 1844

Another local school was called Rock Spring Academy. Anderson Cates, who was a public-school teacher and a member of our church, mentions that he was educated there. It was established in 1858. The initial ad appeared in the _Recorder_ on July 14, 1858 and announced the fall session beginning on August 11 and concluding on December 24:

ROCK SPRING ACADEMY.

THE First Session of this Institution will commence on the 11th of August, and close on the 24th of December, 1858. The Academy is situated ten miles south west of Hillsborough, and twelve miles west of Chapel Hill, in a moral and healthy community. We propose to prepare students for College, or for the ordinary business of life. The terms are as follows :

Classical, or Scientific Course,	$20 00
English, Higher Branches,	15 00
Elementary,	10 00

Board can be had for $7 per month.

T. D. Oldham and J. Moore are living convenient, and will take boarders. For further particulars address, **W. P. OLDHAM, Principal,** Oaks P. O., Orange Co., N. C.

July 14 — 2t

Opening of Rock Spring Academy
***Hillsborough Recorder* July 28, 1858**

T. D. Oldham, born in 1799, was a member of our church and was probably Chairman of the Deacons for a period. He was also our Clerk. The principal of this school was T. D. Oldham's son, W. P. Oldham. The school apparently continued to operate for some years. After the Civil War, in 1867, another *Recorder* ad (July 17) says:

"This school offers the advantages of health, church advantages, and beautiful location. Special favors granted to disabled confederate veterans."

By 1867 the elementary course of study at Rock Spring had been split into "intermediate" and "primary." The principal was now H. M. Cates, a graduate of Wake Forest. We have no record of how long Rock Spring Academy continued in operation. The fact that T. D. Oldham lived nearby suggests that the location may have been across Cane Creek in the neighborhood of the old Apple Mill. However, it is also possible that its location was closer to the present intersection of Bradshaw Quarry Road and Buckhorn Road for it is near here that the original spring known as Rock Spring is located.

There is no indication of any formal connection between Rock Spring Academy and Cane Creek Church. If there were a connection, it would have most likely appeared in the church minutes for 1858, the year the Academy was established. Unfortunately, no minutes survive for the period 1850-1863 so we cannot tell for sure. The wording, "church advantages," and the fact that the principle, H. M. Cates, was also our Church Clerk, at least hint at a connection. The 1867 ad in the *Recorder* is the last trace we have of Rock Spring Academy.

In October 1895 our church called J. F. (Julius Ford) MacDuffie as its pastor. MacDuffie had been born in South Carolina in 1856 and was educated at Daughton Academy in Wake County (by J. C. Hocutt, who later served Cane Creek as pastor) and had studied at Wake Forest. He had withdrawn from Wake Forest for health reasons before completing his degree. He married and settled down to the life of a farmer but could not shake the feeling that he ought instead to be preaching the gospel. He was ordained in 1888 and launched himself into a new career that combined his two loves, preaching and teaching.

J. F. McDuffie and Wife

Two years after beginning his service with Cane Creek, and perhaps prompted by the memory of Rock Spring Academy, the Church convened a special meeting in June 1897. N. A. Cates announced that the purpose of the meeting was "to establish an Academy at this place." The following resolution was passed:

> "That we donate so much of our church lot for the use of an academy and school as may be required for its establishment and use so long as it may be used for this special purpose.

> "That the name of this academy is Rock Spring.

> "That the Church elect annually five trustees to cooperate with the pastor of Cane Creek Church and these to elect two others in the community and that the Mt. Zion Association appoint three trustees to cooperate with us. These eleven shall constitute the Board of Trustees of Rock Spring Academy."

The congregation then elected D. F. Crawford, A. P. Cates, W. F. Dodson, N. A. Cates, and T. M. Dodson as the first trustees.

It is curious that the name Rock Spring Academy appears in the minutes since the school established by Rev. MacDuffie is remembered in the community as Orange Grove School (a name that does not occur in our minutes until 1906). Apparently, the school went through at least one and perhaps two name changes. It was likely first known as Rock Spring Academy as given in the Church minutes. This notion is reinforced by the recollection of Ina Andrews (born in 1886) who reported that her family moved to the community so that she could attend Rock Spring Academy. We also have the testimony of another church member who was born in 1895 that, "Mr. MacDuffie changed the name of the school." The new name was probably Orange Grove Academy. Rebecca Crawford owned a bible given to her father, a graduate in 1898, and it is inscribed, "Orange Grove Academy, May 1898."

The school published an annual brochure that outlined the course of study. The earliest surviving copy is from the 1898-99 school year and here the name is given as Orange Grove School, the name it kept until the school closed in 1912.

The academy building was constructed during the summer of 1897. The first class enrolled for the fall term in 1897. Surviving photos show a neat white one-story building in the shape of a cross. It contained two classrooms, with the short arm of the cross housing a small vestibule. A cupola with a school bell stood atop the vestibule. The picture below shows the school. Our old church is on the right. The school was located approximately where the Educational Building now is.

The Original Academy Building about 1900

Our library has school catalogs for '99-00, '01-'02, '06-'07, '07-'08, and '08-'09. We also have commencement programs for '07, '08, '09, '10, '11, and '12. The materials were originally collected by Rebecca Crawford and Virginia Perry. The quotes below are taken from the catalogs and give us a glimpse of school and community life from a century ago.

 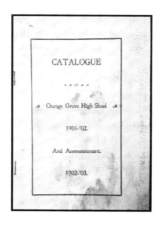 

Academy Catalogs for 1899-00, 1902-03, and 1906-07

1899-1900:

"The establishment of this school is the direct effect of strenuous efforts put forth by Rev. J. F. MacDuffie, who began to agitate the subject about four years ago and who was successful in getting his people to cooperate in establishing and carrying out the work ... The first session began October 1897, which was successful beyond all hopes ... Our building consists of a two-roomed academy. This though, even from the first, has not been sufficient to accommodate the number in attendance [seventy students are listed] ... The location of the school is a most admirable one. It is among the delightful hills of Orange County being in one of the most healthful sections of all North Carolina. It is on the old historic road along which Cornwallis passed with his men."

1901-02:

"The school has been in operation for five years and we have never had an occasion to send for a doctor for a student. We have no doctor nearer than ten miles of us. We would like to have one settle among us but the amount of practice is not sufficiently encouraging for one to locate here. The school is located among a sturdy class of farmers who, conscious that their duty toward their children is their first duty, are rallying to the support of the school. It is among picturesque hills of the old renowned County of Orange where the nightingale sings, and the sparkling rills of water twine their silver threads among the red hills. A locality to be envied by everyone in search of health, away from the attractions of vice and temptation ... Every student in our school is recognized as a lady or gentleman and so long as they maintain this high position, they know no law. We have no code or regulations. The only rule is "right doing and right living" and when this rule is violated the offender will be dealt with according to the nature of the case. We employ corporal punishment only as a last resort" (Note: The catalog lists 101 students.)

The school prospered and grew. In 1906 a much larger building was constructed. Indeed, the fall term of '06 was delayed to allow for the finishing touches to be put on the building. It was a large two-story building with classrooms on the first floor and a spacious auditorium on the second floor. It stood just to the southeast of the present church. The two stories to the right from local newspapers describe the school. Both are from *The News* for August 1906.

1906-07:

"Orange Grove has been in successful operation nine years ... Already numbers of young men and women have been sent forth into the battles of life, and they have shown by their character and success that Mr. MacDuffie's work has not been in vain... Mr. McDuffie is still pastor of the church ... and leads the community in the erection of a new building which will meet all the demands of a large and growing school... Country location has always been considered by leading educators as almost requisite for the successful conduct of a boarding school.

"Our location is happy, nestling among the hills of the Occoneechees on the old Raleigh Stage Road. The Orange Grove School will be found in one of the most select neighborhoods in Orange County. Now that the telephone and free mail have been extended into the county, the morning paper may be read at the dinner hour. The country around Orange Grove has more than 600 feet elevation. Malaria is almost unknown, and fever is rare.

Some of our people were busy hauling logs to the saw mill last week to help out the school building. It is to be 38 x 60 feet located at Cane Creek. There is talk of the Masons organizing a lodge there when it is completed. Good.

Prospects for a large and flourishing school are fine. The music department, which is something new in the high schools of this State is attracting much favorable attention. Parents looking for a school would do well to look into the merits of each department.

The Music Department, under the directorship of of Prof. Chas. E. Redman, who had charge of the music department at Bingham School last year, will embrace work in almost all branches of music. The instruction will be of a high order of excellence.

The business department will embrace the regular courses given in any business college. Prof. Bynum, who is a graduate of the Massey Business College will have charge of this department.

The preparatory department will be in charge of the Principal, who will try to keep the standard of work to a high order of excellence.

The teaching force consists of seven teachers, all of excellent standing in their profession. For further information address the Principal, Walter S. Crawford, Hillsboro, N. C., R. F. D. No. 3. (1 in.)

"Board in the homes in the community furnishes a distinct advantage. The mothers and fathers of the community are earnest God-fearing people so interested in the welfare of the school that each will constitute himself a guardian of the welfare and conduct of each pupil. The teachers are high class. Almost all are Baptists; one is a Presbyterian. But broad non-sectarian ideas will prevail.

"The moral and religious conditions of the community are of the highest order. No more serious-minded Christian people can be found than those around Cane Creek Church. None are more interested in education. There is no whiskey, no rowdies, no drunkards, no profane swearing in the community and the parent will find the fewest possible evil influences to corrupt his child.

"Tuition ranges up to $30 per term and board can be obtained for $8-10 per month. Total yearly costs per student should not exceed $125."

The bulletins for 1907 and 1908 list the student body. In both years the number is just over 100 with boys slightly outnumbering girls. Some of the students came from other counties, mostly Alamance, Chatham, and Durham, but these make up only about 15-20% of the student body. The rest were from Orange County and came from families in the neighborhood as attested by the familiar family names of Brewer, Cates, Crawford, Cheek, Dodson, Kirk, Lloyd, Ray, Sykes, Snipes, and Thompson.

In the Church minutes for December 1906 (just after the new building had been completed) we see that the Church passed a motion to allow the Academy's Trustees to sell the original school building to the County along with a small parcel of land. The building sold to the County was destined to become part of the developing Orange County public school system.

1908-09:
"Orange Grove School was founded nine years ago by Rev. J. F.MacDuffie. The school ran for many years under his wise superintendency. Last year, a new building, at a cost of approximately $4000 was erected to accommodate the growing patronage of the school. This additional accommodation affords ample room for society halls, commercial rooms, recitation rooms, office, and a large chapel... Our location is happy... ten miles southwest of Hillsboro, nestling among the hills of the Occoneechees on the old Raleigh and Guilford stage road in one of the most select neighborhoods in Orange County.

The catalog for 1901-02 had said that, "we have no code of regulations" other than "right doing and right living." By 1908 this had changed. Here are the new rules printed in the catalog:

"Students must respond promptly to all bell signals and must obey cheerfully all minor regulations made known during the school year. Attendance upon all school duties is rigidly enforced. Any damage such as marking on the walls or desks, or fracturing window glass must be made good by the party guilty of such offense. Students are held responsible for the condition of their rooms and also for the conduct in their rooms. The time for recreation is from 4:30 to 7PM. After that hour all students are expected to be in their rooms and at work. Young ladies shall not be allowed to leave the grounds or receive calls from young men without the consent of the principal. During the day from 8:45 to 4:30, all students will study in the school building or in their rooms unless excused specially. All profane and indecent language, playing cards, quarreling, fighting, and smoking about the buildings or on the grounds is strictly forbidden."

The teachers at the school were young men and women mostly in their twenties. All had some advanced training at such places as Shenandoah Collegiate Institute State Normal and Industrial College, Wake Forest, and the Georgia-Alabama Business College. A few had earlier been students at Orange Grove. One rather amazing characteristic of the teaching staff is that their stay at Orange Grove was brief. Of the seven teachers mentioned in the 1906 bulletin, only one appears in next year's bulletin. Of the five teachers mentioned in the 1907 bulletin, only one is listed the next year. And in these three years there were three principals, Walter Crawford, Henry Loy & James Greason, and William Flick.

The education offered at Orange Grove was the typical four-year course that prepared students for college or business. There was a "Literary" course that concentrated on Latin, Greek, English, mathematics, and history. The Music course offered training in organ, piano, and various other instruments. The Business course offered bookkeeping and business mathematics. A Scientific curriculum added in 1908 included chemistry, physics, psychology, botany, physiology, and geology.

Rev. MacDuffie served the Church until October of 1907. Thereafter, he served other churches in the county, including Bethel, and created another academy located near Bethel Baptist Church. Meanwhile, Orange Grove Academy continued in existence. We find little mention of the school in the Church minutes beyond the election of a new Trustee, John Suitt, at the November 1909 meeting. At the January 1911 meeting, the Trustees were empowered to dispose of an unnamed "school matter." The "school matter" was possibly its closing. We must therefore explore this problem. Why was a school that was so successful in 1908 closed in 1912? The answer may involve the increasing competition from public schools. We have a graduation program dated 1912. I presume that this is the last year of operation.

Thursday Night, April 22

BY INTERMEDIATE AND PRIMARY GRADES

Chorus	Welcome Song
	By School
Recitation	Welcome
	By Otto King
Recitation	The Wish of a Small Boy
	By Hally Garrett
Chorus	D Blue Jay
	Intermediate Grades
Recitation	The Dead Doll
	By Mary Dodson
Duet	Playmates
	By Bank Lloyd and Alpha Snipes
Dialogue	The Bashful Boy
	Intermediate Grades
Pantomine	The Blossoming Parasols
	By Twelve Girls
Recitation	The Teacher's Pet
	By Banks Lloyd
Recitation	Grandpapa's Spectacles
	By Alpha Snipes
Song	Old Mother Moon
	By Three Girls
Dialogue	An April Fool
	Intermediate Grades
Song	The Night Cap Song
	Smaller Grades

Friday A. M. 10:30

DECLAMATION AND RECITATION CONTESTS

Address of Welcome	Grady Aldridge
Popping the Question	Nellie Turner
The Orange Grove of To-morrow	Edgar Snipes
The Wedding Fee	Mettie Garrett
MUSIC	
Painting a Picture	Glen Dodson
A Leak in the Dyke	Beulah King
Patriotism in School	Bryant Carr
Jerry	Erma Andrews
MUSIC	
An Ex-Soldier	Bennie Lloyd
The Red Jacket	Clera King
John Morgan	Clem Cheek
The Ride of Jennie McNeil	Leta Cheek
MUSIC	
Out of the Harbor Into the Sea	Paul Cheek
College Oil Cans	Hattie Dodson
Is Life Worth Living?	Lemuel Cheek
Station Signal	Adenia Wagoner
Liberty and Union	Hight Perry
MUSIC	
The South	Gilbert Ray
Kentucky Bell	Thelma Andrews
NOON — RECESS	
1:30 P. M. — Educational Address	
By Mr. J. A. Williams, of Mebane	

Commencement program, 1912

Unfortunately, the only picture I have been able to locate of the school building was taken as it was being torn down. After the school closed in 1912, the academy building reverted to the Church, which used the building for Sunday School and for community get-togethers until it was pulled down in 1949.

The Demolishing of Orange Grove Academy in 1949

There is a tradition in the community that may shed some light on Rev. MacDuffie and his school. It is said that he graduated from Wake Forest in the same year as J. A. Campbell and that both men had the burning ambition to establish a school. Campbell University now stands as a monument to Campbell's success. MacDuffie is said to have harbored ambitions to turn Orange Grove School into a college and that when he felt that community support was lacking, he stormed off in a huff.

A few years ago, I learned from Harry Byrd a finishing touch about McDuffie's feeling toward our community. Harry was our preacher from 1953 to 1957. Harry's father, C. E. Byrd, preached for us from 1921 to 1924. Harry wrote me that his father used to tell the story of what MacDuffie once said to the Cane Creek congregation. The occasion was C. E. Byrd's invitation to MacDuffie to address his old church after an absence of about 15 years. McDuffie said:

> "Since the time I drove my buggy on this church yard there were some people who fought me, and they fought me until I left." He then went on to tell what J. A. Campbell has done at Buies Creek. He said, we could have done the same thing here at Orange Grove if everyone had cooperated." He then turned around and said to my father, "And you wouldn't be here today."

Below are a few other school photographs.

Rev McDuffie (bottom center) and his Faculty

The Orchestra in 1908

Academy Students

The baseball Team

The Orange Grove School Student Body

Many of today's local residents have ancestors who attended either Bingham School, Rock Spring Academy, or Orange Grove School. All these were private schools, and the cost of tuition and board could amount to as much as $100 or more for a year, a sizable amount at that time. For families of more modest means, education could only be obtained in a public school. We look at public schools next.

Public Schools (Called "Common Schools" in the 19th century)

We now regard a good education as a birthright, and we accept the idea that it is proper for the state and county to provide this education and levy a tax to support it. But it was not always this way.

In the early days of our Republic, it was not at all self-evident that government at any level should take responsibility for education below the University level. A debate on education began in North Carolina early in the nineteenth century and continued for decades. Nowhere was the anti-common school sentiment better stated than in a letter to the editor in the _Raleigh Register_ in 1829:

> "To the members of the legislature: ... you will probably be asked to render some assistance to the University ... I hope you will strenuously refuse to do this. I submit that ... our good old-field schools are abundantly sufficient for all our necessities... College-learned persons give themselves great airs, are proud, and the fewer of them we have amongst us the better...

"You may be solicited to take some steps with regard to the establishment among us of common schools. Should so ridiculous a measure be propounded to you, ... treat it with the same contemptuous neglect which it has met with heretofore ... Would it not redound as much to the advantage of young persons ... if they should pass their days in the cotton patch or at the plow or in the cornfield instead of being mewed up in a schoolhouse where they are earning nothing? ... I hope that you do not conceive it at all necessary that everybody be able to read, write, and cipher. If one is to keep a store or a school, or to be a lawyer or physician, such branches may perhaps be taught him ... but if he is to be a plain farmer or a mechanic they are of no manner of use, but rather a detriment. Should schools be established by law, any prudent, sane, saving man desires his taxes to be no higher."

It is a curious side note in early North Carolina that churches played a role early on in the public education of children, particularly those children who fell in a particular niche: those who did not have parents who were well enough off to be able to hire a tutor, but who clearly saw the value of learning to read and write. These children, in the early nineteenth century, could attend a Sunday School, sometimes referred to as a Secular Sunday School, that was run by volunteers at Orange County's churches and supported by donations. They were not today's Sunday Schools. Instead, they taught reading and writing. An ad in the _Hillsborough Recorder_ for 1822 asks for funds to support such an effort and says that sixty to eighty children have already been served "some of whom perhaps would never have learnt to read."

Within a few years this effort had grown and in 1825 the Orange County Sunday School Union petitioned the Legislature for funds, 25 cents per pupil, to support its efforts, claiming that more than 800 children were being taught in 22 Sunday schools throughout the county, children "who would otherwise have been brought up in utter ignorance and vice." The Legislature turned them down.

After years of debate, in 1839 North Carolinians finally had the opportunity to vote on the issue of public schools. The issue passed statewide, and Orange County was one of the counties that stood in favor of tax-supported public schools. Counties that voted for the law were required to create school districts, each to be served by a single school, and to levy a tax that would raise $20 per district. To this was added another $40 from the state's so-called Literary Fund (this fund had been established in 1825 and received money from whiskey taxes and the sale of swampland). At first the schools were ill-housed and the teachers ill-prepared. But improvements were made steadily, especially after the appointment of a State School Superintendent in the 1850s. t By the time of the Civil War, North Carolina had become known for the excellence of its schools. But the war and Reconstruction devastated the school system, and it was not until the early twentieth century that the public school system again reached the levels it had attained in 1860.

Community memory of these old schools has faded, and we remember the location of only a few. It is likely that they did not change materially from those shown below for the year 1922. This map is adapted from one in a master's thesis by Cordelia Cox. Note that there was no Orange Grove Road on the map.

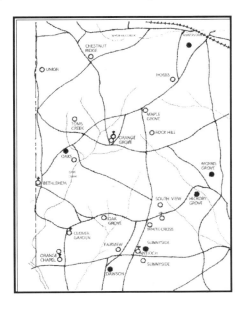

Public Schools (o = White Schools; ● = Black Schools)

Two of these schools are shown below.

Rock Hill School

An Unknown Local School

Each school was in its own school district, with district lines drawn at creeks so that children would not have to risk crossing them to get to school.

Toward the end of his life, one of our church members, Anderson Cate, who was baptized at Cane Creek in 1833, left a short autobiography in which he describes his career as a teacher in one of Orange County's common schools:

> "In the fall of 1857 I went five months to my uncle William Cheek at Poplar Springs. I studied English grammar, arithmetic, geography, etc. In the spring of 1858, I went three months to M. B. Jones at Cane Creek. I then went before the Board of Education, and it granted me a license to teach in the public schools in Orange County. I began teaching in the fall of 1858. My first school was taught in the Chestnut District about two miles south of Efland. From 1858 to 1896, my main occupation was that of teaching although I did run a little farm, teaching in the fall and tending crops in the spring and summer.
>
> "I completed my education by attending Rock Spring Academy for ten months, which school was taught by William Oldham. My additional studies while attending this school were Latin and algebra. I had made arrangements to prepare for college but the war coming on broke up the school.
>
> "My profession of teaching kept me from going to the war at first, and after the conscript law was passed, taking all persons up to 35 years of age, I was exempt from going by being a militia officer which kept me out until the fall of 1864. And at that time, the militia officers were organized into the Home Guard. I belonged to Company K of the North Carolina fourth Regiment and was second Sergeant. I was in the service for about 90 days but was never in any battle."

We are also fortunate to have a firsthand description of Anderson Cate's old school left by James Cheek in his autobiography, _Footprints of a Human Life._ The period he writes about was in the 1880s.

> "The school we attended was called "Chinquapin Rough" located in Toms Creek District. From the ridge on which the school stood, it was a quarter of a mile to the spring where we got drinking water. Of course, most of us wanted the pleasure of going to the spring; anything to get out of school... The schoolhouse sat in an opening on a ridge the size of a small baseball diamond. The building was made of logs, about twenty-by-twenty feet square, with rafters of round pine poles and a roof of what we called clapboards about three feet long, riven with a froe. The west window was an opening about ten feet long and eighteen inches high, covered with a hinged board. Then on the north and east sides there were two small sash windows with panes. The floor was made of wide undressed boards and the seats of slabs from the sawmill showing plane marks of the saw teeth on their surface. We boys had worn them slick, sliding back and forth to whisper or to engage in mischief. The girls had their fun, too. One

day Susie Nicks threw gravel and hit Mr. A. P. Cates, the teacher, right on top of the head. He tried hard to find out who threw it, but Susie looked to be the most innocent child in the room, and no one told on her.

"There was a fireplace with an extremely large hearth, about four feet by seven, made of large rough stones, which would hold a five-foot log. We would fill the fireplace half way up to the arch of the chimney and get the fire to roaring, so it would counteract the cold air, which blew in through the cracks of the floor and walls ...

"For a writing desk, we had a table twelve feet long, made with a board in the center twelve or fourteen inches wide for the ink, then on each side of this was a board of the same size, slanted a little, where we put our copy books and did our best to write like the copy before us. There was room for about sixteen to write at a time, eight on each side ...

"...the school at Chinquapin Rough enrolled about sixty pupils and one teacher handled them all... I do not know how they did it but, as Benjamin Franklin said, 'Necessity is the mother of invention'."

The old one room schoolhouse conjures up a romantic image of the good old days when one could get a sound education consisting of "reading, riting, and 'rithmetic." It is interesting, therefore, to look at a description of Orange County's schools just after World War I when educational reformers were trying to put an end to these schools.

The schools were often in a poor state of repair. Some had leaky roofs and missing windowpanes. A few were still heated by open fireplaces. The sanitary facilities were wretched outhouses. The poor state of Orange County's roads made it almost impossible for the County Superintendent to visit all 78 schools (50 white and 28 black) in a single year. The fact that many schools were situated well off traveled roads as far as a half mile down foot paths or rough wagon roads made conditions even worse. A 1919 study of the county's schools, said:

"In the main the quality of teaching is poor. Teachers were formal, bookish, listless, vague, careless, confined to the text in their teaching... a great many were merely going through the motions."

"Less than 80% of the school age children were actually enrolled and of these, only about 70% were in attendance on any given day.

"A business run on such a basis is bound to turn out a crude, rough, unfinished, inferior product." [See UNC Record Extension Series and Cox's Master's thesis, 1925].

The answer, of course, was school consolidation. The UNC Record report used Bingham Township as an example and suggested that all the old schools should be shut down and that two new schools should be built, one at White Cross and one at Orange Grove. In 1924, this is exactly what was done. It is probably the case that Orange Grove was selected as the site of a fine new brick school because of the community's well-known support of education, and because Cane Creek Church had sold its original academy building to the county in 1906 to be used as a public school. The site of the new school is where the Activity Center is now located.

In 1943, records show that the principal of the Orange Grove public school was Mrs. Helen Carr, who presided over a staff of three teachers, one of whom was Mae Crawford who died recently at over a hundred years old. This school and the one at White Cross replaced the eleven schools that had existed for almost a century. When the school burned in 1943 (local lore alleges that it was arson), local children were bussed to White Cross or to Hillsborough. Following World War II even the White Cross school was closed as the consolidation movement crested. Presently, the children in the community are bussed to schools several miles to the north.

We have just two pictures of Orange Grove School and its teachers:

Orange Grove School just constructed in 1924

Three teachers (including Mae Crawford) in the 1940s

17: PAYING THE PREACHER

Why does a pastor need to be paid for his labors? After all, he is doing God's work, isn't he? Why should he have to be paid for the joy of serving him. Paschal (Vol II, p. 208) has a delightful passage that captures the feeling he had often heard in the more remote regions of western North Carolina a hundred years ago that undoubtedly reflected common thinking almost everywhere in earlier times.

> "Since their minister was one whom they had ordained from their own number, the church felt no obligation to pay him anything for his services... He usually had a farm and was as able to make a living for himself and his family as any other member. On this account, he enjoyed a measure of independence for which he could thank God. It was almost a creed in some churches that while the minister preached on Sunday, yet Sunday was the Lord's day, so why should he be paid for what he did on a day on which he owed his services to the Lord? The members also had their duties on Sunday, one of which was losing as much time as the preacher to be at the church and sit and listen to his sermon. If the pastor attended the church meeting on Saturdays, so did the members."

It was common in the 18th century for the pastor of a church to receive nothing for his labors except the occasional love offering. Our first preacher, Thomas Cate, was no exception. He lived to the south of the church, owned land, and farmed it for a living. The personal property listed in his estate inventory does not differ from that of other farmers in the community. There was no mention of a bible.

There was certainly ample evidence of the evils of paying ministers. In colonial times there was the despised Church of England, which was imposed on the citizenry by law and which was supported by a tax levied by the local Vestry Committee. Everyone had to pay the tax regardless of whether they belonged to the Church of England. In the view of the colonial authorities, the parish minister should not have to toil for a living but should be able to devote himself full time to the needs of the church and its members. This tax infuriated most people. Why should ordinary citizens have to imitate this vile custom of paying the preacher in their own churches?

But it was not long after the formation of Baptist Associations that the argument in favor of paying preachers began to be heard on behalf of Baptist ministers. How could a minister tend to his flock if he had to tend to his fields and animals to feed his family?

The change toward paying Sandy Creek preachers may have been prompted by the "Circular Letter" sent out in 1835 by the Association at the time of the annual meeting. Here are excerpts:

"There is one evil arising from a spirit of covetousness, which has long prevailed to the serious detriment of our Churches, and of which it is high time to complain. This is the refusal of our people to give their ministers any adequate support. ... Ministers have a right to support from the people for whose souls they labor and ... those people commit a sin who refuse him a reasonable support. ... We hope, brethren, that you will take this exhortation in good part and seriously consider whether the curse of God is not blighting our churches for their ill-judged and unscriptural conduct in refusing Ministerial support."

The first record in our Minutes of a preacher from outside the community attending to the needs of our church on a regular basis is in 1830, when Stephen Pleasant says that he will "attend to our church agreeably for the ensuing year." No mention is made of money in our minutes until 1838, when the Minutes state, "a committee was appointed to settle with Bro. Oldham as [collecting] for the minister." Thomas Oldham was later elected the Church's first treasurer. This passage suggests that even by 1838 he was looking after financial matters. Perhaps he was in charge of collecting funds to pay Stephen Pleasant for his services.

Pleasant lived in Caswell County near Yanceyville. He would leave his farm on Friday afternoon, spend the night on the road, and arrive in Orange Grove Saturday morning in time to give a short sermon and preside over the church business meeting. On Saturday night he would stay with a family of the congregation and take meals with them. Then on Sunday after preaching he would mount his horse and travel the rest of the day homeward. The next weekend he would be off to another church. As many as four weekends during the month would be devoted to his calling. At other times he would travel to Association meetings. It is a wonder that he could also pursue an occupation and still be able to answer the call of the Lord.

After Pleasant, the next pastor was G. W. Purefoy. He was a prominent man in Baptist affairs in the state but by the time of his call at Cane Creek (1839), he was already a member of our congregation. So, this may be a case, as cited above by Paschal, of the flock's calling one of its own. It is not until December 1841 that we have hard proof that Cane Creek paid its pastor: "the Church called G. W. Purifoy for next year and agreed to give him $50." For comparison, an acre of land in 1840 was selling for between $1.50 and $3.00, meaning $50 would buy about 25 acres. These salaries do not seem very substantial by today's standards, but one must remember that most preachers maintained a circuit of four churches, rotating to each one once a month. Thus, the above salaries should be multiplied by four to derive the preacher's annual income from preaching.

Soon our church settled into a regular procedure for raising money to pay the pastor. This is indicated in April 1842, when a motion was made "to change the usual way of collecting for the minister." We are not told what the usual way was, but it probably involved voluntary contributions by the more prosperous church members.

The new method, adopted in 1843, was to appoint some of the more active men to sit as a committee to determine what each person's share of the pastor's salary should be. Apparently, women as well as men had an obligation in this regard although it may be that only single women and widows of means were so obligated. The money would then be collected privately, and the church would know nothing of the business unless a difficulty arose. In November 1846 that finally happened. At this meeting the Deacons felt obliged to make public the names of those who had failed to pay their share of the pastor's salary. Presumably, the threat of public humiliation loosened their purse strings.

This "apportionment" method of collecting for the pastor's salary continued for years with the same problems. During the war year of 1864 the Church found it necessary to spread across the Minutes the names of six men who were "delinquent." At the next meeting those who still had not paid were excluded, the first time, as far as we know, that such a thing had happened. In 1869 the Church voted to withhold a letter of Dismissal from any member who had not paid his share of the salary. (A letter of dismissal was given to members who moved out of the community while in good standing in the church. It was a ticket of admission to another Baptist church.) In January 1869, the Minutes duly recorded that Jordan wished to be paid in advance for each quarter.

When F. M. Jordan, our Civil War pastor, elected to move on late in 1869 the Church called W. R. Gwaltney at a salary of $150. He accepted our call. As the century waned, so too did the fortunes of the community. The pastor's salary began a steady decline. In 1880 James Mason was reduced from $150 to $125. He preached his last sermon at Cane Creek in 1881.

We are fortunate to have an old record book (owned by Virginia Perry) kept by the Clerk, D. M. Sykes, during the 1890s. Below is a portion of the list from 1892. In it we find such a list as the committee would have made out. There are 126 names on the list. The largest amount paid by any individual was $5.00 by E. H. Stubbins. The smallest amount was $0.25, which was the most common amount among the 38 "sisters." The total amount raised was $200.

An 1892 Accounting for the collection of the pastor's salary

In 1895 a move was undertaken to alter the method of collecting for the pastor's salary. The congregation voted to "let each member pay as he pleases." Optimistically, they agreed to call Rev. McDuffie for 1896 at a salary of $125. The new free-will method must have fallen flat for in August a motion was passed to "call out the amount each member is to pay for the pastor's salary."

In 1904 the Minutes for September report the adoption of the "envelope method" for collecting the pastor's salary and for missions. We do not have the details of the technique, but it probably asked people to put their offering in an envelope and sign it on the outside. It enabled the clerk to keep track of who was paying what amount. In October 1905 the clerk was asked to read out the list of how much each person paid for the pastor's salary for each of the two preceding years.

In 1909 W. O. Petty was hired "at the usual price of $150," the same figure used since 1897. Petty was then asked to preach twice a month for $300 and it was decided to pay him monthly using a pledge method for raising the funds.

In 1911 the Church called R. C. Hilliard at $175 and transportation to the train station. For this the Church tried again to use the "envelope method." The apportionment method was kept only for special expenses, and in 1913 when the Church apportioned the amount needed to repair the building, it had to "suspend" 13 members for non-payment. A few months later the delinquents were threatened with exclusion and those who were behind on their share of the pastor's salary were threatened with having their names read in church.

By 1920, as the church considered calling R. S. Lennon at a salary of $225, the method of raising the funds reverted to the old tried and true apportionment method. This method was continued for several years, until the church began to collect an offertory as part of each Sunday service. We do not know when the church began to include a regular time of offering at the Sunday service. The first bulletin we have is for Homecoming in 1950. There is a line in the program that says, "Tithes and offerings."

We also do not know when our church first started to agree upon an annual budget for the upcoming year. Our budget records go back to 1970 so that may have been the first year.

All the above reflects the evolution of the role of the pastor. Originally, he was a member of the community selected to lead the church because of his spiritual gifts and his ability as an orator. He farmed for a living and received no pay for his services. Then, about 1840, it became the practice for rural churches to pay a pastor who arrived from outside the community. Now, a pastor would attend to up to four churches in his "circuit." He had to spend much time just getting to each of his churches. He probably ran a farm but needed compensation for the time he spent on his churches and thus lost to farming.

By the 20th century it became possible for a pastor to make a modest living just by preaching. And as the century went on, it became possible for some rural churches to pay a pastor well enough that he could devote all his time to one flock. From the minutes and the surviving church budgets we, we have the following salaries:

Year	Salary	Benefits	Comments
1840	$50	0	Preaching once a month
1850	$100	0	This is an estimate since our records are missing
1860	$200	0	
1870	$150	0	
1880	$125	0	
1890	$150	0	
1900	$150	0	
1910	$300	0	Preaching twice a month begins

1920	$300	0	
1930	$400	0	
1940	$400	0	
1950	$700	0	
1960	$3,480	0	Preaching every Sunday begins
1970	$4,900	$650	The parsonage comes into use
1980	$10,100	$2,195	
1990	$19,800	$10,380	We paid Social Security this year only
2000	$29,895	$5,800	
2010	$37,200	$9,804	
2020	$28,606	$33,452	Housing allowance added

Beginning in the 1970s, we began to provide fringe benefits. These have come to include travel & visitation expenses, professional development expenses, life insurance, health insurance and retirement. In the 2010s, the pastor no longer lived in the parsonage, and since then we have provided a housing allowance.

I want to mention another aspect of Cane Creek Church that has a long tradition. That is our practice of hiring only pastors with a college degree. Because of our limited supply of money, we often called pastors fresh out of divinity school.

The first pastor that we know of who could be called "educated" was George W. Purefoy. He sprang from humble origins and never attended college, but he became quite prominent in Baptist affairs and wrote the definitive book on the Sandy Creek Association. Later, in 1870, UNC granted him an honorary Doctor of Divinity degree.

After that, starting with F. M. Jordan, in 1865 (and perhaps earlier if we could learn more about those who served us between 1852 and 1865) all our pastors have been college educated, most at Wake Forest until recently.

18: GLIMPSES LIFE IN OLD CANE CREEK

As we rush about our modern daily lives, driving sleek shiny cars and pickups, watching television beamed down from satellites, and observing gigantic green John Deere tractors harvesting crops, we seem far removed from the slower, simpler life of bygone years. A few of us are old enough to remember when the road by the church was unpaved, when lighting was done by kerosene lamps, and when water was drawn from a well by bucket. But there was a time when our ancestors gave thanks for a decent dirt road and a hand dug well. Their grandparents could talk of the time when the roads were frequently impassable and water came from a spring. We all know a little bit of what life was like in the old days from conversations with our parents and grandparents, but many of the interesting details of what life was like get lost over the generations. Below, I hope to recapture some of these long past images to give a hint of what life was like in olden days of Cane Creek.

Robert Kenzer has published a study of the pre-Civil War period in Orange County. At this time, a hundred years after the arrival of the first settlers, geography, transportation, religious institutions, and marriage patterns all combined to create eight relatively isolated self-contained, tightly knit rural neighborhoods in Orange County: Eno, Little River, Flat River, Cane Creek, New Hope, Durham, White Cross, and Patterson. His history (we have a copy in our library) can help us understand life in old Cane Creek.

He tells us that the rural neighborhoods were virtually self-sufficient. They had to be because travel was so difficult. Country stores were established, often at the site of a gristmill, to provide the residents with what they needed. There was little need to venture beyond the reach of the neighborhood. Thus it was that a century after the land was first settled, most people resided on the same land that their ancestors had obtained through land grants.

The same close-knit structure of the old neighborhoods is also illustrated in marriage patterns. It was the exception rather than the rule that marriage partners came from beyond the neighborhood.

Because there were so many blood ties linking families within a neighborhood, it was these family ties, more so than anything else, that helped residents find their places in society. In contrast to modern times, where one might tend to identify himself as a member of the middle class and to associate with friends of roughly the same economic level, in the decades before the Civil War family ties trumped economic status. Thus, a poor tenant farmer barely scratching an existence from a small plot of land might feel kinship and affection for a cousin who resided in a large house, farmed a huge tract of land, and had all his material wants satisfied.

Before taking a closer look at local life. I would like to insert an important 19th century event, our joining the new Mt. Zion Association. A Baptist Association is a group of churches that occupy a local area and share beliefs and attitudes, especially those concerning missions.

Our first Association was the original Sandy Creek Association, which we joined in 1806 when we became a Baptist church. Our second was the Beulah Association, which we joined during the controversy over "benevolent institutions," the primary one being missions. This debate divided North Carolina into two groups, missionary Baptists and primitive Baptists. We were with Sandy Creek for 31 years and with the Beulah for 33 years. Each change was prompted by changes in attitudes and approaches to religion and evangelism.

In the years just following the Civil War, another set of issues led to our meeting at Lystra Baptist Church with twelve other churches to consider forming a new association. The issue at hand pitted traditionalists against progressives. We were in the progressive camp. Progressives wanted the annual association meeting to be primarily a short business meeting. Traditionalists preferred the old practice of a four day "camp meeting" with sermons twice a day, hymn singing, and fellowship. The 'business' part of the meeting was almost an afterthought.

Progressives also wanted the association to focus on establishing new Baptist churches within its bounds. Additionally, they wanted to actively encourage each member church to establish a Sunday School program, to form temperance societies to combat the widespread use of whiskey, and to foster the education of the young people.

This informal group of churches discussed the issues and looked favorably on forming a new association. On September 23, 1870, they met at Mt. Moriah Church to make it official. Our former pastor, G. W. Purefoy, was elected moderator. The new Mt. Zion Association started with 1,588 individuals spread across 13 churches. When the historian, J. H. Waugh, Jr., wrote a centennial history in 1970, he reported a membership of 14,000 individuals in 36 churches. Today membership is roughly 10,000 with 37 churches. We are a charter member and have been with the association for 152 years.

Over the years, we have helped establish several churches: These "daughter' churches are:

> 1806 Haw River Mountain (now Antioch);
> 1834 Mars Hill;
> 1851 Sandy Field (now Bethel);
> 1877 Hickory Grove;
> 1882 Betheden (now Crossroads);
> 1887 Mebane; and
> 1936 Oak Grove.

Returning to a look at life in old Cane Creek, I would like to begin with two matters of importance: county government and county roads.

Government

Today, we have a commissioner form of county government, but under the original North Carolina Constitution of 1778 counties were run in a way that preserved many of the features of colonial government. Primary authority lay in the county court, which was composed of Justices of the Peace appointed by the Governor. These were usually prominent planters or businessmen. The Justices of the Peace came together four times a year in Hillsborough to conduct business. Here all the important matters within the county were decided: roads and bridges, schools, taxes, legal disputes, and such. The Sheriff was empowered to enforce the rulings of the court and to collect taxes. Under him were a number of magistrates, each in his own district, who represented the Sheriff's authority in the neighborhood in which he lived.

Only the sheriff was elected by the people. Since the Justices of the Peace were empowered to nominate men to be appointed as new Justices of the Peace, the whole power structure came to be a self-perpetuating system run by a small group of prominent and influential citizens of the county. Compared to today, ordinary citizens had little say in the daily workings of county government. It is little wonder that there was general suspicion of the so-called "courthouse gang," a group of lawyers, hangers-on, and their cronies, all who knew how the complex apparatus of county government worked and how to bend it to their own desires.

At the State level, the Constitution of 1778 produced a form of state government similar to what we are familiar with today. There was a governor and a legislature composed of two houses, the Senate and the House of Commons. Unlike today, however, there were severe restrictions on who was eligible to serve and who was eligible to vote for members of the legislature. Of course, Blacks and women were not allowed to vote. But, in addition, a white male had to own enough property to be a taxpayer to vote for a member of the House and had to own at least 50 acres of land to vote in a senate race. A member of the House had himself to own at least 100 acres and a member of the Senate had to own land valued at a minimum of £1000.

The American founding fathers did not envision political parties and made no provision for them in the national Constitution. But parties soon arose and ever since have played a dominant role in American political life. It was perhaps inevitable for it is natural to have a difference of opinion on important issues and it is also natural for those of like mind to band together in opposition to those of a contrary opinion.

The first issue to crystallize two opposing camps occurred after the Revolution and concerned the matter of states' rights versus the powers of the new national government. In general, North Carolinians were leery of vesting too much power in the hands of a central government and had held out for the addition of a strong bill of rights to the Constitution that insured individual liberty against a possibly tyrannical central government. Those who thought that the nation would need a strong central government to protect itself in a hostile world were called Federalists. Those who preferred that power to be left in the hands of the individual states were called Anti-Federalists.

Orange County, in general, and its farmers in the rural areas, were staunchly Anti-Federalist. When a state convention met in Hillsborough in July 1788 to consider ratification of the federal Constitution, all six Orange County delegates voted against it. One observer of the time placed the blame on the farmers' "extreme individualism." This view softened a bit over the next year, but, even after the addition of the Bill of Rights, a majority of the Orange County delegates voted against ratification in 1789. Most of the support in favor of the new American constitution came from the more conservative planter class in the eastern part of the state. Orange County, then considered more of a frontier county, was a hotbed of radical belief, which, on this issue, centered on a suspicion of centralized authority and a firm belief in property rights and individual liberty.

The Anti-Federalist party disintegrated after the war of 1812, when it became obvious that the country did need a strong central government. Party politics waned for a time. By the time things sorted themselves out again, there were two new parties vying for power, the Democrats, and the Whigs. One of the central issues that divided people into two opposing camps was the matter of "internal improvements:" Canals, bridges, roads and a national bank. Should the government involve itself in internal improvements supported by taxes, or should these matters be left to individual citizens who would build things that the public wanted, such as toll roads and bridges, to make a profit while serving the people?

Democrats were, in general, against the federal government's involving itself with internal improvements. They also favored low tariffs and free trade. This sentiment was especially strong in the South since its economy depended upon the ability to sell agricultural products to foreign countries. If the nation imposed high tariffs on imports to protect northern manufacturers, this would encourage foreign countries to retaliate with high tariffs against southern cotton and tobacco. Thus, as long as these crops were important to the south, the south's politicians were against high tariffs. And southern Democrats were also hopeful that, in the election of 1824, Andrew Jackson would do nothing to jeopardize the institution of slavery.

The Whig party, formed in 1834, endorsed the government's role in internal improvements and also favored having a government-run national bank. In North Carolina, allegiance to these new political parties amplified a divide that was growing within the state. The eastern part of the state – controlled largely by prominent planters who had run the state and the colony since before the revolution – favored the

Democratic position. The interior of the state tended to favor such things as better roads and leaned toward the Whig party.

Local politics were even more impassioned in the 1800s than they are now. Election day was a huge social event with large crowds gathering at the polling places. Rival parties would hand out food and whiskey to get people to vote for their candidates. This was called "treating" and it became more intense and scandalous with each passing election.

The issue came up at the 1829 Annual meeting of the Sandy Creek Baptist Association. The following motion was passed:

> "Resolved: That this association concurs with the Savannah River, the Bethel, the Moriah, and the Pee Dee Associations in their disapprobation of the practice of candidates for office, treating the voters with spirituous liquors, and will cordially unite with said associations and other friends of reform, to put down said practice."

Orange County was about equally divided between Whigs and Democrats, but each of the neighborhoods mentioned by Kenzer was strongly for just one party. White Cross was known as a strong Democrat precinct due largely to the influence of the Lloyd family. Cane Creek, on the other hand, was strongly Whig.

Roads

The other issue I want to discuss is the matter of roads. They were a big problem for the first settlers. They began as horse trails that closely followed old Indian footpaths. Some re-routing was done to suit horses and mules, which are not able to navigate sharp turns and steep slopes quite as nimbly as humans. Later, the paths were widened and relocated again to allow for the wagons used by the first settlers coming south from Virginia and Pennsylvania. Even before Orange County was created in 1752, a British form of county government was instituted that put the main "Public" roads under the jurisdiction of the County courthouse.

In the 1760s, Colonial Governor Martin wrote that the roads in Orange County "were the most wretched he had ever seen" and that the region west of Hillsborough was "the most broken, difficult, and rough country he had ever seen." It took a long time for things to improve.

There were two sorts of roads in the early days. Private roads were put in wherever a land owned wished. They connected a barn with the fields or connected one farm with another. Their location and upkeep was in the hands of the local landowners.

Public roads were meant to help people go longer distances. Their location was determined by where the towns were located and where the rivers and creeks could be crossed with fords and ferries. The earliest public road in our neighborhood that I know of came south from Hillsborough along what is now Orange Grove Road, then cut southwest about where Sugar Ridge Road now is, then ran back of Tommy Holmes' house, joined the present Bradshaw Quarry Road at Cane Creek, and headed on toward Woody's Ferry and Saxapahaw, where the Haw River could be crossed. On the other side of the Haw River, it joined the Fayetteville Road, a major east-west road connecting the back-country with the closest point for river navigation. The other main road that went through the community was the Greensboro Stage Road, which I have already mentioned. There is a faint community memory that General Cornwallis marched his troops along this road on the way to do battle at Guilford Courthouse.

Public roads were under the jurisdiction of the County Court. All taxable men between the ages of 16 and 50 had to devote three day's labor a year (six days in Colonial times) to road maintenance. Anyone who did not appear for work had to supply three other workers in his place or else forfeit five shillings a day. At each quarterly session it was common to have citizens designated as responsible for a certain stretch of road. In the minutes of the session for March 1785, we find that James Ball was appointed overseer of the road from Cane Creek to Meadow Meeting House with the following hands: Henry O'Daniel, Barnard Lasley, William Kirk, John Pickard, Thomas Lasley, James Christmas, James Moore, and seventeen others, presumably men who owned land along the road.

A hundred years later, this same procedure was still in effect. In James Cheek's autobiography (p. 35) we have a description of roadwork in the 1880s:

> "The county roads were kept up by sections according to law. An overseer was appointed for each section and the men of a neighborhood would work on their own section. When an overseer thought it was time to go over the road, he would go from house to house or send word as to what day they would begin work. That was called 'warning the road hands in.' There was no grading, the road being left flat, except for diagonal ditches, which were made across the road to carry the water off. Mr. Tommie Dodson would bring his black mule where plowing was needed in our section. When I did my first work on the road, a man by the name of Joe Murray was overseer. He had a certain by-word he often used as he worked, which I could never forget. He was a great worker. When he picked up a mattock or spade, it meant there was going to be something done, and every so often he would use his cherished by-word."

This arrangement continued into the 1890s. But by this time, Hillsborough Township had decided to levy a tax to support roadwork and within a few years this idea found acceptance throughout the county. In the two-year period 1891-92, the seven-cent road tax raised $440 in Bingham Township of which $187 was actually spent on road maintenance.

Roads, however, were still pretty dicey things in bad weather even into the 1920s during North Carolina's so-called "good roads" era. Road maintenance, especially in rural areas, had become the top county expenditure and Orange County, like many other North

Carolina counties, was becoming deeply indebted just to keep up with the demands of its citizens for better roads. In 1931, North Carolina did a radical thing. It took over jurisdiction and maintenance of all county roads. In spite of this, it was not until Governor Kerr Scott's administration in the early 1950s that his two hundred-million-dollar program to pave "farm-to-market" roads program finally got us out of the mud.

The next two pages show local maps made in 1925 and 1930. Note that Orange Grove Road was extended south, in this timespan, to what became NC54.

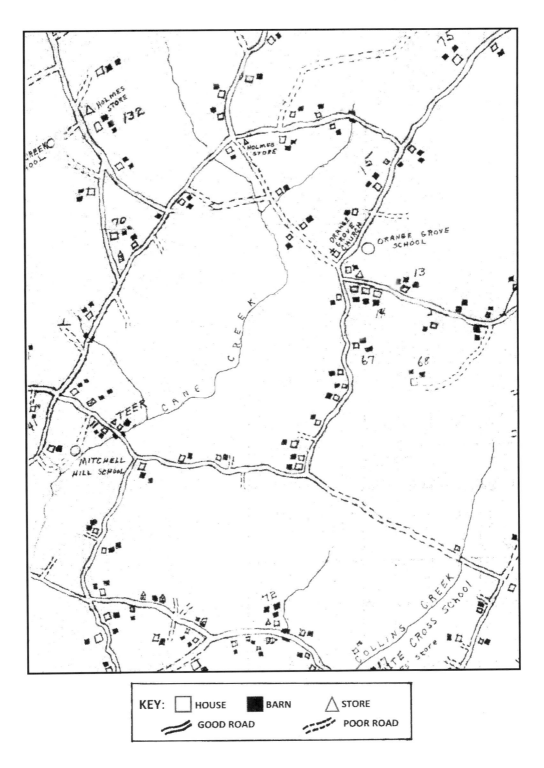

The Moore Map from 1925

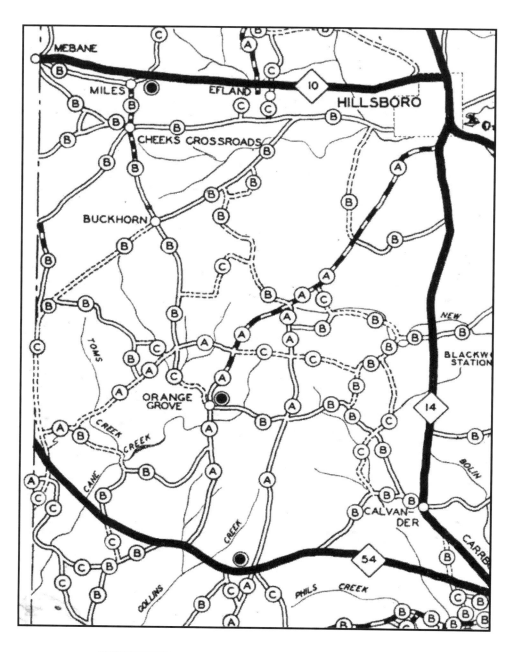

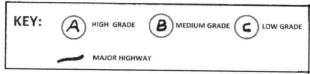

State Highway Map from 1930

Daily Life in Cane Creek

Now that we have looked at how our local government operated and at how roads were handled, we can get closer to home by seeing what a few local people wrote about their experiences in Cane Creek. One is Anderson Cates, who was a deacon for more than 20 years at Cane Creek after the Civil War. Toward the end of his days, he wrote a brief sketch of his life.

The second is James Cheek, whose book I have already quoted several times. Lastly, we have a 1990 term paper written by Gretchen Case, a student at UNC. The topic is the farm that was run by Cecil Crawford and his sister, Mae.

We begin with Anderson Cate's story. He speaks of being "bound" to various people as a boy. This refers to the practice of apprenticeship. A boy would be 'bound" to a tradesman – such as a blacksmith, a miller, or a weaver – who would house, feed, and clothe the boy and gradually teach him his craft. Sometimes the boy's father would have a handshake agreement with the tradesman. Other times there would be a formal contract that might, for example, require the tradesman to see that the boy was sent to school. Here is Anderson Cate's story.

James Cheek's Photograph of the Anderson Cate House

"I was born on December the 11th, 1834 in Orange County one- and one-half miles northwest of Cane Creek Church on the public road leading from Hillsboro to Saxapahaw.

"My father's name was Richard Cates, and my mother's name was Kesia Cates, daughter of Solomon Cates. From this union sprang forth 12 children, I being the youngest one. My father died in May 1837, and my mother died in 1844 in Randolph County and was buried at Prospect Church. I was living with my mother when she died, after which I came back to Orange County.

"My mother was married the second time to David Cates. I lived a while with my brother, Thomas. I was then bound to David Williams and lived with him until he died. I was then rebound to my eldest brother, James F. Cates, and lived with him until I was 18 years old. At that time, I bought my time for 30 dollars, but he was to send me to school six months or at least board me while I went to school; all of which he did according to the contract, and from the time I was 18 up until now I have been my own man.

"From 18 to 23 I worked at various places on the Cape Fear navigation, the railroad, and finally at the Blacksmith Shop with David McBane for one year. After this, I worked on the farm until 1857 at which time I decided to go to school and prepare myself for teaching.

"In 1868 I was elected Clerk of the Township Board of Trustees for Bingham Township which office I held for four years. I was appointed a magistrate in the year 1882 and held said office for eight years in succession. Since then, I have been a private citizen.

"Since 1896 I have been running a little farm. I have never lived at but three places besides the one I now live at since I was married on May the 30th, 1861.

"I have been a member of the Baptist church for at least 40 years. I have been a Deacon in Cane Creek Church for at least twenty years. I have read through the Bible five times during my life.

"My wife, Mary E. Lloyd, was born on March the 6th, 1835 two miles East of Cane Creek Church. She was the daughter of Frederick and Mary Lloyd. Her mother was a Thrift. She was raised by her father and her mother until she was married in 1861. All those who attended our marriage have long since been called to their reward above and yet we are the spared monuments of His amazing goodness and mercy. Our union has been pleasant, agreeable, and fruitful.

"Mary was a member of the Baptist Church for 60 years. She joined the church at or near 16 years of age and was baptized by Brother John Wilson in Hopson's old millpond. We raised a family of eight children till all were grown and married except one who is not but has gone to his reward. We have thirty living grandchildren."

Anderson's oldest brother was Thomas S. Cates, born in 1823 and, like Anderson, a grand-nephew of our first preacher. His house was on Buckhorn Road where Hight and Virginia Perry lived. He and his wife Adeline appear in *A Cane Creek Tapestry* on page 104. There is a direct line of descent from Thomas S. Cate to daughter Luda Cate, who married A. A. Perry, to their son Hight Perry, to his son, H. M. Perry, Jr., to his daughter, Denise, who married Scott Hudson, and on to their children, Curtis and Clayton. Thus, there are seven generations from our first preacher to our current youth.

Anderson was elected a Trustee of Bingham Township. During Reconstruction, occupying union forces imposed a Pennsylvania-type of local government on North Carolina counties. They created townships and gave township Trustees considerable authority. After Reconstruction ended, the system was abolished. The Union forces had also instituted commissioners at the county level. This did work. Anderson was appointed a Magistrate by the Legislature and they, together with the Commissioners, ran the county until 1892, when the Commissioners were first elected by popular vote.

Note that Anderson Cates' mother had been born a Cates. She married a Cates, and when he died, she married still another Cates. It sounds almost incestuous, but it was not because of the huge number of Cates then living in our community. F. M. Jordan, our preacher from 1865 to 1869, wrote:

"This church was noted for having a great many members by the same name. Cates was the largest. They would call the role on Saturdays, and it was Cates, Cates, Cates. It was said in that country, if you met a man and called him Sykes and happened to miss it, just say 'I am mistaken, this is Mr. Cates, and you would be certain to hit it."

The second person I quote is James Cheek. His father moved the family back to the community in 1876 and settled on James' grandfather's place, which I judge to have been somewhere along Toms Creek not far from Oak Grove Baptist Church.

"When I think of grandpap Moore, I remember the old Chestnut Ridge Methodist Church of which he was a prominent member. In my early boyhood they still had camp meetings there. A row of log cabins was built fifty to one hundred yards from the church. In these cabins, some of the families would stay through the meeting, one member going back and forth to take care of the stock at home.

"I thought it was great to spend the night there with Cicero Jones. His folks had a cabin and stayed during these fall meetings. Mother was a member of this church and father was a member of Cane Creek Baptist Church. They would go to camp meeting for the day and I would sometimes stay over with Cicero. We ate at the camp table, which had a charm for me that I cannot express.

"Not far from the church there was an arbor under which they held meetings when the weather was suitable. It had a high pulpit, mourners' bench, and straw all around in front of the pulpit. One day, Cicero Sykes, Mr. John William Sykes' son, had been to the mourners' bench and had prayed through and had shed enough tears to wet his handkerchief, which he showed to me as we walked down the long hill to the spring. A great many of us would go to the altar every year and get renewed. Somehow, the circuit riders did not preach about a faith that would hold good from one end of the year to the other.

"In my mind's eye, I can see those old circuit riders mounted on their horses, with their saddlebags. They would ride up to a tree, dismount, hitch their horses to a swinging limb and walk slowly and reverently through the grounds shaking hands with the brethren. I especially remember one preacher whose name was Pickens. His general appearance and preaching style appealed to me. He was popular with everybody at the Ridge. We had another preacher who was very peculiar, called "Monkey Dick Mischeaux." He was well liked and was one of the cleverest men in the Conference. His brother, John, also a preacher, was more precise, but Dick, with all his peculiarities, was considered a better preacher and was popular amongst Methodists and Baptists alike ...

"The old Cane Creek Baptist Church was about four miles from our house over a rough hilly road. The circuit riders came once a month, preaching Sunday morning with a business meeting on Saturday before preaching.

"David Sykes was clerk of the church and I remember so distinctly seeing him sitting at the little table with the church book before him. He had a resonant voice and it resounded in the church as he called out 'John Dodson, Charles Kennedy, William Cheek, Billy Cates, Anderson Cates, John W. Holmes, Chesley Andrews, Henry Lloyd,' and many others. It was a rule of the Baptist church in those days that if a member missed three meetings, he would be 'brought up before the church.' Sometimes they would 'bring them up' for being drunk or going to dances.

"In the late summer months, we would have our protracted meetings at Cane Creek Church. The people throughout the district would come, walking, or riding in wagons and buggies or on horseback. Many took dinner, and two of the main dishes served were fried chicken and fried ham. When morning service was over, an effort was made to see that everyone on the grounds had something to eat.

"The buggy used in the days of slavery was made with pieces of iron extending over the rear axle. On this was a wooden seat where the servant boy rode, in order to serve his master and to look after the horse.

"As boy of about fourteen years old, I was convicted of my sin and when the call for seekers was made, I came to the altar. Some of the church leaders came and talked to me and I surrendered to Jesus. I especially remember Mrs. Wilson Dodson who was one of them. I rose with a light heart, and as I looked around on the swarthy faces of our neighbors, they looked better than I had ever seen them. The dingy unpainted walls of the old church looked better than they ever had before... I was baptized in Thompson's millpond.

"The church where I was saved was one of the prominent landmarks of that section of Orange County and had the appearance of being close to a hundred years old at that time. It was torn down years ago and has been replaced by two other church buildings."

The "rough hilly road" that James Cheek had to travel over to get to the church would have been the Greensboro Stage Road, which had to climb and then descend Thunder Mountain and cross Cane Creek below the old Crawford house. His discription of our 1874 church is the only one we have. It was torn down in 1890 following the completion of the church that stood where the basketball court now is. Jame's notion that the church "had the appearance of being close to a hundred years old" is contradicted by the fact that we bought our current tract in 1852 and would probably have built the church soon thereafter. James was baptized in Thompson's mill pond. This is the mill pond on Buckhorn Road where I live.

Here are other excerpts from James Cheek's book that describe some details of daily life at Cane Creek.

"When I was two years old, we moved to Grandfather Cheek's place. We could hear the baying of foxhounds, the blowing of fox horns, and the noise of coon hunters along the creek. This creek ran about three quarters of a mile through our farm. Along its banks lived the opossum, raccoon, muskrat, and mink. In the creek were perch, hornyhead and other small fish. Our neighbors would go along the creek with their seines and catch fish that way, but we children fished with hook and line. (p. 13)

"We used to go bee hunting. There was an art in locating bee trees. A good hunter would go along a watercourse and see on which side of the water the bees were drinking. Then he would watch them rise. If the tree were nearby, they would not fly high, but if it were quite a way off, they would rise high in the air, and the hunter could get their course and follow them. Before the honey could be removed from the tree, it was necessary to smoke the bees so they would not sting. (p. 14)

"When I was growing up, there were many moonshine establishments hidden away up the little streams and in other secluded places. Some of them were most crudely built. One moonshiner lived close to Mebane. It seemed he was determined to make whiskey. He would be caught and jailed and as soon as he got out of jail, he would go right back to his whiskey making. (p. 18)

"One day mother did something which displeased me. I was standing beside Grandpa's chimney at the lightening rod and I said 'Ma is mean.' I do not know how she heard about it so quickly, but she came out with a switch and when she was through with me, I was completely cured. Somehow, I got completely turned against talking that way. (p. 25)

"Very often, our mothers would have quiltings and the neighbor women were invited to help. The quilt would be stretched on frames ready for quilting when the crowd gathered and, in the meantime, a big dinner was prepared. The quilts made then would last a lifetime or longer. (p. 34)

"Our mothers used to bake in an oven on the hearth. They would draw out coals from the fire, set the skillet or oven over them, put their corn pone or biscuits in and cover with the lid on which coals were heaped. Potatoes and corn ashcake were often baked in the hot ashes. Boiled foods were cooked in pots swung over the fire on a crane. This was back-breaking work, but they were always glad to have a crowd of the neighbors come in and eat with them. I remember Aunt Nan's old kitchen and the fireplace in it, which was at least seven feet wide. On a cold morning, I have seen a boy sitting on each end of the log while the fire blazed in the middle. Before I was grown up, stoves and steel ranges were used throughout the country. (p. 52).

"There were plenty of deer in Orange County at that time and grandpa told us a fanciful tale about an inexperienced man on a deer hunt. This man had been told to stay where the deer runs crossed and shoot the deer as they came along. Finally, a deer with big antlers approached, but the man did not shoot. Then the other man asked him if he saw a deer. He replied, 'No, I didn't see a deer, but saw a man coming along with a chair on his head.'(p. 44).

Lastly, we have this description of the Crawford's farm. Cecil and Mae Crawford (along with Settle) were the children of Luther and Mary Bell ("Mit") Crawford. A family picture is on page 112 of _A Cane Creek Tapestry_. (Page numbers in parenthesis below refer to pictures in _Tapestry_.) The farm lies on parts of two old land grants. The southern half was part of a 1756 grant from the Earl of Granville to Alexander Mebane, the first sheriff of Orange County. I do not know the original grantee for the upper half, but in 1768 it belonged to John Cate. By 1810 the entire farm was owned by William Hopson who may or may not have been the builder of what came to be known as Hopson's Mill (I lean toward the mill's having been built by a Cate in the 18th century). In 1884-5, the farm belonged to C. E. Gower (page 31), one of our pastors. Gower sold the farm to W. H. Lloyd, and it then descended to Mr. Tommy Lloyd (page 15) who sold the farm to the Crawfords in 1909 for $1,225.

In 1990 Gretchen Case wrote a term paper for a UNC Folklore course. She got most of the information from talking to Cecil and Mae. Here are some excerpts.

"The land on which these buildings stand tells the history of Orange County. At first there was the Hopson cotton plantation, with its old gristmill and slave cabins. The stagecoach road from Raleigh to Greensboro ran just to the north of the house. Cecil points out that trains put an end to the old stagecoach road, and all that is visible now is a tree-lined gully. During Civil War times, Union troops marching from occupied Raleigh to do battle at Guilford Courthouse, stopped to rest here. [This is an error. The tradition is Cornwallis' troops in 1781.]

"The farm passed from the Hopsons to the Lloyds and then to the Crawfords. But its traditional crop remained cotton. Mae says that prior to 1941 "we did the big cotton" - nine acres producing up to nine bales a year in Depression years. Although they were growing an abundance of cotton, prices had plummeted. The Crawfords recall that one year their father held the cotton back until he could get eight or nine cents a pound, rather than the six he had been offered. The money they received was used to purchase things the Crawfords could not provide for themselves. They did not buy many groceries since they always kept a garden going, churned every day, and had cows, hogs, and chickens for meat. Octagon soap and sugar were two of the small luxuries in town. Some tools and farm equipment also had to be bought- Cecil fondly remembers the days when a good heavy knife was only 25 cents! Though the Crawford women did most of their own sewing, they bought shoes, men's suits, and winter coats. Cloth was also often store-bought. Another alternative for cloth though, was the brightly printed feedbags in which many farmers received chicken and dairy feed. These were of sturdy material, often with bright patterns that made them desirable for making dresses. (p. 88).

"The original one room cabin, now the kitchen, is apparent only from the rear of the house. The cabin dates back to the early nineteenth century. The Crawfords cannot pin down an exact date, but they do know that it and the smokehouse to the south were constructed at least as early as 1835 by "Old Man Hopson." Hopson, his wife, and young son are buried out just to the west of the Crawford's' old granary. The flooded Cane Creek now covers the land that held the cotton plantation's old gristmill and numerous slave cabins. At the top of the hill, the cabin that is now the Crawford's kitchen served as the "big house." The cabin and the smokehouse are both of solid, simple construction: hand-hewn logs with wooden pegs holding the joists together.

"Luther and Mary Bell Crawford wanted a new house to raise their family. The cabin was still solid, but the front structure was dreary and aging. Before any building could be done, though, they had to establish their new farm. In the next few years, they had three children: Cecil, born in 1910; Settle, in 1912; and

Mae, in 1915. Finally, in 1917, they were ready to raise a new house. The decision of what style to build was easy: The I-house was obviously the style of the times, as Mary Bell's two sisters had each just built an I-house on nearby property. Building the new house was a community project. The head carpenter, and the only professional involved, was Mr. Ed Cates (shown on page 117 of _Tapestry_), a man from the neighborhood. He and Luther Crawford did the brunt of the work themselves. The lumber for the house came from the backyard. Luther cut the timber with a handsaw, and then took it to a nearby sawmill to be made into planks. The framing timber was procured from a neighbor, at the price of 20 cents per 100 square feet- even in those days a negligible sum. Mr. Cates was paid $2 a day for his labor. Neighboring farmers who put in days of labor on the Crawford's' new house were repaid through the barter system. There was always plenty of hard work to be shared: fields to be cleared, crops to be gathered.

"Perhaps most important, is the ethic of preservation that lies behind these buildings. Nothing was torn down if it could be improved or put to another use. The old garage became the woodshed; an insufficient carport was widened. There is a lesson in all of this for our throw-away society: adapt instead of abandon. Mae summed it up best when she said, "If you just take care of yourself, you'll live to be old." Simple but true, as is evident in the buildings the Crawfords have taken such good care of and grown old with."

The Cane Creek or the Orange Grove Community?

Finally, I would like to discuss the issue of where our community gets its name. When I began writing the historical sketches for the church's webpage a few years ago, I asked folks to make suggestions about topics for me to write about. The most frequent question was, "Where did the name "Orange Grove" come from?"

My suspicion is that our community has had three names. I suspect that we were first known by our church name, Cane Creek. The basis for this guess comes from Stephen Pleasant's letter, quoted in Chapter 10, to Samuel Wait, the founder of Wake Forest, in 1833. In it he writes:

> "Very Dear Bro. Wait: I have just returned home from Cain Creek and found you had wrote me a letter... the people about Cain Creek are well ... things go on quite comfortable there..." [in the early days "Cain" was a common spelling; indeed it was used much more often than "Cane."]

We do not know for sure whether he was referring to the church in particular or the community in general, but, in all my readings about the history of the community, I have come across no other name for our neighborhood in those old days except the occasional use of "Cane Creek" instead of "Cain Creek." I should also note that I have inspected

North Carolina maps dated 1770, 1775, 1808, 1833, and 1861, which give no indication of any community name.

In doing a land trace on my property on Buckhorn Road some years ago, I found that the old gristmill on my property had been constructed in 1813 by Bernard Cate. The next year, 1814, James Kirk sold a huge tract (462 acres) adjacent to the mill tract to John Thompson. Thompson then acquired the mill tract in 1836 and the Thompson family operated the mill for a long enough time that it became known at Thompson's Mill. By 1868 the Thompson property that surrounded the mill tract had grown to about a thousand acres and was referred to in the deed books at Hillsborough as _Rock Spring Farm_. I think that the actual spring lies on a branch of Turkey Hill Creek just north of Bradshaw Quarry Road. There was a post office nearby known as Rock Spring Post Office. Letters coming through this post office would have been stamped "Rock Spring."

Scott Hudson had a book of old Civil War maps. One map shows this part of the state and clearly locates Rock Spring southwest of Hillsborough, though the scale is a bit distorted. More precisely, it is located at the intersection of present-day Bradshaw Quarry Road and Vernon Road (along the old Greensboro Stage Road).

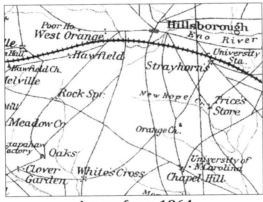

A map from 1864

One of the last references to Rock Spring is in 1895 when the church, under the leadership of J. F. MacDuffie, voted to build a school to be known as _Rock Spring Academy_. The school opened in 1897 under that name. The name must have been selected so that people would know exactly where the school was located. For some reason, the name was soon changed to _Orange Grove High School_ and then to _Orange Grove School_. We have a catalog for the High School for 1902-03. In the back are listed the names and hometowns of all the '01-'02 students. Of 101 students, 63 list their place of residence as Rock Spring.

One possibility for why the school changed its name from Rock Spring to Orange Grove is that there had once been a Rock Spring Academy on the west side of Cane Creek in the mid-19th century. So, the name might have caused some confusion. In any event, the presence of Orange Grove School, and the community's close identification with it, may have had something to do with the name "Orange Grove" becoming attached to the community and not just the school. In the school's catalog for 1906-'07 the final section is headed "How to get to Orange Grove," which I take to refer to the community and not just the school. So, the community changed its name sometime between 1897 and 1902. But as to who changed it and why "Orange Grove" was selected still remains a mystery. I do, however, recall that Ina Andrews, who died at age 95 in 1985 and who attended the school, once said, "Mr. MacDuffie changed the name of the school." This may tell us the "who" but does not tell us the "why" "for the choice of the "Orange Grove" name. The word "grove" is used as a common place name in rural Orange County. Close to us are spots still known (or once known) as groves: Oak Grove, Maple Grove, Hickory Grove, and so on, Perhaps "Orange Grove" was intended to indicate a community – or *the* community? – of Orange County?

Now that I have quoted some of the old descriptions of life at Cane Creek, I turn to modern times to describe life here now.

19: CANE CREEK TODAY

When I say "today" in the title of this chapter I really mean "within the memory of our oldest members." I will thus begin with our fifth church building, whose first service was held in 1950, just over 70 years ago. We have a few members still with us who attended that service. It is scary to write a history of our recent years because there are people still alive to say that I have made a mistake or to let me know that I have forgotten to include a topic they hold dear. `

Part of the difficulty of describing our recent history is the loss of some of our recent records. The best source of information is our old business meeting minutes kept by the church Clerk. After every meeting, he (sometimes "she") would write the minutes in a large book. This stopped in 1993 when desktop computers and printers made handwritten notes seem tiresome and laborious. After that, all the minutes were typed on individual sheets of paper. A copy of each set of minutes should have been preserved, but no one oversaw this new responsibility so that the preservation of minutes became haphazard. Things only got worse in 2006, when the church became a non-profit corporation and the position of Clerk was abandoned. Now, the job of keeping minutes belongs to whoever is secretary of the Deacon Board. The result is that we have a limited collection of minutes from 1993 to the present.

Fortunately, another source of historic information began when we acquired a mimeograph machine and began to publish a newsletter. This began in 1968, when Fred Reid was our pastor. We are fortunate to have an almost complete collection of newsletters up until about 2014, when we started to use an internet homepage to keep church members updated about church activities. We also have the minutes of the Church Council, which was active from 1989 to 1994. But before I write about the church in the current era, I will begin by describing the community and how it has changed over the past 70 years.

Development and Transformation of the Community

In 1950, Orange Grove was still a rural agricultural community with most of the large farms devoted to dairying. Only a few roads were paved. The countryside consisted of forests, pastures, and crop land. The crops were grown to provide feed for the cattle, mostly Holsteins, known for providing a lot of low-fat milk.

As the years went by, the daily routine of rural life changed. More roads were paved, which meant that going into town became a routine trip instead of being something special. The arrival of electricity in 1937 brought about better lighting, indoor plumbing, refrigerators, electric stoves, radios, and television. Later came home computers and cell phones. All these changes could have resulted in church life becoming less and less the center of community activity. But, as it turns out, this has not been true. Church life is now more active and alive with opportunities to get together than it ever was.

Historically, the most important institution in a rural community was the church, but a close second was the general store. Ours was run by Manley Snipes. It was mostly a male institution. Folks could stop in for a quick snack or a game of Rook. One could learn what was going on in the community and exchange opinions about politics and how the county was being run. This is the place that county politicians would visit during their campaigns for public office.

Snipes Store about 1950

In 1973 another local institution was created: a volunteer fire company. It grew and prospered and has a history of providing the community with excellent fire protection and emergency medical services. It has been manned by local men and women, many of them church members. All the corporation presidents have been church members as have most of the fire chiefs. Everyone in the community supports the fire company through local fire taxes but the cost is offset by an even larger savings in the cost of fire insurance because the fire company is so well equipped and trained.[1]

Another major development was caused by Chapel Hill's rapid growth and its increasing need for water. In the 1970s, the town's water system, originally built and operated by the University, came to be operated by the Orange Water and Sewer Authority (OWASA). They immediately set their eyes on Cane Creek as a good clean water source for a growing town. In the early fall of 1976, they invited the community to a meeting at the Activity Center to present their plans. They expected Cane Creekers to heartly endorse the plans for a reservoir and to ask for shovels so they could help. Nothing could have

---

[1] *Editor* – The author was too modest to mention that he was one of the key figures in establishing the Orange Grove Volunteer Fire Department and served as its President from 1974 – 1994.

been farther from the truth. Local people stood up in angry opposition to what they feared would be a lethal blow to their way of life. The meeting ended in total confusion. The community created an opposition group called the Cane Creek Conservation Authority (CCCA).[2] The CCCA raised money from ham and egg suppers, farm-city days, and personal contributions from local residents and hired an attorney. He found that OWASA had neglected some legal details and CCCA called them on it.

The cases languished in court for many years. It was a very intense and tiring effort to raise money to keep the legal battles going. Eventually, in 1986, the owner of the dairy farm where OWASA wanted to build its dam fell under a diagnosis of cancer. The family decided to sell its land to OWASA. This was the critical event that led to the defeat of CCCA and OWASA's successful acquisition of all the land it needed for the reservoir. The bottom-land hardwood forest along Cane Creek was cleared, two old rock gristmill dams were pushed down, and the lake began to fill in the early 1990s. Our fear that the presence of a large reservoir would destroy a way of life soon faded and we found that things went on about as they always had. OWASA and the community have become good neighbors.

But other forces were at work that would change the nature of the community. The farms, which were its very heart and soul, began to abandon dairying. This was due partly to the huge amount of work necessary to sustain a large dairying operation and partly to the lack of a younger generation willing to follow in their parents' footsteps. Additionally, new people were moving into the community who had work ties to the University or to the Research Triangle.

Now, there are no large pastures filled with Holsteins. Only a few farmers remain. They raise beef cows and grow crops to feed them. Fortunately, these few farmers rent most of the old fields and tend them with the use of large machinery and hired help, much of it Latino. One family, the Nutters, continued in the dairy business and created a sizable operation called Maple View Farm that went from field crops to cow feed to raw milk to pasteurized milk and ice cream. They built an agricultural enterprise that sold milk throughout Orange County and attracted customers by the hundred to their local ice cream store. In 2021, they shut down their dairying operation and the fields have recently been planted in grape vines. But the ice cream store still operates, getting its milk from another dairy.

Development and Transformation of the Church

Until the 1950s the preacher was present at Cane Creek Baptist Church just once a month. There was a Saturday afternoon business meeting that perhaps included a short sermon and a bit of hymn singing and praying. The main event would be on Sunday, with a service that went longer than today's one hour service. Following the service, if the

[2] Editor – As with the fire department, the author failed to mention his own critical role here, as he long served as the [•] of the CCCA. [Do we know what his official role/title was?]

weather allowed, there may have been "dinner on the grounds," a picnic-style lunch on roughhewn tables beside the church.

In 1944 we were in good enough financial position to afford preaching twice a month. James Wright was the first one to do this. In 1953 we called Harry Byrd and were able to go even farther and have weekly Sunday services. Jim Ballard was our first preacher (in 1959) who actually lived in the community. This was before we built the parsonage in 1969. We rented the Ed Cates house on Orange Grove Road to serve as a parsonage. We not only had weekly peaching but now had a local pastor who was able to visit those who were sick or shut in and to address other issues that needed sound spiritual judgment.

There was also a regular annual revival, originally called a "protracted meeting," that was held in any season except winter. There would be preaching every night for a week by a visiting minister. This was a time when many young people in the community would come forward as candidates for baptism. A revival in 1968 resulted in 16 baptisms. Revivals continued until 1990.

We have long followed a practice of hiring young pastors at the beginning of their careers. Beginning in 1854 with Stephen Gilmore, our new pastors have had theological training, from Wake Forest until recently and from other theological schools more recently. We have also encouraged our young pastors to study for advanced degrees while they are with us. Recent pastors to do this include Jim Bouseman, Tommy McDearis, and Gregg Hemmen.

When we were served by a pastor once or twice a month, the pastor's main duty was to deliver us a good sermon and to preside over a business meeting. But once we had a full-time pastor who lived in the community, we realized how much more a full-time pastor could do. He visited us when we were in the hospital or sick at home. He counseled us about our marital problems and our troubled relations with other church members. He attended committee meetings when invited and was at every deacon's meeting. He met with and guided those considering becoming a Christian. He helped us with our spiritual concerns.

Church Programs, Events and Activities

One treasured document in our library describes our church in 1959. It was put together by James Ballard at the request of the Grange. This is how the Ballard Report describes our church program:

> "In addition to Sunday School and preaching every Sunday morning, prayer meeting and choir practice are held every second, third, and fourth Wednesday nights of each month. The first Wednesday night of each month is devoted to meetings of various church groups, During the first week of every month our Senior Circle of the WMU meets on Monday night and the

Young Adult Circle meets on Wednesday night. The RAs and GAs have two meetings a month and the YWA meets once a month. The Sunbeams meet every second Sunday morning during worship service. The observance of the Lord's Supper is usually held on the last Sunday of every quarter.

"In the line of special activities during the year, we would include our Homecoming Day on the third Sunday in May. Next, a Thanksgiving program was held on Thanksgiving Day and our Christmas program was held the Sunday night before Christmas."

Today our church program has grown significantly. There are now more opportunities for enrichment, service to others, and fellowship. But some things have remained almost as they were in the old days. One example is our Sunday morning service. Below is the order of events for a service in 1960 and in 2020.

February 21, 1960	January 19, 2020
Musical prelude	Musical prelude
Call to Worship	Welcome and announcements
Choir song	Welcome hymn
Hymn	Invocational prayer
Scripture reading	Choral call to worship
Pastoral prayer	Psalter reading
Hymn	Hymn of praise
Tithes and offerings	Children's message
Doxology	Prayers of the people
Choir song	Offertory hymn
Sermon	Offertory prayer
Benediction	Tithes and offerings
Musical postlude	Choral music
	Sermon
	Hymn of response
	Benediction
	Musical postlude

In the 1950s, the sermon would usually take up the second half of the Sunday service. Today, there are more events, e. g., a children's message, so the sermon now lasts about 20 minutes.

Every successful church spends much effort on its youth program. This is vital since the youth will become tomorrow's church leaders. Besides Sunday School, there are lots of things going on with our youth. Our youth program had its beginning with the Women's Missionary Union (WMU), which was begun in 1888 in Baltimore, Maryland by Annie Armstrong, who had a strong interest in mission work. Local chapters spread from church to church throughout the south. At Cane Creek, we date the beginning of WMU to 1903, when the annual meeting of the Mt. Zion Association held its annual meeting here. A young church member, Mae Reynolds, was elected president. WMU was active in our church until she left the community. After that, our WMU chapter went through several periods of inactivity. That spark came again in 1944, when the wife of our pastor, J. M. Wright, recreated the program.

In the early 1950s, the GAs (Girls Auxiliary), the RAs (Royal Ambassadors) began and were quite active for several years. We have members today that got their start in church activities in these youth groups. Unfortunately, the WMU was subjected to male bias that hindered its development. It was not until 1920 that the WMU annual report at the SBC convention was allowed to be given by a woman. Then, when the conservative takeover of the SBC was completed, women were again denied the privilege of speaking at the convention. Finally, in 2009, the North Carolina chapter of WMU withdrew from the NCSBC when it refused to provide any more money to WMU to support its program. Since then, the WMU has had to subsist on voluntary contributions. Presently, there are no WMU chapters at local Baptist churches. The GAs and the RAs also no longer exist.

Royal Ambassadors 1950s

Sunbeams 1959

In the years that followed the golden period, the 1950s, of WMU at Cane Creek, the youth program declined. More recently, we have found leadership talent within our congregation and have also paid for professional talent to reinvigorate our youth program. We now have a youth minister who is in charge of the church program for our younger members. Children attend Sunday School as they always have, but there are more opportunities than there used to be. In the summer there is a week-long Vacation Bible School open to any child in the community. Since 1973 there has been an "Easter Parade" from the Activity Center down to the church. At Halloween there is a "Trick or Treat" gathering at the Activity Center. For older youth, there are annual trips to Camp Caswell south of Wilmington for spiritual advancement as well as fun in the sun on the beach. Additionally, there have been trips to West Virginia in the winter for skiing as well as trips to the Nantahala River for rafting and tubing.

Another important feature at Cane Creek is our musical program. We can date the first improvement in our musical program to 1907, when a young woman who had just joined the congregation, Inez Reynolds, was asked by the Deacons to undertake fund raising to buy an organ. It took until 1920 to raise the money. It is a push-pedal organ that is now displayed in our new history display room just off the sanctuary. We also bought a piano in 1927. In the 1950s we had a church choir, a men's choir, and a youth choir under the able direction of Rebecca Crawford, our pianist and organist, and Martha Barbour, our choir director.

In 1983, we decided to hire a part-time choir director and found a young man, Kraig McBroom, who was choir director at Broughton High School in Raleigh. It was a brilliant choice. Kraig turned our little country church choir into a thing of beauty. Every December he leads the choir in a Christmas cantata that is truly inspirational. There were also Easter cantatas and always inspirational Sunday morning singing. Kraig is still with us. He now lives in Myrtle Beach and must make the long trip each week to direct the choir. Now, almost 40 years later, the music continues to be outstanding.

Kraig McBroom and the choir in 1985

There are also special events throughout the year for adults (with children usually invited too). The foremost one is our annual Homecoming celebration on the third Sunday of May. Anyone who has ever been connected with our church is invited. The sermon is often provided by a beloved former pastor. The church service is followed by a potluck dinner "on the grounds" (although in recent years it has been at the Activity Center).

Homecoming 1981

Another set of events is our Wednesday night suppers. When the church was given the Community Building in 1988, it was first used only for special events. Then in 1989, we began to have fellowship suppers on one Wednesday night each month during the school year. Members of the congregation contributed desserts and a kitchen crew prepared the main course. In the beginning, the cost was $3 a person. In recent years we are more likely to have catered meals and the cost has risen to $7.

A Wednesday Night Supper

There is also an evening Bible study group that meets on Wednesday nights to discuss and study particular parts of the Bible and to read books that have had a religious impact such as *To Kill a Mockingbird*.

At Easter there is a sunrise service held behind the Activity Center, with a broad view of the rising sun as it comes up over the Snipes' fields. At Christmas there is a special service at which Kraig McBroom and the choir present a cantata that always attracts a large crowd. There is also a special luncheon for the elderly members of the congregation. In past years there have been special get-togethers at the Activity Center that were lots of fun. Among these were the womanless weddings, the "not-so-newlywed" game, young-at-heart suppers, ice cream socials, talent night, the "who-act" play, old timers' day and the Christmas craft fair. We also once had a vigorous sports program for young people. We had both boys, men's, and women's softball games on the ballfield by the Activity Center and participated in a church and community basketball league. Later we did a few years of volleyball. In recent years it has become almost impossible to maintain an athletic program because of conflicts with other interests and activities.

Over the years, the manner of dress at the Sunday service has shifted toward the informal. In the early 1950s, the men wore coats and ties, and the women had their hats. Below is Harry Byrd with church members in 1953. Now, there are no hats and few coats and ties. Today's attire can be seen in the picture of the 2020 congregation at the end of this chapter.

Harry Byrd with Church Members in 1953

Another development in recent decades was the church's decision, in 1983, to make women eligible for the deaconate. This ended the ancient custom that said that a woman could never be allowed to have authority over a man in church affairs. The first female deacon was Pat Griggs, who was elected in 1986.

Not only has our church program been enriched over the years, but our church facilities have also changed:

1959: The Education Building is constructed
1969: The parsonage is constructed
1972: The pews used in the old church are replaced with new ones
1973: Central air conditioning is installed in the Sanctuary
1973: The brick sign out front is erected
1977: Central air conditioning is added to the Education Building
1977: The church gets its first computer
1977: The church buys its first copy machine
1979: A steeple is put on the sanctuary
1989: Acquisition of the Community Building (called the "Activity Center" since 1994)
1995: Central air conditioning is installed in the Activity center
1996: The church buys a fourteen-passenger van
1998: A new organ is installed
2002: The church creates an on-line website
2006: The rear of the sanctuary is expanded and a baptistry is installed.
2009: A sound system is installed in the sanctuary
2015: A video system is installed in the sanctuary.

Church Publications

Over the years, the church has produced several publications to raise funds or to preserve our history. The first came in 1993 and was a cookbook containing old family recipes from many local folks. The next one was in 1999 and was a project led by Susan Trollinger, who directed the church youth in researching our stained-glass windows, each of which was financed in 1949 by a local family who dedicated the window in memory of a recently deceased loved one. The book explains the meaning of all the religious symbols in the windows and tells about each of the memorialized church members.

In 2003 the church published A *Cane Creek Tapestry*, a picture history of our church and community. It contains many old family photographs collected from throughout the community. In 2008 this was followed by a book of old family pictures owned by the late Ruth Holmes Patton, who grew up in our community and belonged to the church. In 2014 the church published a set of 35 historical sketches. Each sketch fills the front and back of a single page and tells about a particular bit of community history such as the new Year's day murder of William Thompson in 1877. Copies of these books are in our library.

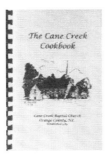

Church Publications

Another thing that has changed over the years is our basic governance. There is little visible consequence to the average church goer, but the changes have been necessitated by the increasing need to be legally correct and up to date. In most Baptist churches, the final authority lies with the congregation in a conference meeting. The deacons do most of the day-to-day decision making, but major decisions, including the annual budget, must be approved by the congregation.

To guide this decision making, there was for many years only one document that identified the fundamental principles of the church. This would have been the Articles of Faith that likely appeared on the first page of our early Minute Book (of which we have no more record; *see* the discussion in Chapter 9).

There was no other set of rules that governed how we were to behave at business meetings until 1841, when George Purefoy became our pastor. He insisted that before he answered our call we had to write and approve a set of "Rules of Decorum" (*see* Appendix 3) for how church business meetings were to be conducted.

These Rules of Decorum guided us through the next century and a half. Then in 1989, the 200th year of our existence, we created a constitution and a set of bylaws. The constitution replaced the old Articles of Faith and listed our basic principles of belief. The new bylaws replaced the old Rules of Decorum and laid out how we were to conduct ourselves in business meetings. Basically, we followed Roberts Rules of Order.

In 2006, to protect our church leaders from lawsuits, we became a non-profit corporation. Non-profit organizations have a charter issued by the North Carolina Secretary of State. The charter replaced our old constitution. We kept our old set of bylaws but collected a great number of procedures and regulations drawn up by various church groups (for example the Memorial Association's Bylaws that dated to 1934) and put them into a *Policies and Procedures Manual.*

Starting in 1973, the church has published five church directories that present pictures of all our members and gives addresses and phone numbers. It is an excellent way for church members to be able to contact one another. Copies of all these publications are in the church library.

Church Directories

1973

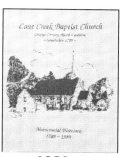

1989

2001   **2010**   **2019**

Another way to track recent church history is through our Sunday bulletins. Before about 1950, no bulletin was handed out at the Sunday service. There was little need for one because the service followed a standard routine, with the only thing to change being the title of the sermon and which hymns were to be sung. In the front of the sanctuary there was a large board on which the current Sunday's hymn numbers were posted. The digits were large enough to be read even from the back row.

The first Cane Creek church bulletin I have been able to locate was for the first Homecoming service in our new church in 1950. The next one was for the official church dedication in 1954. These were one-off printings done professionally in Hillsborough. After that, we had no regular church bulletins until 1959, when the church bought a mimeograph machine.

The First Church Bulletins

These early bulletins were printed on special forms that we bought from the Baptist Bulletin Service. A new batch would be mailed to us each week. It would have a picture on the front and a message on the back. The church secretary would type the interior two pages onto a special stencil. One page was devoted to the schedule of the Sunday service and another gave announcements, future events, and recent births and deaths. Then she would wrap the stencil around a drum on the mimeograph machine, pour ink into a tank, and crank out one copy at a time by turning a handle round and round. It was a messy and laborious process. Correcting typing errors on the stencil was a nightmare. The secretary was often left with ink-stained hands.

The earliest bulletin that we did ourselves was printed in 1960 and is shown below. Later we acquired a duplicating machine and still later a desktop computer and printer, which allowed us to create more imaginative bulletins. In 2014 we created an official church logo that now adorns our bulletins as well as our website. The logo portrays our church with "Cane Creek" symbolized by a curving swath descending from the front door.

1960-1984

1986 - 1991

1991 - 1995

1995

  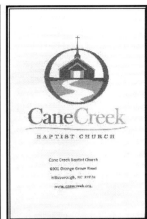

1996 – 1997   **2002 – 2013**   **2014 - Present**
Later church Bulletins

In our current bulletins, there is usually an extra sheet. One is devoted to prayer requests and concerns within the community, and another gives a financial summary and a record of attendance for the last four Sundays.

<u>Church Baptisms</u>

Since 1789, our church has baptized new members in Cane Creek, at Thompson's Mill, in Watery Fork, local farm ponds, and at neighboring churches that had indoor baptismals. In 1974, we began to regularly use an old swimming hole in Turkey Hill Creek, downstream of the old Thompson millpond.[3] It is a peaceful and beautiful site that may have been used by the Church as early as the 1870s. The congregation sits on one side in folding chairs. On the other side are the pastor, the choir, and the baptismal candidates. When we added a baptistry to our sanctuary in 2006, our new members could choose whether to be baptized inside or in the "living waters."

---

[3] *Editor* – This site is on property where the author lived.

Gregg Hemmen baptizing at Turkey Hill Creek in 2004

Church Finances

It takes money to run a church these days, but it was not always like this. In 1789 money was not an issue. The preacher was a local farmer and received no pay. Upkeep of the church was done by the congregation. Occasionally, there would be a "love offering" to help a destitute widow.

The earliest set of budget figures come from the account book of D. M. Sykes. He ran the mill where I now live, and he was also out church clerk. He kept mill accounts and church accounts in the same book. The figures below are for the year 1897. A close inspection shows that the only accounts kept in those days were what we now call missions.

Church finances for 1897

Another set of our financial figures can be found in the Mount Zion minutes for 1918. It is not so much a budget as it is a record of collections and expenses.

Pastor's salary	$175.00
Sunday School	18.00
Association Minutes fund	2.00
Mt. Zion missions	8.90
Home missions	24.70
Foreign missions	12.80
Baptist orphanage	16.95
Christian education	5.60
Ministerial relief	4.65
Total	**268.60**

The first reference I have been able to find of an actual church budget does not come until the 1950s. Our library collection of annual budgets begins with 1970. Below is a chart of the amount of our annual budget since then. The bottom line in the chart represents actual dollar values for the total budget. This line is somewhat misleading since part of the increase in our budget is due to inflation. The top line shows the same budget figures adjusted for inflation. Thus, the 1970 budget of $9,837 would have been worth $68,880 in 2021 dollars.

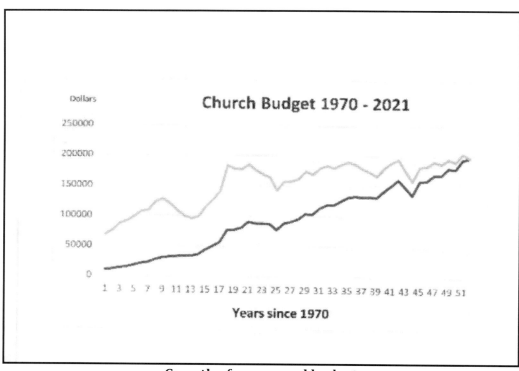

Growth of our annual budget

Church Missions and Community Support

An important part of our budget has always been an amount given to support missions. The first indication of mission giving in our old minutes comes in 1830, when we sent $1.50 to the Sandy Creek Association. We are ignorant of the early mission giving by our church because the topic is not mentioned in our minutes. The figures for 1918, shown above, indicate that 17% of our collections went to missions and another 6% went to the Baptist orphanage. The first actual church budget that has survived is the one in 1970. Out of a budget of $9,837, we devoted $1,050 to missions or 11%. In 2022 our budget is $203,000 and the line item devoted to missions is $14,000, or 7%.

Our "good works" have not been confined to budgeted mission giving. We, like many other churches, find ways to put our Christian beliefs into action. Each fall we hold a Harvest Fund offering and the church decides how to distribute the funds. Some goes to Orange Congregations in Missions, some to local prison ministry, and some to other causes as recommended by our Missions Committee. At Christmas, we have an "Angel Tree." On it are the hopes and desires of indigent Orange County children who otherwise would receive no Christmas presents. A card on the tree might read: "Boy, age 10. A pair of sneakers." Individuals in the congregation select an angel card, buy the desired present, and return it to the church a week in advance of Christmas. The individuals who receive presents are selected by Orange Social Services. Altogether, these off-budget offerings amount to about 3% of our budget, so our mission giving is quite close to a true tithing.

Since 1997 we have participated in the Appalachian Service Project. This was first proposed as a project with University Presbyterian Church in Chapel Hill, by Diane Hemmen, wife of our then pastor, Gregg Hemmen. Each summer volunteers from each church spend a week in a needy community in the southern Appalachians. Our group is assigned a local needy family and fixes up their often-dilapidated house. We may put on a roof, build a handicapped ramp or a new porch, or replace rotted-out floor joists. The people we help are thrilled at what we do, and, in turn, our volunteers benefit from helping people in need. This is truly an ecumenical project. As one Cane Creeker put it in a 2004 newsletter, "isn't it great that we have the downtown Presbyterians and the rural Baptists working together on a Methodist mission?".

Appalachian Service Project work on a trailer

We have also formed a relationship with the Bob and Hope Carter mission in Zambia, Africa. The Carters have visited us several times to describe what they do, and we have sent our contributions on an irregular basis.

Another important part of our mission work is called Backpack Buddies. It helps children at Central Elementary School who depend upon the school lunch for their main meal of the day. Backpack Buddies provides these children with a bag of food that will tide them over each weekend when they may have no chance to eat a good meal.

In 2013 Mary Lin Truelove and Katherine Andrews became interested in the process of patch-work quilting. They thought it would provide an opportunity for fellowship and that the quilts they made would benefit our shut-ins. They recruited several other members of the congregation, and they meet twice a month to socialize and to collaborate on the making of patch-work quilts. This soon became so successful that the quilters began to raffle quilts in order to be able to buy more materials. A quilt is given to each new pastor, to elderly members of the congregation, to residents of worn-down houses on the ASP mission trip, and to those whom we ordain. They are also for sale at our annual craft fair in December. Altogether and much to the delight of the entire congregation, they have made over 100 quilts and have been able to contribute proceeds to other church activities.

A New Quilt in 2021

Our outreach to help others is also shown in other ways. In 2005, a local farmer, Kieth Trollinger, was hospitalized in a farm machine accident and was in danger of losing all his crops. Members of our church quickly showed up to harvest all his crops and save him from possibly losing his farm.

All that I have written in this chapter is a testament to what a caring and loving congregation we have at Cane Creek. We have been fruitful in our Christian walk so far, but what lies ahead?

The Congregation in 2020

20: WHAT LIES AHEAD?

Predicting the future is a risky enterprise. Unexpected events may occur that push the future in an unexpected direction. For example, in 1991 the Orange County Planning Department looked at the 1990 census figures and forecast that by 2010 Bingham Township would have a population of 17,000. The actual number turned out to be less than half of that, only 6,500.

Our church's future depends on community trends, national trends and events occurring within the Southern Baptist Convention (SBC). I will discuss SBC issues first and then go on to look at the other trends later.

The Southern Baptist Convention

It would be misleading to overlook our role as a church-member of the Southern Baptist Convention. For the last few decades it has been in a crisis that is reminiscent of the battle over missions in the first half of the 19th century. That battle broke congregations and Associations apart and created new alliances that led most Baptists in a new and vigorous mission-oriented direction. Baptist churches that did not follow were left on their own. The new crisis may have far different implications.

The current battle within the SBC is between fundamentalists and moderates. Fundamentalism was born in the United States in the years following the Civil War. Most scholars describe the movement as being a reaction to scientific developments, including Darwin's Theory of Evolution and disputes over the age of the earth. Couple this with the fact that some scholars, beginning in the 1790s, had begun to study the Christian religion as they would the works of Shakespeare or _The Iliad_, so that some felt that Christianity was under attack. The reaction to all this came after the Civil War, when some Christians revolted against these scientific and scholarly ideas and sought to focus on what they considered to be the fundamental tenets of Christian belief. Early on, they rejected the new scholarly approach and focused attention on a literal interpretation of the Bible, which included a seven-day creation in opposition to Darwin's idea that it took many ages for man to have evolved. They also had pronounced beliefs about the Noah story – his ark and the flood, which they claimed had engulfed the entire world. These are still active issues in fundamentalist beliefs, but today they focus more on other issues.

Fundamentalist belief is characterized by a highly rigid frame of mind, but since most Southern Baptists are conservative by nature, it is useful to try to distinguish just what it is that characterizes modern fundamentalists and why it is that moderates are so alarmed. A fundamentalist tends to think in terms of black and white. Most of us seem to get along quite well in a world that is mostly shades of gray. However, in an uncertain world there may be comfort in believing that X is always true and that Y is always false. Thus, if one sits on the Foreign Mission Board that must act on the application of someone who wants to become a missionary, the problem of what to do if the applicant has been divorced is a simple one. The fundamentalist position is that divorce represents a Christian failing that cannot be tolerated. The application would be rejected. A person of more moderate tendencies would want to know if there had been mitigating circumstances, if the applicant had put the tragedy of divorce behind him, and so forth.

There is also a distinct opinion on the role of women in the church. Fundamentalists believe that women should be honored and encouraged to participate in church life, but that they must have no authority over men. Thus, it is wrong, they say, for a woman to be a pastor or ever preach from a pulpit. Additionally, only men should be deacons.

Perhaps the primary identifying belief of the fundamentalist is belief in the inerrancy of the Bible. The scriptures represent the word of God and so are without error or ambiguity. The more moderate belief is that while the message of the Bible may have been divinely inspired, the message has been filtered through imperfect human minds and has been subjected to numerous translations from one language into another, each translation adding another layer of confusion to the original message. Therefore, reading the scriptures requires much effort and prayerful attention. If the message of the Bible were straightforward and clear, then there would be no possibility of a dispute over interpretation. But one passage may contradict another. Does one exact "an eye for an eye" or "turn the other cheek?" As Chris Gambill put it in a 1992 newsletter, "It seems that now most of us would rather argue about the Bible than actually spend time and effort reading it."

Another difficulty involved the separation of church and state. Conservatives do not mind seeking to influence American political life. Jerry Falwell founded the Moral Majority in 1979 and favored the election of one candidate in the presidential election. The Moral majority no longer exists but fundamentalists continue to favor conservative candidates.

In 1996 our pastor, Gregg Hemmen, reported that, "I recently was invited to attend a meeting of local pastors and the topic of discussion was a particular candidate for governor. The sponsors of the meeting were asking the pastors to influence their congregations to vote for that person. I was turned off by the whole meeting." Gregg thought about the role of pastors in politics and decided that his task was "to help, but not force, the congregation to share a genuinely Christian conscience."

Historically, there have been several attempts by fundamentalists in the various Protestant denominations to take over the operation of their denomination. Until the take-over of the SBC, all previous attempts had failed. Beginning in 1979 and continuing each year since then, the SBC at its annual meeting has elected a President who was a self-described conservative or fundamentalist. In the early 1980s, this turn of events was not a cause of great concern. Fundamentalist beliefs were known to be strong in the Gulf States and it was thought that moderate Southern Baptists would eventually find their voice. But by the late 1980s, many moderates were beginning to wonder if they would ever be able to participate again in the leadership of the SBC. It is generally perceived that fundamentalists are in the minority among Southern Baptists but have the advantage of being better organized and willing to fight for what they believe in whereas most moderates would rather not get involved in controversy.

The annual Baptist convention in the summer of 1990 seemed to many to be a watershed event. Once again a fundamentalist won election, and following this election there was a purging of moderates in important positions of the SBC and the fundamentalists cemented control of all SBC governing bodies, including the Foreign Missions Board, The Cooperative Program, and the Boards of Trustees of all the theological seminaries. Chris Gambill, our pastor, attended the convention and wrote in our newsletter:

> "Returning from this year's SBC in New Orleans, I feel a deep kind of grief over the loss of our once familiar Southern Baptist faces, voices, events, and practices ... I was shocked and grieved over the events and attitudes I witnessed in New Orleans ... What we once were is no more."

The congregation at Cane Creek has, from the very beginning of the church, participated in mainstream Baptist affairs. Its citizens have taken part in the civic affairs of the county and state and have been known for their interest and encouragement of education. It is a rural and essentially conservative congregation, but it is relatively sophisticated in its approach to social and political affairs. This is not the sort of environment that breeds a fundamentalist frame of mind. Thus, the congregations at Cane Creek, almost to a person, is traditional and moderate in outlook. The congregation has been dismayed to see the SBC advance a fundamentalist agenda. This is illustrated by another pastoral comment from our 1992 newsletter that said, "our soul freedom is being threatened by those who continue to call themselves Baptists while at the same time are working vigorously and often unscrupulously to bring uniformity of belief and practice to our denomination."

But how has the difficulty within the SBC affected our church life? In 1992 the church formed a Denominational Relations Committee to consider what our place should be within the Baptist community. We decided to not move away from the SBC. We still send moderate delegates to annual meetings of the Mt. Zion Association and the State Baptist Convention, In the 1990s we revised how we distribute our missions giving to reduce the amount sent to the SBC and to begin funding the Cooperative Baptist Fellowship because, as was stated in a 1993 newsletter, "many no longer wish their offerings to solely support increasingly narrow and fundamentalist dictated SBC causes." In addition, we have had preaching by women from our pulpit. Since 1986, we have had female deacons. Lastly, we have adopted a practice of insuring that each new pastor is moderate, not fundamentalist.

All in all, the ongoing controversy has had little effect on how our church functions and in attitudes within the congregation. The controversy is seldom mentioned. It takes a good ear to discern the occasional reference to the controversy in our Sunday sermons.

Still, it is not impossible to look a few years into the future and see our possible departure from the SBC. Other churches may follow suit and what remains of the original organization will depend on the popularity of fundamentalist belief. Already, we see a decreasing number of baptisms among Southern Baptists and a slow decline in membership. Currently, the vagaries of an uncertain world make many people seek shelter where beliefs seem simple and clear cut. But times change and when they do, many members of the SBC may begin to look for a richer and more inclusive spiritual home.

National and Local Trends in Church Participation

Now that I have discussed issues within the SBC, I will turn to the other factors that will affect our future as a vital and energetic congregation. There are trends on a national scale that have been going on for decades. Nationally, church membership has been declining. The Gallup Poll organization published, in 2021, the latest in its 80-year-old inquiry into the religious affiliation o Americans. The question they ask is, "Are you a member of a church, synagogue, or mosque?" For the first time ever, the "yes" answers fell below 50%. Here is the graph.

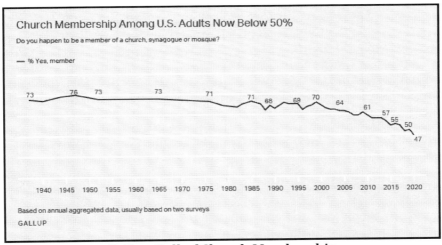

Gallup Poll of Church Membership

For a long time, the Evangelistic churches bucked the trend and enjoyed continued growth, 234ha SBC membership peaked in 2006 at 16 million and has now seen 15 years of steady decline. By 2021 the decline has amounted to 13.6% from the peak total.

In Christian history there have been other times when there was a lack of religious fervor. One came in Europe in the 18th century, after most of the issues around the protestant Reformation had been settled and people began to relax. This period of "spiritual coldness" was followed by the Great Awakening in the 1750s. The next one came in the early 19th century and was called the Second Great Awakening. Will the current spiritual coldness result in a third awakening?

I would like next to focus on our community, to see what local trends are shaping our community. In a 1974 newsletter, our pastor, Jim Bouseman, noted that, "slowly we are changing from an agricultural community to a suburban neighborhood." This was quite perceptive because, in 1974, we could look around and see a rural community with large thriving dairy farms. But from the perspective of the 2020s, it is obvious that the community has changed and will continue to change. We are no longer a farming community featuring large dairies. Slowly we have shifted toward becoming a bedroom community for Chapel Hill and the Research Triangle. Our township is not yet a fast growing and bustling one – thank goodness, I say – but extensive growth could lie in our future. We still have plenty of families that are in their third century of living at Cane Creek, but new people trickle in.

So, what lies ahead? One thing that will keep our population growth down is the presence of the Cane Creek Reservoir. Under County zoning regulations, the minimum lot size is two acres within its 30 square-mile watershed. Close to the water's edge, the lot size is five acres. This will keep population density down and will discourage crowded developments such as trailer parks. Instead, newcomers will have to be able to afford large building lots. But an opposing possibility lies in the large fields now devoted to crops and grazing. What will happen if the few remaining farmers abandon farming? We don't know what the future holds, but it is likely that abandoned agriculture fields will come to hold something that changes our community.

I would now like to consider how these societal changes will affect the future of Cane Creek Baptist Church. I fear that these trends may threaten our continued existence. I am reminded of the old story about a frog in a pan of water. The pan is being heated on a stove and the frog can hop out at any time. But the frog doesn't notice the warming because the temperature is climbing so slowly. Then it's too late. The frog is cooked.

There is a possibility that our congregation is like the frog. We are doing things the same old way from year to year and failing to notice the changes around us. The most alarming one is the decline in our membership. Below is a chart of our membership since 1937, the same period as shown in the Gallup poll chart above. Nationally, membership has been in decline since 2000. Our own decline began in 2010.

Cane Creek church membership since 1940

When you go to a Sunday service you see many old faces and not enough young ones. You can consider our declining membership and our increasing budget needs and conclude that we depend on an ever-increasing amount of financial support from each member. This is a trend that will be difficult to sustain.

Perhaps local churches should face reality and re-examine what their true mission is. In the old days a person might attend church to keep his soul from everlasting torment in Hell after death. This idea has lost much of its power in recent American history. Not that many people believe in a literal Hell anymore.

Look at our own Mission and Vision statements shown in the Introduction. There is no mention of hellfire and brimstone. Instead, it includes these words:

> "Jesus taught, in the Great Commission, to make disciples. Being a disciple means we must be in a relationship with others, those who have been long with us as well as those who have just walked through our doors."

If churches refocused their mission to emphasize love, compassion, and justice along with fellowship and service, they could begin to again appeal to the spiritual needs of the population. So, instead of appealing to people by offering an alternative to frying in Hell, it might instead offer a way to live this earthy life in a rich Christian way and to offer opportunities for enrichment, fellowship, and ways to help those in need. I think that this already characterizes our church life at Cane Creek. So, we may well be hiding our light under a bushel. If more people realized what we are about, they might want to be a part of it.

How can we reach out to others? Somehow, we must find a way to let the non-churched people in our community know what we are all about. We have a webpage (www.canecreek.org) which could become a valuable outreach tool if we can keep it fresh, informative, and up to date. It could let people know that our Sunday service is available live. For this to be an effective way to get our message out, we need to find a way to let people know about our website and be curious enough to check it out. Perhaps we ought to create an out-reach committee that would focus on getting our message out to the community.

A Closing Note

But enough of discouraging trends. I would like to close on a hopeful note by quoting a letter sent to us in 2020 by Colin Kroll. He came to us in 2018 as an interim pastor. We ordained Colin in the fall of 2020. A few days later he sent us this note of appreciation that is as good a description of our congregation as I have ever seen:

Dear Cane Creek Baptist Church,

As I sit here a few days after my ordination sipping some wonderful cinnamon tea out of my new CCBC mug, I am reminded once again of what this community has meant to me. It means forgiveness. When I first came to Cane Creek, my heart was still broken from my experience at a different church. The last thing that I wanted was to be seen and known in such a vulnerable way. Yet, through your hospitality, support, and kindness, I found the grace to forgive myself for my shortcomings as a minister and to forgive the church for the strain it had previously put on my health and relationships. This community means peace. I have had the honor to witness both worship and business meetings in my time with you, and I have seen all that you do, you do with love. Peace shows up at the sacred corner of mercy and trust, where we come together in light of everything we are and everything that God is calling us to become. You trust one another and you have even trusted me, and you treat one another with dignity and grace when life together isn't simple or easy.

Finally, Cane Creek means home. This community's commitment to generosity and hospitality is truly second to none. I can point to so many examples of how I've felt Christ's love through your welcoming spirit, but two are especially on my heart today.

First, I want to thank you for the love you showed to Sarah and me on Saturday. From the moment we arrived for my ordination council, your intentionality in helping me feel safe and at home was on full display. I honestly broke down in tears when I walked into our beautiful hotel room and found a gift basket filled with tokens of love from the church. I unpacked cards, candies, gift cards, gifts from the church, and gifts from your homes, I felt my heart completely overflow with gratitude for the sacrifice of one community.

Second, I want to thank you for the hospitality you showed my friends and family on Sunday. The service was so meaningful, but I continue to hear the same thing from my family and friends this week: "We see what you mean. That's a special church." They saw your hospitality firsthand in how you welcomed them and made sure that they felt safe throughout the service. They saw your generosity as you gifted me with a beautiful new Bible and a breathtakingly intricate quilt. They saw your loving spirit as you prayed over Sarah and me so personally and thoughtfully. I am so grateful for each of you, for this community, and for the witness to Christ that you have borne in my life. I will continue to carry you in my heart and prayers until we are able to be together again.

With love and gratitude,

Colin

Colin has described our greatest strengths: 238 hat we are a loving, caring, and compassionate congregation. There is real benefit in belonging to such a group. In 1996, under the urging of Gregg Hemmen, the Deacons made a list of goals that our church should strive for. One of them was that we should "invite new people we meet in the community to join us at Cane Creek." If we can do this, our future is secure.

APPENDIX 1: Short Histories

These are the short histories of our church that we are aware of. The first was written by A. G. Crawford in 1933 at the request of the Mt. Zion Baptist Association. It is followed by historical notes added by Mae Crawford in 1969. The second history appeared in the 1951 minutes of the Mt. Zion Association. The author is unknown.

B. **G. Crawford's History, 1933**

From the "History of the Sandy Creek Association" (by Elder Geo. W. Purefoy) we find that Cane Creek Church was represented at this Association which met at Unity Baptist Church, Randolph County, Oct. 24, 1807, by John Workman and Thomas Gates. From its origin in 1758 to 1805 the minutes of the Sandy Creek Association were recorded in a book which was burned together with the home of Bro. William Lightfoot in 1816.

In 1805 this Association met with Chambers Church in Montgomery County, and Cane Creek Church was not represented at that Association. In 1806 no meeting of the Association was held. From these facts we would conclude that the Association in 1805 in Montgomery County was too far away for delegates to attend, therefore, we are older than the records of the Sandy Creek Association.

From history handed down by former generations and given by Brother Jas. H. Lloyd (now deceased) we get this history given below. "The present building is the fourth. The first two being located about one-half mile west of the present building." The only thing remaining at first site is what former generations designated "The Meeting House Spring."

Tracing events backward to the beginning we find: The present Church was begun in 1884. The Church just preceding this and on same location was either built prior to 1829 (the beginning of our recorded minutes) or no record was made of this Important event—moving the location and constructing a much better building. Therefore, if the third building was constructed before 1829, and two buildings were used before this time, it would be reasonable to suppose that this Church is as old as the Independence of the United States—1783. Brother Lloyd gives 1790 as about the date of first Church which was a Primitive Baptist Church.

The first roll of Church members is dated May 31, 1829— Enoch Crutchfield, Clerk— containing eighty-nine members. The pastor at this time was a Brother Roberts (no initials given). Stephen Justice, Enoch Crutchfield and Thos. D. Oldham were very influential members in the affairs of the Church. In 1830 Stephen Justice became Clerk and Stephen Pleasant was called as Pastor, but a Brother Andrews did most of the preaching.

The first record of money paid to the Association was in 1830, the amount being $1.50.

Rev. J. P. McDuffie states that Antioch Church was constituted by this Church. In September 1831 "Antioch sent a petition praying for two brethren to be sent to assist them in their business. Brethren T. Oldham and John Workman were sent.

From 1834 to 1845, T. D. Oldham served as Clerk. Geo. W. Purefoy was called to the pastorate Oct. 1839. We do not know when this pastorate ended, as we have no recorded minutes from 1849 to 1867. Thos. J. Gates served as Clerk a part, or all of this time, but in 1867 H. Mc. Gates was serving as Clerk and F. M. Jordan, pastor. We presume that F. M. Jordan and Geo. W. Purefoy served as pastors during this time—1849 to 1867.

In 1869 David M. Sykes was serving as clerk and Rev. U. R. Gwaltney was called as pastor.

In April 1870 the Church withdrew from the Beulah Association and joined the newly formed Mt. Zion. The Association met that year at Lystra and T. D. Oldham, Wyatt Cates and D. M. Sykes were appointed delegates.

In 1871 James T. Mason was called as pastor and served to January 1882. In 1882 R. A. Moore was called as pastor and served one year—salary $100.00.

In December 1882 twenty-three were granted letters of dismission and since these names are familiar to the Cross Roads Church section (formerly Betheden) we infer that this Church was also constituted by Cane Creek.

In December 1883 Rev. C. E. Gower was called and served one year.

The first record of an organized Sunday School was In May 1883, though we presume there had been one before this time. K. A. Cates, Supt., D. M. Sykes, Asst. Supt., Jack Crawford, Sec., and A. P. Cates, Treas.

1884	present Church was begun.
1884	C. E. Newton called but did not accept.
1885	P, A. Furguson called as pastor.
1885	C. E. Newton again called but did not accept.
1886	the Church was without a pastor.
1887	Rev. 0. Churchill called and served one year.
1888	Rev. J. C. Hocutt was called and accepted the work and later in the year the call was extended indefinitely,
1892	Rev. J. W. Watson was called and served two years.
1894	Rev. J. C. Hocutt was called and served two years.
1896	Rev. J. F. McDuffie was called and served seven years.

In June 1897, through the efforts of Rev. J. F. McDuffie and the hearty cooperation of a number of the Church members and others, Rock Spring Academy (now Orange Grove School) was begun.

In 1897 Brother McDuffie built a home and moved near the Church.

In September 1903 the Church asked that Brother A. C. Hamby be ordained as a minister at the Association which met with this Church.

In 1903 Brother Edward Sykes was granted license to preach. In May 1905, Brother S. W. Bynum was elected Clerk.

In Jan. 1907, Brother McDuffie offered his resignation but was not accepted.

In January 1907, Brother J. L. Cheek was elected Clerk.

1907	Rev. J. C. Hocutt called as pastor and served two years.
1909	Rev. J. F. McDuffie called.
1909	Dr. Petty accepted Principalship of School and called as pastor.
1909	R. E. Clark called and served one year.
1910	C. E. Billiard called and served one year.
1911	W. T. Baucham called and served two years.
1913	L. R. Dixon called and served five years.
1918	H. G. Dorsett called and served one year.
1919	C. R. Lennon called and served two years.
1921	C. E. Byrd called and served four years.
1925	B. L. Gupton called and is still serving in 1933, with Brother W. M. Snipes as Clerk.

Since writing the above we find from a list of pastors prepared by someone that in 1849 J. C. Wilson was serving as pastor; 1850 Thos. J. Yarborough served as pastor, but records were lost until 1862 when Stephen Gilmore was called and served one year. 1863 Samuel Baldwin was called and served two years.

Adopted in Conference on Saturday before the third Sunday in April 1933.

B. L. Gupton, Moderator   W. M. Snipes, Clerk
Compiled and written by A. G. Crawford

SUBSEQUENT HISTORICAL DATA, DERIVED FROM CHURCH MINUTES, BULLETINS, ETC.

Rev. B. L. Gupton continued to serve as pastor until March 16, 1941.
Rev. Frank H. Marshall was called in 1941 and served through September 1943.

Mr. Otto A. King was elected Clerk in 1944.

Rev. J. M. Wright was called in May 1944 and served Through September 1947.

The church bought approximately five acres of land, which was formerly the Orange Grove School grounds from Orange County in May 1947. In 1948 a plot of land lying between the cemetery and the paved road was sold to Mr., W. Manley Snipes; also, a plot east of this road was sold to Mr. James M. Snipes, Jr., and Mr. W. Banks Lloyd.

Mrs. John W. Kirk, Sr. served as Clerk a few months in 1947 followed by Mr. Norbert K. Andrews in the same year.

Rev. James C. Rittenhouse was called in November and served through September 1952.

A new church building was built during the pastorate of Rev. Rlttenhouse in the winter of 1949-1950. This was the fifth such building to be erected and the first to be constructed of brick. The ground-breaking ceremony followed immediately the morning worship service Sunday September 18, 1949. The first service in this building was May 7,1950. The dedication service was held on Home -Coming Day, May 16, 1954.

Mr. Charles W. Snipes was elected Clerk in 1951.

Rev. Harry Byrd was called February 22, 1953, and served through September 1957.

A system for the rotation of Deacons was established in the middle nineteen fifties.

A Baldwin organ was bought in 1954.

The Church began full time ministry in January 1957.

Rev. James H, Ballard was called December 1957 and served through August 1959.

Rev. J. G. Wooten, Jr. served as Interim Pastor from October 1959 through August, I960.

During the ministry of Rev. Byrd the Church became aware of her educational responsibilities and started to plan for an educational building which was constructed under the leadership of Rev. Ballard in the winter of 1958-1959 with the interior being completed in I960 during Rev. Wooten's ministry. It was dedicated on Home Coming Day, May 21, 1961.

Rev. John B. Bay was called in September I960 and served until September 11, 1966.

A church library was begun in 1963.

On October 4, 1963, the church deeded an acre of land entitled "Orange Grove Community Building Lot" to the trustees of the Orange Grove Community Center; this to be used as the site for a community building.

Miss B. Mae Crawford was elected Clerk in 1966.

Rev. Fred W. Reid, Jr. was called as Interim Pastor December 18, 1966. On April 30, 1967, he was instated as Pastor and served until January 26, 1969.

A building program for a parsonage was initiated in 1967. The publication of a quarterly Church newsletter was started in 1968.

Adopted in Conference Sunday, February 23, 1969.
        Charles Snipes,
        Moderator   B. Mae Crawford, Clerk

Compiled and written by B. Mae. Crawford, assisted by Fred W. Reid, Jr.

****
Historian's Report
Minutes of the Mt. Zion Association for 1951

Cane Creek is the oldest Baptist Church in the Mount Zion Association. The first record we have of it was the deed of August 20, 1789, when Thomas Durham deeded one acre of land for 20 shillings to Thomas Cate, minister and eight trustees on which to build a meeting house. The trustees were Thomas Cate, Richard Cate, Joseph Cate, Bernard Cate, Robert Cate, John Workman, John Strader, and Mary Christmas. All were landowners and four owned slaves as is shown in the tax lists for 1790. Their wills indicate that they possessed Christian characters.

However, Cane Creek was not then an organized Baptist Church for it was not listed in 1790 as belonging to the Sandy Creek Association. It was supposed to be an arm of Haw River Church located near Bynum. Elnathan Davis was pastor of Haw River. Among his assistants, licensed preachers of several arms of Haw River, was Thomas Cate. It was an organized church before August 20, 1806, for on that date, Antioch was organized from an arm of Cane Creek. All minutes of Cane Creek before May 1829 have been lost and the minutes of Sandy Creek Association to 1805 were burned.

There is a tradition that there was a meeting house named Cane Creek as early as September 1781. If this tradition is true, the meeting house was on private property for in colonial times a Baptist Church could not own property for a meeting house. The supposition would be strong that there were Baptists along Cane Creek from the time of Shubal Stearns, either converted by visiting Sandy Creek or Cane Creek being visited by Shubal Strearns or some of his many converts who became licensed preachers.

Cane Creek joined and remained in the Sandy Creek Association until 1837 and belonged to the Bulah Association until 1870. She joined the Mount Zion Association at its organization.

In March 1833, the pastor, Stephen Pleasants, was received by statement into Cane Creek Church after he had been excluded by Ebenezer Church in Person County, for favoring benevolent principles, viz. Bible, Temperance, and Missionary Societies. There arose a difference between Cane Creek and Ebenezer Churches and Sandy Creek and County Line Associations. When Cane Creek on the advice of Sandy Creek sent a committee to Ebenezer Church, it was not received. There is no record of any member of Cane Creek going with the Primitive Baptists.

Preaching in 1829 was done by Armstrong V. Roberts, Levi Andrews, and Stephen Pleasants. It is not clear who was pastor. However, in 1830 Stephen Pleasants was called to preach two times every two months at a salary of $50. Later, he was called every month preaching. Enoch Crutchfield was clerk in 1829 but he moved the next year and Stephen Justice acted as clerk. We do not know when Enoch Crutchfield became clerk nor when he began his long career as a Baptist preacher.

George W. Purefoy, the next pastor, served from 1839 to sometime after the war. Frank M. Jordan and S. R. Gwaltney served two years each. Next was James T. Mason from 1871 to 1881. Then came R. A, Moore, C. E. Gower, P. A. Ferguson, and O. Churchill. John C., Hocutt served at three different times. J. W. Watson was pastor for two years. J. L. McDuffy was pastor from 1896 to 1907. Then followed W. O. Petty. S. C. Hilliard, W. T. Baucom, L. K. Dixon, H. Grady Dorsett, Rufus S. Lemons, and C. E. Byrd, each serving from one to four years. B. L. Gupton was pastor from 1925 through 1940 and was followed by J. H. Marshall, J. M. Wright, and James Rittenhouse.

The clerks after Stephen Justice were Thomas D. Oldham from 1834 to near the Civil War. Thomas J. Cates was then Clerk for a few years. D. M. Sykes was then the next clerk and served thirty-five years, followed by June L. Cheek from 1907 to 1921. Then W. M. Snipes was clerk until 1944. Otto King was clerk for three years and Norbert K. Andrews is serving at present.

At least four churches have been formed from Cane Creek. In 1806 Haw River Mountain, now Antioch, was organized from an arm of Cane Creek. In 1830 Stephen Justice and John Reeves, deacons of Cane Creek, received a deed from John J. Freeland for two acres to build a meeting house two and one-half miles north of Hillsboro on the road to Goshen. In June 1834 an arm of Cane Creek was formed and in September letters were granted to form an independent church called Mars Hill.

In April 1874, Chesley Moore and others with the missionary of Mount Zion Association were authorized to sit in conference at Moore's schoolhouse to receive and baptize members. In May 1878, nineteen member letters were granted to form Moore's Chapel Church.

In December 1882, twenty-two members were dismissed by letter to form the new church, Betheden, now, Crossroads Church.

Cane Creek has lettered members to the churches of Chapel Hill Durham, Hillsboro, Mebane, Swepsonville, Graham, and Burlington. While she has baptized over one thousand two hundred into fellowship, over four hundred of these have gone to swell the ranks of the Lord's children in other fields.

Appendix 2: The Preachers of Cane Creek Baptist Church

We know of at least 45 preachers who have served our church. The exact number is in doubt because our minutes for the first 40 years were destroyed in a fire. Thanks to the hard work and diligent research of Rebecca Crawford, we are fortunate to have pictures of 36 of these preachers. These are the photographs that line the hall of our history display room in the sanctuary.

Thomas Cate: preached 1789-1814(?); born 1747 – died 1814.
Thomas Cate was our first preacher. Born of Quaker parents in Virginia, Thomas Cate migrated, along with two brothers, to Orange County in the 1750s. Asplund's Register lists a Thomas Cate as a licensed preacher at Haw River Baptist Church in 1790, but a Thomas Cates received several land grants along Cane Creek from the Earl of Granville in the 1750s. These grants contain, I think, Cecil Crawford's land or perhaps was the tract just to the south. We are not sure when he stopped preaching because our early minutes are missing. We are also unsure of his immediate successors. It may be deduced from other sources that Thomas Cate was followed by William Farthing, Randolph Mabry, Levi Andrews, and Armstrong Roberts, not necessarily in that order.

William Watkins Farthing:　preached before 1829; born August 25, 1782 – died November 6, 1826
The only evidence that William Farthing preached at Cane Creek is in the N. C. Baptist Historical Papers 1905-09 in a sketch of Enoch Crutchfield that states that Crutchfield "was baptized into the fellowship of Cane Creek Church by Elder W. W. Farthing." This source also says he was born in Wake County (although another source says he was born "near Durham"). He fathered 14 children, two of whom became ministers. Farthing was a traveling minister for the Missionary Society of N. C. His wife was Polly Halleburton. He moved to Watauga County just before his death.

Randolph Mabry:　preached about 1815; born 17?? – died 18??
Randolph Mabry is shadowy character. He may have been a preacher at Cane Creek in about 1815 [see Purefoy]. Later he was found to be doctrinally "in error" and Sandy Creek published notices against him in several newspapers. Still later he showed up at Cane Creek seeking restoration, was received, and later excluded again for "opposing the benevolent institutions of the day." There is no file for him at Wake Forest.

Levi Andrews: preached 1829; born c1798 – died 1868,
The Sandy Creek Association Minutes, 1878 (pp. 13-14) describe Levi Andrews as follows: "A North Carolina native, he grew up in very modest circumstances. He joined the church while still young, was impressed by the churchly life but only reluctantly answered the call to do God's work. He served as a licentiate until 1833 when he was ordained. He achieved much good with little education. His career as a preacher was short, too short to show what he could have accomplished." Andrews married Elisabeth Brewer, daughter of Ezekiel Brewer of the Cane Creek community. His father had been a preacher.

Armstrong Roberts: preached 1829; born 17?? – died 18??.

No record can be found of Armstong Roberts, who is listed in our Minutes as preaching at Cane Creek in 1829.

Stephen Pleasant: preached 1831-1839; born January 12, 1779 – died November 28, 1852.

The first preacher for whom we have a photograph is Stephen Pleasant. He was born in 1779 of Quaker parents and served us from 1831 to 1839. He was a man of some distinction. He began with several churches in the County Line Association but was excommunicated because of his support of missions. He found a new church home at Cane Creek. He was a founder of the Beulah Association, which Cane Creek joined in 1837.

G. W. Purefoy: preached 1839-1852; born January 29, 1809 – died April 17, 1880.

G.W. Purefoy was, perhaps, the most famous of our pastors. The son of a Baptist preacher, he was ordained in 1834. Although he was deprived of advantages in childhood and never earned a college degree, he was one of the best educated men in the State. He made up for his lack of formal education by a close and persistent study of books. He was not an eloquent or showy preacher but had few equals as a strong and faithful one. He was a prolific writer of church history and church tracts. He became involved in many controversial issues of the day and wrote many tracts in defense of his positions. He was seldom if ever in doubt and expressed himself forcefully. In recognition for his outstanding scholarship and service, the University of North Carolina awarded him an honorary DD degree in 1870. Three of his sons became preachers. He wrote a centennial history of the Sandy Creek Association in 1852.

J. C. Wilson: preached 1852-1856; born July 23, 1820 – died 1894.

Born in Chatham County, J. C. Wilson studied at Wake Forest, the first of many Cane Creek pastors to do so. He was ordained in 1849. He also preached at Mt. Pisgah, Lystra, and other churches in the Raleigh and Mt. Zion Associations. For many years he was the Moderator of the Mt. Zion Association. His obituary in the Mt. Zion Minutes says that "his preaching was of a high and sound order ... He did not preach with enticing words of man's wisdom but in demonstration of the spirit and of power."

Thomas J. Yarbrough: preached 1856-1858; born June 6, 1827 – died November 27, 1860.
Born in Caswell County, Thomas Yarbrough worked as a boy with his father, who was a millwright. He was exceptionally talented at mechanical things and at the age of 15 and without any supervision, constructed a sawmill that ran successfully for many years. He married Elizabeth Terry and went to Covington, Kentucky for theological training. He was ordained there in 1852. On returning to North Carolina, he founded and ran a seminary at Mt. Vernon Springs in Chatham County. At his untimely death at the age of 33, he left a wife and four children. Note: his name also appears as "Yarbro" in some records.

Stephen Gilmore: preached 1858-1863; born 1828 – died 1902.
We know little of Stephen Gilmore. He was married four times and thrice made a widower. He was the father of two sons and two daughters. He attended Wake Forest and was ordained in 1857 by George Purefoy, Stephen Gilmore, and J. C. Wilson, all pastors at Cane Creek. His other churches were in counties to the south. His obituary states that "he was an orthodox preacher and loyal to the institutions of our denomination."

Samuel Baldwin: preached 1863-1864; born 1803 – died November 10, 1879.
Samuel Baldwin was born in Chatham County and was baptized at Antioch in 1832. He was ordained in 1842 and was the father of one son and one daughter.

F. M. Jordan: preached 1865-1869; born June 4, 1830 – died 19??.
F. M. Jordan became a prominent preacher, and after his service with us, went on to lead churches in Greensboro and Raleigh. He became an evangelist and "baptized in almost every river, creek, and pool ... and in the Atlantic Ocean." We have a copy of his book, "The Life and Labor of F. M. Jordan" in our library.

W. R. Gwaltney: preached 1870-1871; born September 9, 1835 - died 1907.

W. R. Gwaltney was born and reared on a farm in Alexander County. He attended Wake Forest and was a student when the Civil war broke out. He volunteered as a chaplain. He was ordained in 1863 and served as a regimental Chaplin until ill health forced him to resign in 1864. He returned to Wake Forest and graduated in 1867. He married A. E. Staley in 1866 and became the father of six daughters and four sons. His first preaching was done in Hillsborough, but he was so ill at ease and his delivery so poor that he considered quitting the ministry. But the wife of ex-Governor William Graham took him under her wing, encouraging and coaching him until he gained confidence. He became our preacher in 1870. He helped form the Mt. Zion Association, which we joined. After serving us, he led churches in Statesville, Winston-Salem, Greensboro, and Raleigh. At his death, he was described as one of the three most notable Baptists in the state during the period following the Civil War.

James P. Mason: preached 1871-1881; born March 13, 1827 - died June 24, 1893.

James Mason was a native of Orange County and was educated at Wake Forest. He married Mary Morgan of the well-known Orange County Morgan family in 1854 and settled down on what was to become known as Mason Farm southeast of Chapel Hill. He preached at Mt. Pisgah, Mt. Carmel, Mt. Moriah, Antioch, Bethel as well as at Cane Creek. He was described as "always an acceptable preacher being plain and lively and warm." He was a successful preacher but successful, as well, as a planter. He said that "no person can flourish that loves the bed of a morning." In 1882 typhoid fever took both his daughters and almost killed him. He never regained robust health. He ceased preaching in 1886 but tended his farm until the end. Several of his diaries are in the Southern Historical Collection at UNC.

R. A. Moore: preached in 1882; born September 20, 1838 - ied January 31, 1921.

R. A. Moore served as an interim pastor. Born in Person County, he studied at Wake Forest, fought in the Civil War, and was awarded the Cross of Honor for his valor at Gettysburg. Twice married, he was the father of eight children by his second wife. After leaving Cane Creek, he was pastor at Raeford in Robinson County, where Moore's Chapel is named in his honor.

Claude E. Gower: preached 1883-1884; born July 30, 1854 - died 1914.

Claude Gower was our preacher when we made the decision to construct a new church building. He was born in Wake County, graduated from Wake Forest in 1881 and then spent a year at the Southern Baptist Theological Seminary. We ordained him in 1883. He also preached at Graham and Mebane. While here, he bought and lived in the house once owned by Cecil and Mae Crawford. In 1890, he suffered a nervous breakdown and seldom preached after that. At the time of his death, he was living in Jacksonville, Florida. The picture above shows the Wake Forest graduating class of 1881. The picture was taken at a time when it was thought fashionable to have people staring at various points in the room and not at the camera. Unfortunately, we don't know which one is Rev. Gower except that he is not the man standing at the far right.

P. A. Ferguson: preached 1885

Ferguson was an interim pastor during the hard times when Cane Creek was trying to build its fine new building. I have been unable to find anything about him.

Oren Churchill: preached 1887-1888; born October 19, 1819 - died October 23, 1893.

Oren Churchill was born in Dorchester, Massachusetts. He married Rhoda Shackleford in Danville, Virginia in the 1850s while he was a Baptist circuit preacher. During the Civil War he served as a Regimental Chaplain in the Confederate Army. His early education and opportunities for development were limited, but with hard study and diligent application he became informed on many topics. He was a humble and unassuming man. He approached a sermon hesitantly and trembling, but once warming to the task became a forcible speaker. He denied himself and his family many of the luxuries of life that he might concentrate more on the saving of souls.

J. C. Hocutt: preached 1882-92, 1894-95, and 1907; born November 7, 1849 - died August 4, 1912.

J. C. Hocutt was born in Johnston County and studied first at Rocky Point Academy and later at Wake Forest. He was licensed at the age of 23 and ordained at 27. He served us three times: 1888-92, 1894-95, and 1907-09. Never in good health, he nevertheless toiled ceaselessly for his churches. According to J. F. MacDuffie, "he made mistakes but always of the heart, not the head." He also worked for the Mount Zion Association. During his third tenure with us, he became Orange County Superintendent of Schools. The fact that the old Orange Grove Academy building eventually because a public school was perhaps an outcome of this new position. He once wrote a letter to Washington Duke protesting the new practice of including pictures of pretty girls in packages of cigarettes. Duke was so moved by the letter that he ordered the practice stopped. He did much work under the auspices of the Executive Board of the Mt. Zion Association and was responsible for the construction of many church buildings. He was also a pastor in Burlington, and he helped found Glencoe Baptist Church near Haw River in 1896.

James W. Watson: preached 1892-1894; born July 2, 1860 - died October 31, 1916.

James Watson's picture was taken from a group picture of the Wake Forest graduating class of 1886. He was ordained in 1889 in a ceremony led by J. C. Hocutt. He also led the congregations at Antioch, Bethel, and Lystra. During his stay with us, he attended UNC. While at Lystra, he founded Fairview Academy. It is possible that Watson laid the foundation for what our next preacher accomplished.

J. F. MacDuffie: preached 1896-1907;
born 1856 - died 19??.

J. F. MacDuffie was born in 1856 in South Carolina. He led the church into the field of education. In June 1897, the church resolved "that we donate so much of our church lot for the use of an academy and school as may be required ... The name of this academy is Rock Spring." As soon as the resolution passed, MacDuffie purchased the house where Allan and Chris Green now live, and the academy opened its doors in 1898. By 1900 it was known as Orange Grove Academy. Legend has it that MacDuffie was in competition with a Wake Forest classmate named Campbell to establish a school. Although Orange Grove Academy no longer exists, Campbell University prospers. MacDuffie's wife, eleven years his senior, died in 1907. He later married Ella Cheek. After leaving Cane Creek, MacDuffie started another school at Calvander, which was associated with Bethel Baptist Church. During his lifetime, he served 25 of the 54 churches in the Mt. Zion Association. Curiously, it is almost impossible to discover any information about this man on the internet.

R. E. Clark: preached 1909-1910born 18?? - died 19??

R. E. Clark was born in Apex and served us from 1909-10. The Wake Forest annual, the _Howler_, for 1910 says, "Here is an ardent believer that, 'there is a divinity that shapes our ends, rough hew them as we will.' A promising minister of the gospel, whose mild manner, graceful and eloquent delivery, will sway audiences gathered together from the 'highways and hedges,' hamlets and cities. Self-confident, enterprising, with the hermit's love for seclusion and the devotion of a great man to his duties, he promises us that that old age shall not find him like the belated virgins nor over eager to accomplish the impossible. Content with the present only when it gives promise of a better future, he seems to the stranger, eccentric and cranky; but to those who know him best, he proves himself an unassuming gentleman." In 1913, Clark was awarded a PhD in Sociology from the University of Pennsylvania and taught at various colleges. He died in Florida in 1970

S. C. HILLIARD: preached 1910-1911; Born 1886 - died 1918, S. C. Hilliard served us in 1910 and 1911. A 1912 graduate of Wake Forest, the *Howler*, said this about the then 26-year-old Wake County native: "This is the biggest man of the class. Of a towering physique and weighty intellect, he towers far above his fellows. A keen student in affairs of state, possessed of a tongue that could convince Prof. Lannau that the moon was made of green cheese, he is a debater of parts. It is told that those Davidson debaters listened in fear and trembling to the mighty roaring of his voice and it is a matter of history that the judges fell over each other to hand him their decision, and that a half hour later a fair damsel in the audience delivered him her decision, also favorable. On the gridiron he has used his mighty brawn while the multitude looked on in wonder and amazement. He is a ministerial student, and since his sophomore year has held down with great effect the pastorate of divers churches. His success is so clearly assured that it is useless to waste words in prophecy." Tragically, he did not have the opportunity to fulfill this prophecy. He died in the influenza epidemic of 1918.

W. T. Baucom: preached 1911-1912; born 1883 - died 1972. W. T. Baucom served us from 1911-12 while a student at Wake Forest. The *Howler* for 1913 says the following: "Baucom is old enough [age 30] to be somewhat 'sot' in his ways. But generally, he is 'sot' on the right side of every question, and it takes a Socrates and Demosthenes combined to move him. He has a clear conviction on what his life's work shall be, and is one of the few members of the Ministerial class who makes all-round college students. For three Saturdays and Sundays in the month, during his last three years at college, Baucom has used his melodious voice to expound the truth to the 'brethren' of three of the country churches, and in this way, he has succeeded in paying his way through college. Still, when the athletic games come on, he is always there and stretches his lungs to their fullest capacity in rooting for his Alma Mater. Baucom will go to the Louisville Seminary next year to continue his course of preparation for the ministry, and we predict for him success." Baucom was an army chaplain in World War I.

Lemuel Richard "L.R." Dixon: preached 1913-1917; born 1863 – died 1922.

L. R. Dixon was licensed in 1886, was ordained a year later, and preached primarily in the Sandy Creek Association. He had a "circuit" of four churches and traveled to each one once a month. Evidently, he would show up at Cane Creek on horseback having ridden up from Chatham County. This is the entire entry on the "findagrave.com" website: "Baptist minister, teacher, farmer, husband of (1) Sarah Catherine Womble (11 children), (2) Mollie Ellen Stinson (1 child), (3) Sallie McKay Dowd (5 children). To say that he enjoyed life might be an understatement: he was known (despite his calling) to take a nip now and then, he had an eye for the ladies (as the number of wives and children might attest) and he rode his circuit on horseback with a pistol strapped on. He claimed that the pistol was to protect him from highway robbers, but rumor has it that it was really to protect him from jealous husbands."

A. C. HAMBY: preached 1918; orn 18?? – died 19??.

Although A. C. Hamby is among the preachers pictured in our historical display room, there is no evidence to indicate that he was ever officially our preacher (although we did ordain him). He was born in Siler City and attended UNC in 1911.

Henry Grady Dorsett: preached 1918-1919; born September 15, 1881 - died 1960.

Henry Grady "Tip" Dorsett was born in Florida. The family soon moved to Siler City. Dorsett attended N. C. State for two years (playing on the baseball team) and later earned a law degree from UNC in 1911. Soon he felt a call to the ministry and was ordained in Mebane in 1914. He resigned to attend Southwest Baptist Theological Seminary in Fort Worth. Returning to North Carolina, he served us in 1918-19. He then moved to the town of Wake Forest to build and operate a hotel while practicing law. He retired to Chapel Hill.

Rufus S. Lennon: preached 1919-1921;born March 12,1880 - died December 24, 1954.
Rufus S. Lennon was born in Columbus County. He graduated from Wake Forest in 1911. The *Howler* said, "He knows how to work for the hot sun of many glorious days has tanned his cheeks. The description 'in doctrine uncorrupt, in language plain' is a true index of the innate qualities of this young minister."

C. E. Byrd: preached 1921-1924; born 18?? – died 19??.
C. E. Byrd served us from 1921 to 1924. We know little about the man except that he was the father of Harry Byrd, who served us in the 1950s. It is ironic that the Baptist archives at Wake Forest University in Winston Salem have more information about our 19th century preachers than about our 20th century ones.

B. L. Gupton: preached 1925-1941born 1897 - died 19??.
B. L. Gupton served us from 1925 to 1941, a longer period than any of our other preachers with the possible exception of Thomas Cates, who may have served for as many as 23 years. The picture was made about 1941. He had a booming voice that served him well when he thought the congregation's attention was wandering. He left Cane Creek to become an Army chaplain in 1941 and was sent to Harvard University for training before beginning official duties.

Frank H. Marshall: preached 1941-1943; born 1900 – died 1960.
Frank H. Marshall was born in Bynum and served us in the early World War II years. We were his first church. He had learned about Cane Creek after some friends had visited us to sing Gospel songs. After leaving us in 1943, Marshall moved to Durham, established Immanuel Church and served as its pastor for 13 years. He had an artificial right hand and always wore a glove on it.

James Wright: preached 1944-1947; born 19?? – died 19??. James Wright served us at a time before we had a full-time preacher. Services were held on the first and third Sundays. He re-started the tradition of holding an annual revival each August. He resigned in 1947 because he was unable to support his family on what two churches could pay him. His salary at Cane Creek was $600 per year. He later served at Cross Roads Church.

James C. Rittenhouse: preached 1947-1952; born September 11, 1923 – died September 26, 2002. James Rittenhouse served us from 1947 to 1952 and was ordained at Cane Creek in a service led by his father, the Rev. W. H. Rittenhouse. During his stay, we debated whether or not to build a new church building. He led us in the planning and construction of our present church. He served us twice a month on a salary of $700 a year. In World War II he served in the Marines as a photographer. He flew a reconnaissance mission over Japan just after the bombing of Hiroshima and Nagasaki. He died in Virginia.

Harry E. Byrd: preached 1953-1957; born 1932 - died September 29, 2015.
Harry Byrd was born near Apex. He was a 1953 graduate of Wake Forest. He was our first full-time pastor. He resigned to complete work on his DD degree. Later Rev. Byrd served as a missionary in Guatemala. From time to time he would return on leave and visit us. He preached at our Homecoming in 1975. He retired to Durham.

James H. Ballard: preached 1957-1959;born 1934 –died August 19, 2019.
James Ballard was born in Ashville in 1934. He attended Mars Hill, Carson-Newman, and Southeastern. He served us from 1957 to 1959. After leaving Cane Creek, he spent a missionary year in Brazil. He later served churches in Hendersonville and Charlotte. In 1959 he wrote a report describing our church and its activities. The report is in our library. His wife, Joanne, returned to the community to attend Cecil Crawford's funeral.

John B. Ray: preached 1960-1966;born March 11, 1931– died January 5, 2013.

John ("Jack") was born and bred in Mebane, where he was a member of First Baptist from an early age. He attended Gardner-Webb and Carson-Newman. He was awarded his divinity degree at Wake Forest in 1960. After his years at Cane Creek, he served at Moore's Chapel in Saxapahaw, White Oaks in Johnston County, and Rock Spring (the old Haw River Church) at Bynum. Afterward, he served churches in Pennsylvania until he and Patsy returned to the Cane Creek community. He served as our Pastor Emeritus for many years. He had a deep interest in history, especially church history. We have a copy of Purefoy's _Centennial History of the Sandy Creek Association_ thanks to him.

Fred W. Ried, Jr.: preached 1966-1969;born 19?? – died 19??.
Fred Reid was a Professor of Hospital Administration at UNC Memorial Hospital, where he served as chaplain. In 1970 he was elected president of the College of Chaplains of the American Protestant Hospital Association.

James S. McBride: preached 1969-1971;born 19?? – died ????.
James McBride was born in Maryland and graduated from Mars Hill in 1967, where he was a member of the track team. He served us from 1969 to 1971. He was our first pastor to use the parsonage that was built in the late 1960s. He later was an associational missionary for the Delaware Baptist Association. He worked with immigrants, families of prisoners, seamen, and NASCAR race fans.

James Bouseman: preached 1971-1976; born 19?? – died December 2, 2006. James Bouseman served us from 1971 to 1976. He was working as a power company linesman when he felt God calling him to the ministry. He instituted an annual event at Cane Creek, Old Timers' Day, which went on for three years. In 1976 we used the event to help celebrate the country's bicentennial. Since then, Jim returned from time to time, most notably in 1989 for our church bicentennial and in 1990 for Homecoming. He retired to Garner and died in 2006. On a curious note, Jim is the latest in a long line of "Jims" to serve as our pastor: Mason, Watson, Wright, Rittenhouse, Ballard, McBride, and Bouseman.

Michael Goudelock: preached 1976-1979; birth year unavailable.
Michael Gaudelock was highly regarded at Cane Creek for his faithful visitations with members of the church. He helped our farmers at harvest time and did house repairs for older members. We remember him as always being cheerful and jovial. A sad family situation led to his leaving the ministry shortly after he left Cane Creek. He moved to Lenoir and headed up a farm supply store.

Thomas McDearis: preached 1980-1988; born 1958.
Thomas (Tommy) is remembered as a shortish man with a strong voice, a wry sense of humor, and a cackling laugh. He soon became involved in the developing conflict between Baptist fundamentalism and mainstream Baptists. After leaving Cane Creek, he became minister to a church in Charlotte before becoming senior pastor at Blacksburg Baptist Church in Virginia. He has served as president of the Baptist General Association of Virginia.

Chris Gambill: preached 1988-1993; born 19??.
Chris Gambill has degrees from Wake Forest, Southeastern Seminary, and Capella University. Rev. Gambill is a short man with a big heart. He is remembered as always having a smile on his face. After leaving Cane Creek, he became a campus minister at Appalachian State University in Boone. Unfortunately, he suffered a serious illness there, which impaired his inner ear, leaving him with constant vertigo and loss of balance. Over time he greatly recovered and since 2015 has served at Wake Forest's Baptist Hospital as Director of the Center for Congregational Health. He was our Homecoming speaker in 2021.

Greg Hemmen: preached 1994- 2007; born June 19, 1964
Bucking a 200-year-old tradition, Greg Hemmen was just our second preacher to be born above the Mason-Dixon Line. He is a native of Iowa, where he was following in the family tradition as a farmer when he felt a call to the ministry. He graduated with a MDiv degree from North American Baptist Seminary in Sioux Falls, SD in 1993. When his wife, Diane, was admitted to the Theology School at Duke, Gregg sought a pastorate nearby. Fortunately for us, he found the right combination of proximity to Duke and a charming rural setting at Cane Creek. Gregg earned a Doctor of Ministry degree from Gordon Conwell Theological Seminary, a Boston school that maintains a branch in Charlotte. After serving us, Greg and Diane returned to Sioux Falls, where he serves a church.

Harvey Clayton: preached 2008 (interim); born April 6, 1943 – died June 18, 2019.
Harvey Clayton attended UNC and earned a BS degree in Chemistry. He then went to Campbell University for a degree in Ministry.

Jack Edge: preached 2008 -2012; born March 17, 1954.
Jack was born in Mayock, NC and grew up on the family farm until he entered Wake Forest. He was ordained at Mayock in 1986. Before coming to Cane Creek, Jack pastored the Baptist church in Spring Hope and was active in missionary work. His wife was Pamela Stokes Edge and they have a son, John. After leaving Cane Creek, Jack was pastor at Mill Creek Baptist Church in Winnabow, NC. After Pamela died, he remarried and now lives in Kentucky.

Julian Griffin: preached 2013 (interim); born February 26, 1932 – died January 4, 2018.
Jack Griffin lived in Burlington. He served as pastor of Chestnut Level Baptist Church in Blairs, Virginia. He served as interim pastor at many churches in North Carolina and Virginia. He was our interim pastor on two occasions

David John Hailey, Jr.: preached 2013 – 2017; born February 20, 1
David John is the son of the pastor at Hayes-Barton Church in Raleigh. He earned a Doctor of Ministry degree from Campbell University. We were his first church. His wife is Claire, and they have a child, Abigail. After serving us, he moved to Chicago and is senior pastor of the First Baptist Church of Oak Park, Illinois. David John has a marvelous singing voice.   He always joined in with the choir and sometimes sang solos from the pulpit.

Michael Ramsey: preached 2017 - to the present; born 1974.
Michael Ramsey was born and raised in the mountains in Brasstown, North Carolina. He earned a B.A. in Psychology from UNC, a M.A. in Christian Counseling from Southeastern Seminary, a PhD in Christian Counseling from Cornerstone University and is currently pursuing his D.Min from Duke University. He has served as Interim Pastor at Parkwood Baptist Church in Rocky Mount and before he came to us, was on staff at Bethlehem Baptist Church in Knightdale, NC. Michael's wife Mindi is a speech pathologist at Duke Hospital and they have two children, Makena and Carter

Appendix 3: **Rules of Decorum**

Originally, Baptist meetings tended to be chaotic. No one was in charge and there were no rules to regulate discussion and govern decision making. In 1816, the Sandy Creek Association agreed upon a set of rules. Gradually, this idea crept back to the local churches. In January 1841, our new pastor, G. W. Purefoy, asked for a set of rules to be drawn up. The rules below appear at the front of our second Minute Book started in 1869 (rules marked with an asterisk come directly from the Sandy Creek Association list).

1st. The Church when assembled shall open their business with singing and prayer by the moderator or by some other person at his request.

2nd. The Pastor of the Church shall be moderator and shall open all the business of the Church himself except he may choose to call upon some other person.

3rd. In the absence of the Pastor the Church shall choose some Brother to act as moderator for that meeting.

4th. First business that shall be entered into by the Church shall be an inquiry into fellowship and orderly conduct of the members and if there be any disorder or cause of grief it shall be brought forward and acted upon.

5th. Next a way shall be opened for the reception of members.

6th. Then all references shall be brought forward and acted upon.

7th. It shall be the duty of each member to attend all Church meetings by the hour of 12 o'clock and any male member not prevented by known bodily infirmity failing to attend three meetings in succession shall be cited to come forward and show cause why he has done so and if any female member not prevented by infirmity repeatedly neglects to attend at Church meeting there shall be some person or persons to inquire into the cause.

8th. Any member male or female failing to comply with the above regulation without giving sufficient reasons shall be liable to censure or expulsion according to the opinion of the Church.

*9th. The members shall keep their seats during the meeting, nor shall any male member withdraw without leave from the moderator neither to laughing or talking in time of conference.

*10th. Every member when going to speak shall rise from his seat and address the moderator and members generally.

*11th. No person shall speak on the same subject more than twice without leave from the Church and while speaking shall avoid casting any reflections calculated to wound the feelings of any member and shall confine himself closely to the subject.

 12th. When two members rise at the same time the moderator shall decide who shall speak.

13th. All matters shall be decided by a majority of the members present except in the reception or excommunication in which there must be a union but if there be a minority who have objections unless they can show that their objections are valid and sufficient it be their duty peaceably to submit to the Decision of their brethren.

*14th. Motions made and seconded shall be acted on except withdrawn by the mover.

 15th. It shall be the duty of each member at all Church meetings and times of communion to take their seats, otherwise it shall be deemed disorder.

 16th. There shall be a clerk regularly elected by the Church whose duty it shall be to record the proceedings of the Church to do the reading and to report members as have, by repeated absences, violated the rules of decorum.

 17th. In all cases where it is deemed necessary to receive evidence on such as are not members of our Church the Moderator may appoint a committee of three persons to hear such evidence and report to the next conference.

 18th. It shall be the duty of the Moderator to invite all Brothers and Sisters of other churches who may be present and in good fellowship at home to sit with this Church.

 19th. The Lord's Supper shall be administered at least once in three months.

 20th. The list of male members shall be called over at every conference meeting.

21st. The clerk shall at the close of business read over the minutes of the proceedings that if anything needs correcting it may undergo that correction before dismission.

Annotated Bibliography

Below is a list of my primary references. I have added comments about what each book is about and say where a copy may be found. The locations of these references are indicated with the following abbreviations:

NCC   North Carolina Collection, Wilson Library, UNC-CH
WFU   Baptist Collection, Wake Forest University
SHC   Southern Historical Collection, Wilson Library, UNC-CH
CCBC   Cane Creek Baptist Church library

Asplund, John. Universal Register of Baptists (1781) NCC: VC286 A842 (Also *see* McMurtie, 1943, in NCC: 655.175 M16k). This is an early list of American Baptist Churches.

Benedict, David. Fifty Years Among the Baptists. NCC: 286 B46f. 1860.

Benedict, David. A General History of the Baptist Denomination in America. Vol. 2, NCC: C286 B46g. 1813. The two Benedict works are a valuable source of early Baptist history in North Carolina.

Blackwelder, Ruth. The Age of Orange. Charlotte: William Loftin, publisher. 1961. This is the only history we have of our county. *But see* Lefler & Wager. (CCBC)

Boswell, Ron. The Blessings of Beulah. Roxboro, NC: Beulah Baptist Association, 1984, 240pp. We belonged to this Association for many years. (CCBC)

Boyd, William. William Byrd's "Histories of the Dividing Line betwixt Virginia and North Carolina." Raleigh: The North Carolina Historical Commission 1929. This valuable book contains Byrd's official history of the 1728 survey and Byrd's "Secret History" published here for the first time. (CCBC)

Caruthers, Eli W. Revolutionary Incidents. 2 Vol. Philadelphia: Hayes & Zell 1856. Reprinted in 2010 by Drain Tree Press Books in Wilmington. This Alamance County preacher interviewed Revolutionary War veterans and wrote the only description we have of the Battle of Kirk's Farm. (Vol. 2: CCBC)

Caruthers, Eli W. American Slavery and the Immediate Duty of Southern Slaveholders. Reprinted in 2018 by Jack Davidson at Pickwick Publications in Eugene, OR. Caruthers was quietly antiwar and anti-slavery. This manuscript was written in 1862 but not published until 2018. (CCBC)

Cheek, James. Footprints of a Human Life: A Sketch of the Life of James Cheek. Los Angeles: privately printed, c1946, 216pp. Cheek was born locally and belonged to our church. His descriptions of life in the 1870s and 1880s have been quoted extensively. (CCBC)

Chute, Anthony, Finn, Nathan, & Haykin, Michael. The Baptist Story from English Sect to Global Movement. B&H Publishing Group, 2015. This is a shorter version of the history compiled by McBeth. (CCBC)

Chilton, Mark. The Land Grant Atlas of Orange County, Vol 2: Saxapahaw Old Fields. Privately printed 2015. Chilton was mayor of Carrboro and is now the county's Register of Deeds. This book required an immense amount of work. (CCBC)

Corbitt, David. The Formation of North Carolina Counties, 1663-1943. Raleigh, NC: State Department of Archives and History, 1950. This little-known book includes the legal description of the boundaries of Orange County and how it was subdivided over the years. (CCBC)

Cox, Cordelia. A Study of the Need of Rural Elementary Educational and Vocational Guidance. Unpublished UNC MA thesis. 1925 NCC

Dunaway, Stewart. Orange County Mill Records 1782-1859. Morrisville, NC: Lulu Press. 2009. Dunaway has self-published a lot of old Orange County records. (CCBC)

Edwards, Morgan. Materials Toward a History of the Baptists in the Province of North Carolina.1772. See copy in N. C. Historical Review, Vol. 7 p369f, 1930. (NCC)

Fanning, David. The Narrative of Colonel David Fanning. Privately printed in Richmond, 1861. Reprinted by Joseph Sabin in 1865. This is Fanning's defense of his vicious Tory behavior during the Revolutionary War. (CCBC)

Gwaltney, W. R. Capture of Fort Hamby. Taylorsville, NC: The Mountain Scout 1903 (CCBC in Civil War folder)

Henderson, Archibald. North Carolina: The Old North State and the New. Chicago: Lewis publishing Co. 2 Vol. 1941. Written by a beloved UNC professor, this was an old standard history of our state. (CCBC)

Hendricks, Garland. Saints and Sinners: The Story of Jersey Baptist Church. Thomasville, NC: Charity and Children, 1988. This is the historic Jersey Settlement. This copy was sent to us by the author. (CCBC)

Johnson, Edward. A Cane Creek Tapestry. Privately printed by Cane Creek Baptist Church in 2003 (updated in 2005). This is a collection of old family photographs from the Cane Creek community. (CCBC)

Johnson, Guion. <u>Antebellum North Carolina</u>. University of North Carolina Press, 1937. This is my mother's social history of the lives of ordinary people before the Civil War. (CCBC)

Jordan, F. M. <u>Life and Labors of Elder F. M. Jordan</u>. Raleigh: Edwards & Broughton, 1899.

Kenzer, Robert. <u>Kinship and Neighborhood in a Southern Community</u>. The University of Tennessee Press, 1987. This is a detailed study of communities in old Orange County including Cane Creek. (CCBC)

Lawson, John. <u>A New Voyage to Carolina</u>. London, England, 1709. There are several recent reprints. (CCCB]

Lefler, H. & Newsome, A. <u>North Carolina: A History of a Southern State</u>. University of North Carolina Press, 3rd edition 1973. This is another authoritative history of our state. (CCBC)

Lefler, H. & Wager, P. (EDs.) <u>Orange County 1752-1952</u>. Chapel Hill: The Orange Printshop, 1953, 389pp. This is a collection of topics concerning Orange County on the occurrence of its bicentennial. (CCBC)

McBeth, H. Leon. <u>The Baptist Heritage: Four Centuries of Baptist Witness</u>. Nashville, TN: Broadman Press, 850pp, 1987. This is a recent and widely used textbook used in divinity schools, (CCBC)

Nash, Francis. "The history of Orange County - Part I," <u>The North Carolina Booklet</u>, Vol. 10, 55-75, 1910. (NCC: C970 NB7b).

Nash, Francis. <u>Hillsboro: Colonial and Revolutionary</u>. 1903. (NCC: CR971.68 H65n).

Parker M. E. A. (ed.) <u>North Carolina Charters and Constitutions 1578-1698</u>. Raleigh: Carolina Charter Tercentenary Commissions, 1903. This is the source of my information about the exact wording of our colonial charters. (CCBC)

Paschal, G. W. <u>History of North Carolina Baptists</u> – 2 Vol. Raleigh: The General Board of the NC Baptist State Convention, 1930, 572pp. This is the most authoritative history of North Carolina Baptists up until 1930. (CCBC)

Pleasant, Stephen. <u>Letter to Samuel Wait</u>. (WFU: Samuel Wait papers, PC117, box 2, folder 215).

Powell, William. <u>North Carolina Through Four Centuries</u>. The University of North Carolina Press, 1989. This is another thorough source for state history. (CCBC)

Purefoy, George W. <u>A History of the Sandy Creek Baptist Association from its Organization in 1758 to 1858.</u> New York: Sheldon & Co., 1859. This is *the* definitive history of the first hundred years of the Sandy Creek Association. Purefoy was our preacher in the 1840s. (CCBC)

Turner, Herbert Snipes. Church in the Old Fields. University of North Carolina Press, 1962. This is a history of Hawfields Presbyterian Church, which later moved and became New Hope Presbyterian Church. (CCBC)

Waugh, J. H. <u>History of the Mt. Zion Association</u>. Burlington, NC: privately printed by the Mt. Zion Association, 1970 (CCCB)

Wheeler, John. <u>Historical Sketches of North Carolina from 1584 to 1851</u>. Lippencott, Grambro & Co, 1851 (CCBC)

- END -

Made in the USA
Columbia, SC
08 December 2024

48746791R00152